Leading School Turnaround

How Successful Leaders Transform Low-Performing Schools

Kenneth Leithwood,
Alma Harris, Tiiu Strauss

JOSSEY-BASS
A Wiley Imprint
www.josseybass.com

Published by Jossey-Bass
A Wiley Imprint
989 Market Street, San Francisco, CA 94103-1741—www.josseybass.com

Jossey-Bass books and products are available through most bookstores. To contact Jossey-Bass directly call our Customer Care Department within the U.S. at 800-956-7739, outside the U.S. at 317-572-3986, or fax 317-572-4002.

Jossey-Bass also publishes its books in a variety of electronic formats. Some content that appears in print may not be available in electronic books.

Library of Congress Cataloging-in-Publication Data

Leithwood, Kenneth A.
 Leading school turnaround: how successful leaders transform low-performing schools / by Kenneth Leithwood, Alma Harris, and Tiiu Strauss.—1st ed.
   p.   cm.
 Includes bibliographical references and index.
 ISBN 978-0-470-40766-0 (cloth)
   1. School improvement programs. 2. Educational leadership. I. Harris, Alma, 1958-
 II. Strauss, Tiiu. III. Title.
 LB2822.8.L45   2010
 371.2'07—dc22   2010008084

Printed in the United States of America
FIRST EDITION
HB Printing   10 9 8 7 6 5 4 3 2 1

Contents

Figures and Tables

Figures

Tables

The Authors

Kenneth Leithwood is professor of educational leadership and policy at the Ontario Institute for Studies in Education at the University of Toronto. His most recent books include *Distributed Leadership According to the Evidence* and *Leading with Teachers' Emotions in Mind*. Leithwood is the recipient of the University of Toronto's Impact on Public Policy award and a fellow of the Royal Society of Canada. His current research and writing is about the influence of leadership on student learning.

Alma Harris is the director of the London Centre for Leadership in Learning at the Institute of Education, London. Her research work focuses on organizational change and development. She is internationally known for her work on school improvement, particularly on improving schools in challenging circumstances. Harris first studied as a secondary school teacher and taught in a number of challenging schools in South Wales. Her most recent work has focused on leadership and organizational change.

Tiiu Strauss is a project director working with Kenneth Leithwood in the Department of Theory and Policy Studies at the Ontario Institute for Studies in Education at the University of Toronto. She has published in the areas of leader problem solving, distributed leadership, and leadership in turnaround schools.

Introduction

UNDERSTANDING SCHOOL TURNAROUND LEADERSHIP

The aim of this book is to build on evidence currently available about how to quickly and significantly improve the performance of exceptionally underperforming schools and sustain those gains. Reflecting on the evidence about successful turnaround processes in organizational sectors other than schools, we assumed that the influence of leaders is a crucial feature of this process. This seems a safe assumption. For example, one of the eight lessons concluding Murphy and Meyer's (2008) remarkably thorough synthesis of evidence about successful turnaround processes is that "successful turnaround schools almost always have good, if not exceptional, principals. As a common strand across successful school turnarounds, leadership is crucial. The principal typically sets the turnaround agenda, while leading teachers, involving the community, and building general capacity" (p. 321).

Starting from this general assumption, our purpose was not to make the case that leadership matters—or even estimate how much it matters. Rather, our focus in this book is on the nature of that leadership. What practices or behaviors do successful turnaround leaders exercise? So the book speaks directly to school and district leaders who are facing the task of turning around seriously underperforming schools. It aims to offer practical advice to those leaders—advice firmly rooted in good evidence about what works.

A summary of our own research providing this evidence is provided in the appendix to the book. It is sufficient to explain here that several multiyear studies, both qualitative and quantitative in design, undertaken in the Canadian province of Ontario and in several different sites in England provide the core of this evidence. In addition, we have wrapped around that information from our own evidence much of the relevant research on organizational turnarounds, school turnarounds in particular, as others have reported in the wider literature. This wider literature reflects research carried out especially in the United States; virtually all of the lessons about turning around schools that we discovered in our Canadian and U.K. research are, in our estimation, entirely applicable to schools in the United States.

Although we believe that adopting a wider perspective on turnaround issues can only be beneficial, it is quite uncommon. For example, the most recent and otherwise quite impressive U.S. texts on turnaround schools and their leadership (Duke, 2010; Murphy & Meyers, 2008) reflect little or no evidence collected from outside the borders of the United States.

Sometimes our own evidence is sufficient to justify the claims we make about how leaders turn schools around. But sometimes it serves primarily to illustrate and support evidence others have generated that is relevant to claims we consider important. We draw on several lines of well-developed research that are germane to the turnaround problem as well, for example, research about low-performing schools typically serving highly diverse and economically disadvantaged students (Corallo & Mcdonald, 2002; Harris, James, Harris, & Gunraj, 2006; Muijs, Harris, Chapman, Stoll, & Russ, 2004) and both school improvement and organizational change processes (Fullan, 2006).

Starting Points

We begin with eight basic understandings, assumptions, or starting points for our subsequent account of how to lead the successful turnaround of underperforming schools.

1. Turning "failing" schools around is a prominent focus of contemporary educational policy.

This book, and the research on which it is based, was prompted by what has become a ubiquitous concern across many countries: turning around "poorly performing" schools, a central component in most educational reform agendas. It is, according to one U.S. account (Calkins, Guenther, Belfore, & Lash, 2007), "the emerging response to an entirely new dynamic in public education: the threat of closure for underperformance" (p. 36). This threat has been prompted by educational policy changes over the past fifteen years, which themselves were generated by a substantial increase in concern about the performance of public schools (Anyon, 2005). Indeed, improving the performance of schools, most often those serving students in challenging circumstances, has become the main focus of school reform efforts in most developed countries. These challenging circumstances include high levels of poverty and disadvantage among the student population, which can be exacerbated by issues associated with racial, cultural, ethnic, and religious diversity among students served by the school. But they can also be compounded by a high degree of homogeneity within the student population, where the social mix becomes a barrier to raising improvement and achievement (Thrupp, 2001).

The concept of turnaround has significant roots in the corporate world and is associated with a high degree of intolerance for prolonged failure or downturn, along with an overwhelming bias for action and better results. This bias for action has been accompanied in school contexts by a significant narrowing and simplification of the criteria officially used for judging school performance—typically student scores on tests of math and language skills and formal examination results (Rogers & Ricker, 2006). One of the most important consequences of these changes has been the creation of an underclass of schools labeled and categorized as "in need of assistance," "low performing," "underperforming," "in challenging circumstances," "failing," or "in special measures" (Mintrop, 2004).

Labels such as these quite intentionally serve as descriptors of student performance, usually measured by test scores and examination performance, but sometimes by rates of attendance, dropout, and exclusion (Holdzkom, 2001). These labels are also a call for action—a call to be "turned around" in a relatively short amount of time (Duke et al., 2005). England, many U.S. states, and the Canadian province of Ontario are examples of educational jurisdictions in which policymakers have recently made significant commitments to this end. Schools in England, for example, are placed in "special measures" or "serious weaknesses" categories when they are judged to have poor levels of relative performance against local or national standards and where there is not much chance of improving without external support and intervention. Under the No Child Left Behind Act in the United States, schools that fail to meet their annual targets face a series of progressively more serious sanctions. After five consecutive years of unsatisfactory progress, for example, these sanctions may include conversion to a charter school, replacement of staff considered responsible for the failure, hiring an external contractor to run the school, or some other equally significant alternative (Rhim et al., 2007).

2. Turning schools around is different from "simply" improving them.

Few would claim that improving schools is an easy business, confronting, as it does, a host of personal and organizational variables that often seem to spin out of control with the least provocation. "Herding cats" pretty much captures the feeling many principals experience in their efforts to make changes. But school turnaround, as most conceive it, is quite different from school improvement in both subtle and not-so-subtle ways. Whereas school improvement is typically viewed as a gradual and continuous process in which almost all schools now are expected to engage, school turnaround "focuses on the most consistently underperforming schools and involves dramatic, transformative change—change driven by the prospect of being closed if it fails" (Calkins et al., 2007, p. 17). Many U.S. schools are of this type. For example, in his recent analysis, Duke (2010) cites evidence indicating that of the 12 percent of U.S. schools identified for improvement in 2005–2006, about a quarter of them "had a history of failing to meet state standards for four to six years" (p. 41).

In contrast to the prevailing understandings of "improvement," turnaround processes are typically restricted to a specific subset of schools. They usually garner significant additional resources, have short time lines within which to demonstrate success in reaching unusually precise and public targets, and are accompanied by sanctions for failure almost entirely missing from the environments in which other schools find themselves.

3. Turning schools around is a "wicked problem."

Initially coined by Churchman (1967), the term *wicked problem* is a label for problems that are especially difficult to solve and to resolve. A not-so-distant relative to the unstructured problems of interest to those who study the nature of expertise (Fredericksen, 1984), these are problems that defy routine solutions, mutate over time, and reemerge after we think we have put them to rest. In short, this means that turning around individual organizations is not an easy business. An illustration might help here.

One of the primary sources of evidence for this book is a multiyear, multiphased study of turnaround school leadership carried out in the Canadian province of Ontario (Leithwood & Strauss, 2008). Ontario was a congenial environment in which to be a public school teacher or administrator at the time the study was carried out—for those who were not wedded to the status quo. The Liberal government of the day had made public education one of its main priorities on its election about three years earlier

and had demonstrated remarkable follow-through in the subsequent years. New money had been added to the system following
a decade of diminishing resources and punishing criticism under a
previous conservative government. This made a big difference to
the job school leaders faced. Explained one secondary principal
in our Ontario study:

> I don't think there is anything specific I did to raise morale in
> the school. The tone in education truly had an effect on this
> staff. We had just come through a very difficult time in educa-
> tion with major cutbacks and staffing cutbacks, and when I got
> here, things were just suddenly better. We were just richer, not in
> terms of money necessarily, but richer in resources, and staffing
> and so on. I think the general tone was on the up. So it was easy
> for me to tap into that and to get the staff on board.

Support for educators was apparent, and teachers were considered the solution to improving the system even more in turnaround
settings than in simply "improvement" settings. This was a distinct
departure from the view of the previous government, which had
considered teachers the problem even though it had to depend on
teachers for any changes it wished to make.

More specifically, a sophisticated balance of pressure and
support had been introduced by the government to help underperforming schools gain some traction on their school improvement
challenges. Pressure came in the form of quite specific provincial
achievement targets widely shared by district staffs and widely
communicated to parents and the general public. These were
targets framed by provincial achievement tests, with the results
available to anyone wishing to see them. Support took the form
of additional funding for which poorly performing schools were
eligible. These schools were also given access to technical and
strategic assistance in the form of turnaround teams. Such teams
(which we refer to frequently in this book) consisted of seconded
(temporarily reassigned) teachers, principals, and central office

staff, most with impressive records of achievement in their own organizations who agreed to work with several underperforming schools over the course of one or several years.[1]

Under these circumstances, it would not be unreasonable to assume impressive progress not only on the part of designated turnaround schools but of schools in the province more generally. Certainly the secondary school principal's comments about improved teacher morale quoted above seem to support this assumption. As well, average student achievement scores on provincial tests did rise during this period, seeming to confirm success on a large scale.

But aggregate increases in achievement, while perfectly suitable for provincial accountability purposes, may easily mask important unresolved challenges in large numbers of individual schools, lulling us into thinking that the prevailing strategies are good enough. So we decided to test this reasonable assumption further. Restricting our attention to elementary schools, we dug out the provincial achievement scores of students in the 3,817 schools for which such data were available for the previous three years. These were aggregated reading and math scores at grades 3 and 6.[2]

First, we examined changes across all schools (minus the seventy-three that were part of a government-sponsored turnaround initiative, about which we have more to say later) over three years. We then examined changes in such scores separately for the seventy-three schools that had opted to be part of the province's turnaround project and for which data were available. We were curious to know the patterns of change in achievement in both reading and math over the three years for all schools, as well as how schools in the turnaround project fared in comparison. Table I.1 summarizes these results.

As the left column of Table I.1 indicates, a school could experience an increase (I), a decrease (D), or no change (stable or S) in its achievement scores each year.[3] To make the twenty-seven possible permutations more meaningful, we created six categories

Table I.1   Three-Year Elementary School Achievement Trajectories in Regular and Turnaround Schools (2002–2005)

Achievement Trajectory Patterns	Reading, Grade 3: % Reg (% TA)	Math, Grade 3: % Reg (%TA)	Reading, Grade 6: % Reg (% TA)	Math, Grade 6: % Reg (% TA)	Mean: % Reg (% TA)
1. Temporary failure, longer-term success (DSI, SDI, DDI, DII, SSI, SII)	24.3 (26.2)	29.6 (16.4)	26.2 (25.0)	28.9 (22.7)	27.25 (22.6)
2. Temporary success, longer-term failure (IDD, ISD, EDS, ISS, IID)	19 (16.9)	15.3 (25.4)	17.3 (14.1)	15.9 (21.2)	16.88 (19.4)
3. No consistent direction (ISD, IDI, DID, DIS, SID, SIS, IDS)	41.5 (32.3)	40.5 (35.8)	42.3 (43.8)	33.4 (39.4)	39.43 (37.8)
4. Continuous improvement (III, ISI, IIS)	13 (24.6)	11.1 (20.9)	10.8 (17.2)	16.3 (15.2)	12.8 (19.5)
5. Continuous failure (DDS, DDD, DSD, DSS, SDD, SDS, SSD)	1.5 (0)	2.7 (1.5)	2.4 (0)	3.1 (1.5)	2.43 (0.8)
6. No change (SSS)	0.8 (0)	1.0 (0)	1.0 (0)	2.7 (0)	1.38 (0)

Note: Regular schools, $N = 3{,}817$; turnaround schools, $N = 73$.

of achievement trajectories, described in the left column, and calculated the proportion of schools in the province on each of the six trajectories. The first number in each cell refers to all schools minus the turnaround project schools (% Reg), and the number in parentheses refers to the schools that were part of the turnaround project (% TA).

For the province's elementary schools as a whole (minus turnaround project schools), Table I.1 indicates that

- The proportion of schools within each trajectory pattern was roughly the same whether the comparison was between grades 3 and 6 or between reading and math (school change seems to be a "whole cloth").
- By far the largest proportion of schools (39.4 percent) had an achievement trajectory described as "no consistent direction."
- More than a quarter of schools (27.3 percent), while initially unsuccessful, eventually gained some traction, perhaps through their own efforts to improve student achievement, although we cannot be certain that is the explanation (see Linn, 2003, for other explanations).[4]
- Continuous improvement, the holy grail of school reformers, was rare (12.8 percent). This, you will recall, was in a remarkably promising policy environment, infused with exceptionally sophisticated knowledge about promising change strategies and able to demonstrate aggregate student achievement improvements during this period.[5]
- Continuous failure was the trajectory of a very small proportion (2.4 percent) of schools.

These results suggest quite strongly that continuous improvement is much more an aspirational goal than something a significant proportion of schools should realistically be expected to accomplish. These results also argue, as Linn (2003) has, for judgments about achievement trends in schools to be based on time spans much longer than is typical. Indeed "typical" often means just one year, while the evidence in Table I.1 suggests that three years is likely too short.

For the largest majority of schools in difficulty, the improvement road is filled with potholes. Their common experience is to achieve some success, only to experience a subsequent downturn. They peak and then they trough, and as we will show, much of the cause of such fluctuations arises from factors outside the school. Many underperforming schools are located in areas of high social deprivation, which creates a turbulent and often volatile context for any improvement efforts to be implemented and sustained (Harris, 2009).

Table I.1 also compares schools not considered in need of being turned around ("only" improved), with schools that were more or less actively participating in the government's turnaround schools project. Mean score comparisons reported in Table I.1 indicate that

- Slightly fewer turnaround schools, as compared with regular schools, could be described as failing initially but eventually improving (27.3 versus 22.6 percent).
- Slightly fewer turnaround schools, as compared with regular schools, could be described as initially successful but failing in the longer term (19.4 versus 16.9 percent).
- Almost the same proportion of turnaround as regular schools changed in no consistent direction (37.8 versus 39.4 percent).
- Continuous improvement was achieved by more turnaround than regular schools (19.5 versus 12.8 percent).

But this mean score comparison does not do justice to the subject-specific scores it represents. Differences between regular and turnaround schools in grade 3 reading and math and grade 6 reading all favor the turnaround schools by a large enough margin to qualify as practically significant. Participation in the government's turnaround project, these comparisons suggest, was associated with a greater likelihood of success in improving student performance. But given the lower (much lower in many cases) average scores of students in turnaround schools at the outset, a more dramatic difference would have been a reasonable expectation. This reinforces the evidence showing that turn-around schools may still be underperforming in terms of local and national standards. Nevertheless, any success can be significant, if relative, achievement.

4. Multiple causes, slippery high ground, and issues of scale account for the "wicked" nature of the school turnaround problem.

The best available evidence about private sector turnarounds suggests about a 70 percent failure rate (Kotter, 1995), and the small amount of available evidence does not justify a more opti-mistic prediction for public sector turnarounds, as the Ontario illustration suggests. Underperforming schools present especially thorny turnaround challenges (Kowal & Hassel, 2005) for at least three reasons that have been identified in U.S., as well as Canadian and U.K., contexts:

• *Multiple and external causes of underperformance.* Multiple factors outside the actual organization often influence its ability to turn around. This is especially the case for school turnarounds. In the case of schools, these external factors are often a product of students' socioeconomic backgrounds. Such factors also sometimes include dysfunctional district policies and regulations, inadequate funding, and disincentives to the recruitment of high-quality teachers, for example (Chapter One examines these factors in more detail). Schools facing a large number of these causes of poor performance typically require very different forms of improvement strategies than schools in more favorable environments.

- *The challenge of sustaining improved performance.* While turning around individual schools is not for the faint of heart, it is possible, at least for a short period of time. Evidence demonstrates that school turnaround even in the most difficult circumstances is possible and that schools can succeed against the odds (Harris et al., 2006). However, this evidence also warns us that turnaround can be fragile and improvement short-lived. The high ground of improved performance is a slippery slope. For every success story, many more schools return to their old ways once special resources and additional support have been removed (Duke, 2010; Gray et al., 1999).

- *The added complexity of attempting turnarounds on a large scale.* Although turning around an individual school is no easy task, the current aspiration in many jurisdictions is to solve this wicked problem on a very large scale. For example, this is the goal of the No Child Left Behind legislation in the United States. It is also the premise of the National Challenge in England, a policy aimed at enforcing improvement in over four hundred schools deemed to be persistent underperformers (Harris, 2009). The best evidence available about what this aspiration entails suggests that neither top-down nor bottom-up approaches by themselves work, and that many millions of dollars so far thrown at the problem have largely failed (Fullan & Sharratt, 2007).

Most top-down strategies to date poorly reflect our basic understandings of successful change processes. The almost entirely punitive nature of No Child Left Behind is the poster child for this inadequacy. The evidence from Ontario described throughout this book, however, was collected in a very different policy context, one carefully attuned to evidence about successful change processes. So one important purpose for this book is to demonstrate the viability of large-scale school turnaround under conditions that nurture schools on a carefully balanced diet of both support and pressure, as well as autonomy and central direction. That said, the results reported in Table I.1 argue for conservative estimates about what is possible on a large scale even under exceptionally favorable circumstances.

5. More ambitious estimates about what is possible on a large scale depend on a better understanding of how to turn around schools on a small scale.

As is apparent from earlier observations, we are far from having a well-codified process—or some equally useful advice—for turning around underperforming schools. There is no magic formula or sure-fire way of improving these schools; an added danger is that any improvement will turn out to be temporary. Not enough research has been done in improving schools in serious difficulty to produce a definitive model of improvement for these schools. For example, Rhim et al.'s (2007) U.S.-centric review of such evidence is based on only twenty-six studies carried out in schools, all of which used only case study designs. Evidence from such studies, although rich in detail and possible insights, provides very little certainty about what works. Furthermore, much of the research about school improvement has focused on schools that require a lift in performance rather than radical intervention. So evidence informing the turnaround process is quite limited.

Yet worldwide, large-scale government reform initiatives aspire to increases in student performance that at least implicitly assume such knowledge exists. In England, a number of large-scale attempts have sought to improve schools that continuously underperform. Initiatives like Excellence in Cities Education Action Zones and the latest suite of challenges there (London Challenge, Black Country Challenge, and the National Challenge) have all been focused on raising student achievement in these groups of underperforming schools. All of these approaches share a common model: targeted resources, prescribed interventions, compulsory staff development, constant scrutiny, endless planning processes, and continual weighing and measuring from external agencies.

Over fifteen years, this model has been followed again and again in different guises, but the net result has been the same: some schools change while the new resources remain, but no large-scale change in overall performance occurs. This is an example of the wrong model being used over and over in the vain hope that it will work next time. It is also indicative of the point that relevant evidence is not sufficiently robust to persuade policymakers to undertake a different approach. As the data in Table I.1 also imply, turning around significantly underperforming schools is likely to require something different from or additional to the improvement strategies that work in adequately performing schools.

Especially as the focus of these reform efforts shifts from raising the bar (increasing mean levels of achievement across the entire system) to closing the gap (reducing the discrepancies in achievement between students who typically succeed and those who are typically at risk), this lack of procedural know-how is an albatross around reformers' necks, placing a low ceiling on what it is possible to accomplish and, at the same time, encouraging the replication of failed improvement approaches in different guises. Change, as it has often been observed, is a problem of the smallest unit. If we do not have a good understanding and a robust model of how to turn an individual school around and ensure that improvement stays around, the chances of turning around many schools at the same time seems remote.

6. Poorly performing schools stand virtually no chance of turning around without good leadership.

A considerable body of case-based research addresses the process of turning around failing organizations (Mellahi & Wilkinson, 2004; Murphy, 2008), although relatively little of this research has been undertaken in schools (Paton & Mordaunt, 2004). Much of the evidence can be found in the business literature where turnaround is a business in itself and the idea of turnaround specialists is commonplace. Within this literature, leadership is widely considered to be vital to private sector turnarounds. We are unaware of any documented example of a successful turnaround in business without some change in leadership, and the same seems likely to be the case in schools as well (Harris & Chapman, 2002a). In his study of schools on probation in two U.S. states, for example, Mintrop (2004) concluded, "What schools did under probation largely depended on how principals reacted to the low-performance status" (p. 13). In his truly remarkable book, *Lessons Learned: How Good Policies Produce Better Schools*, Whelan (2009) also concludes from several successful cases that "schools which have run into severe difficulty can be improved, often mainly through the efforts of existing staff and even when the school faced strong external pressures and challenges" (p. 96). And leadership, Whelan claims, is a central explanation for both successful school turnaround and the subsequent sustaining of improved school performance. This is the most obvious lesson from schools that have been successfully turned around.

Evidence from several other recent lines of school turnaround research also indicates a central role for leadership. For example, research in England by Chapman and Harris (2004), and Clarke (2004) highlights the centrality of a change in leadership as the main lever for turnaround and improvement in schools that underperform. This finding is reflected as well in Rhim et al.'s (2007) review of primarily U.S. evidence. Leadership, in sum, is a largely uncontested linchpin in both accounting for an organization's failure and returning the organization to a stable state (Kanter, 2003; Kowal & Hassel, 2005).

7. We know what almost all successful leaders do.

Two particular claims about leadership are quite central to the general claims we make in this book. The first of these is that there is a common core of leadership practices used by successful leaders in almost all contexts. Chapters Five through Eight describe these practices in some detail and summarize evidence about their effects. As you will see, these practices aim to accomplish four purposes critical to leadership success:

- Create a widely agreed-on sense of direction for the organization (Chapter Five).
- Help develop the capacities of organizational members to move the organization in that direction (Chapter Six).
- Redesign or restructure the organization to support people's work (Chapter Seven).
- Manage the "technical core" of the organization. In schools this will be teaching and learning processes or, to use Raudenbush's (2009) term, the "shared instructional regime" (Chapter Eight).

We spend considerable effort justifying our claim about these categories of leadership practices in Chapters Five, Six, Seven, and Eight. For now we simply note that they are almost equally important, for example: in both large and small schools; in schools serving either diverse or homogeneous student populations; schools in Canada, the United States, England, and most other developed countries; and not only in schools but also in non-school organizations. The four categories include fifteen to nineteen more specific leadership practices depending on which of our studies is referred to (Leithwood & Jantzi, 2005; Leithwood, Day, Sammons, Harris, & Hopkins, 2006).

We use the term *practice* as a synonym for the term *function*. Neither the four categories nor the specific practices within them actually describe behavior or activity. Rather, the practices signify the outcome of such behavior. These are proximal or short-term outcomes in a longer-term effort toward organizational improvement. So these practices do not actually capture how leaders do their work, but they do capture what leaders intend to accomplish through that work.

8. We have almost no knowledge about how successful leaders do their work in turnaround contexts.

I would have to say that to be active in the learning process would probably be one of the best things I've done. Particularly it helped because I was a new principal. It was only my second year when we started the turnaround. I told the teachers, "Honestly, you know I'm new at this too. I don't know where we're going with this exactly, but I do know that I will be a better principal by the end of this, and if I'm a better principal, that should mean that you feel more support, you feel you're better teachers, the kids will have a better quality of education, and you'll have a stronger skill set when we're done. And if that means that I have to be uncomfortable, then I'm fine with that." Because it was not always comfortable. There was criticism. There were questions. It was humbling. There were lots of questions that for a principal would take you outside your comfort zone and called you to task, to step up your game and be more aware of things. I think I've gotten better at most of those things—not all of them. If there's things I'm not good at, I think I know what they are now. I think it's better to at least know where your gaps are than to kind of stumble around.
—Elementary principal

We began the discussion of starting point 7 (above) by noting that we make two claims about successful leadership which are quite foundational for this book. Starting point 7 was the first claim (successful leaders in almost all contexts engage in a common core of practices). The second claim is that, such general application notwithstanding, successful leaders are also exquisitely sensitive to the contexts in which they find themselves. Large schools present much different leadership challenges than do small schools. The challenges facing leaders of inner city schools are typically quite different from those facing leaders of schools in the leafy suburbs. And so on.

Now, having a core set of common practices on which to draw (we described them as intended proximal or short-term outcomes) is extraordinarily helpful for leaders, otherwise they are without intention. Furthermore, having such proximal intentions in mind to guide what leaders do still leaves considerable flexibility for leaders to decide how to accomplish or enact those intentions in their own specific contexts. But this raises a "level of specification" question for leadership research—or in the case of this book, an account of what works based on leadership research. What level of detail should descriptions of successful leadership practices provide in order to be most helpful to school leaders and their collaborators?

Our answer to this question is to give descriptions of how leaders successfully work in contexts that are shared by many. Examples of such widely shared but unique contexts are large or small schools, elementary or secondary schools, schools serving culturally diverse or culturally homogeneous student populations and—of course—turnaround versus "simply" improving schools. Accounts of how leaders work in such contexts does not acknowledge the even more unique features faced by each leader. But research cannot be (nor should it be) in the business of trying to describe successful leadership practices as enacted in response to such unique contextual differences as this school versus that school, or differences in leaders' relationships between this teacher versus that teacher.

So our two claims about leadership are: most successful leaders use a common core of practices, but they enact those practices in ways that are sensitive to the contexts in which they find themselves. A significant part of the success of most leaders depends on their creating a sense of shared purpose in their organizations, for example. This is a core leadership practice. But successful leaders of schools in danger of going out of business in six months if dramatic improvements do not take place often "sell" their own views of where their schools should be headed to their staffs and communities. In contrast, successful leaders of schools in no such danger are much more likely to build a sense of shared purpose through highly collaborative and inclusive processes. A major purpose of this book is to uncover and describe how successful school leaders enact the common core of successful practices in turnaround school contexts.

Kowal and Hassel (2005) have claimed that while the "evidence is strong that a school's leader makes a big difference in student learning in all school settings . . . understanding of the characteristics that distinguish high-performing school leaders from the rest is very limited. In addition, there is limited research that describes how the characteristics of high-performing leaders differ in emerging school contexts such as start-up and turnaround schools" (p. 17). Comparable evidence indicates furthermore, that successful turnaround leadership practices vary in response to the unique challenges encountered at each stage in the turnaround process (Slatter, Lovett & Barlow, 2006). Turnaround schools, it would seem, are unique contexts for leadership and require unique enactments of successful leadership practices.

How This Book Unfolds

The ten chapters of the book are organized into three thematic parts. The chapters in Part One address the causes of school failure and declining school performance (Chapter One); a staged conception of school turnaround processes, which serves as an important framework for our subsequent examination of turnaround leadership practices (Chapter Two); and a case study illustration and elaboration of some key ideas associated with those stages from one secondary school in England (Chapter Three).

Part Two consists of five chapters. Four of these chapters provide an extensive description of how each of four categories of leadership practices is enacted by successful turnaround leaders: direction setting is examined in Chapter Four, developing people in Chapter Five, redesigning the organization in Chapter Six, and managing the instructional program in Chapter Seven. Chapter Eight illustrates these core leadership practices as they were enacted by successful leaders in one elementary and one secondary turnaround school in our Ontario study.

The two chapters in Part Three speak to two outstanding challenges. How to sustain a failing school's performance once it has been significantly improved is the first of these challenges (Chapter Nine). The limited evidence available about this challenge indicates that improved performance is usually not sustained, thus calling into question the wisdom of expending the often enormous efforts required for the initial turnaround. This challenge, touched on in earlier chapters, deserves the much further unpacking provided in Chapter Nine. Finally, Chapter Ten describes just how those leadership practices outlined in earlier parts of the book eventually influence student learning. This chapter offers advice to turnaround leaders, based on recent syntheses of research, about how to select those conditions for improvement in their schools most deserving of their time and attention—a major challenge for school leaders confronted with a potential blizzard of things to do but time to do only a few things well.

A Note About Research Contexts

The original evidence for this book was provided by research carried out in England and Canada. While we believe our results are of direct use to leaders in the United States and most other developed countries, a brief description of some of the key similarities and differences among the English, Canadian, and American school systems is provided here for those wishing to draw their own conclusions.

Major responsibility for K–12 education rests at the subnational levels in both Canada and the United States. Canada's constitution cedes responsibility to provinces, and states hold this responsibility in the United States. Unlike Canada, however, the U.S. federal government wields considerable influence on schools through major policy initiatives that schools must implement if they are to have access to the funding these policies provide. As one example, the U.S. No Child Left Behind (NCLB) legislation has been a major influence on how schools and districts think about curriculum, testing, and accountability. The achievement targets set for schools to remain eligible for federal funding have strongly influenced which schools are considered to be in need of turnaround, as well as some of the most common strategies for accomplishing school turnaround. The Canadian federal government, in contrast, has no such influence, and provinces guard their jurisdiction over primary and elementary schools closely.

Districts or boards of education are a key feature of both the Canadian and American school systems, although the exercise of local authority is a stronger feature of the American system. In general, provinces exercise more authority over Canadian districts than states exercise over American districts. In the case of the research carried out for this book, the strong authority of the provincial government was an important part of the story about turnaround schools in Ontario. The authority of states is likely to have less influence in U.S. districts. Nonetheless, the nature of the provincial authority in Ontario was largely based on expertise, not position. So expert-based authority on the part of states in the United States might yield similar results under favorable circumstances.

England has a national educational system with authority strongly centralized and a recent history of significant top-down initiatives such as the National Literacy and National Numeracy Strategies. Although local educational authorities (LEAs) were a powerful source of influence on schools, the Thatcher government and then the Blair government diminished their authority. More recently, subnational restructuring has expanded the responsibilities of what are now called local authorities to include most government services designed to assist children, including education, health, and other social services. Each school has its own elected board of governors with responsibilities parallel to those enjoyed by elected boards of trustees for districts in Canada and school boards in the United States. This more extreme form of site-based management, however, is strongly restrained by a national system of school inspections, public reports of league tables, and centralized responsibility for leadership development in the form of the National College for School Leadership. The Department for Children, Schools and Families has been responsible for the funding of school turnaround initiatives in England and has sponsored particular programs aimed at turning around failing schools.

Key Points

- Turning "failing" schools around is a prominent focus of contemporary educational policy.
- Turning schools around is different from "simply" improving them.
- Turning schools around is a "wicked problem."
- Multiple causes, slippery high ground, and issues of scale account for the "wicked" nature of the school turnaround problem.
- More ambitious estimates about what is possible on a large scale depend on a better understanding of how to turn around schools on a small scale.
- Poorly performing schools stand virtually no chance of turning around without good leadership.
- We know what almost all successful leaders do.
- We have almost no knowledge about how successful leaders do their work in turnaround contexts.

Part One

THE DYNAMIC CONTEXT IN WHICH TURNAROUND LEADERS WORK

1

REASONS FOR SCHOOL FAILURE

> You have to understand the context we work in.
> This is an area of high social deprivation where
> daily existence is difficult enough. Simply getting
> to the school gate is an achievement for many
> of our students. Poverty is not an excuse for
> underachievement, but it is a powerful influence.
>
> *Secondary school principal*

The reasons for school failure are almost as complex as are the reasons we are unable to turn around underperforming schools in vast numbers. These reasons are multifaceted and interrelated, compounding and exacerbating the problem of school failure. Whether in Canada, England, the United States, or any other part of the Western world, there are common factors that make turnaround difficult and render some schools, in certain contexts, less able to raise the performance of their students. Many approaches aimed at improving underachieving schools have served to further disadvantage them, largely by failing to take adequate account of their context and by locating the blame for failure squarely within the school. But reasons for school failure are rarely one-dimensional or singular. Consequently, the polarized debate of "school's fault" versus "society's fault" for failure does not take us very far. Attributing blame detracts from solving the problem.

As always, the truth lies somewhere in between. In some cases, schools are at the heart of the problem. Poor teaching is condoned, weak leadership is tolerated, and the dominant view is, "What can you do with these kids?" driven by low expectations. On the other side of the coin, it is undeniable that the relationship between poverty and underachievement is powerful. The consequences of growing up poor affect millions of young people worldwide (Berliner, 2006). Poverty remains a global, social, and economic issue, and the educational reform agenda in many countries reflects a renewed interest in addressing the relationship between poverty and underachievement. The gap in achievement between children from low-income families and their more affluent peers persists, and in the majority of cases, it actually increases throughout schooling. Although social disadvantage is not an excuse for poor achievement in academic terms, it certainly is a powerful explanatory factor. It remains the case that many failing schools are located in high-poverty contexts.

A substantial corpus of international research into the relationship between poverty and education demonstrates that while the general attainment levels of poor children have improved over time, the gap between the majority of children from low-income families and their more affluent peers has widened (Knapp, 2001; Thomson & Harris, 2004). Children attending high-poverty schools are not likely to achieve as well as their peers in more favorable school contexts. The net effect of poverty on educational achievement is stark. Educational outcomes in deprived areas are worse than those in nondeprived areas, whether they are measured in terms of qualification, attendance, exclusions, or retention rates. Inner-city areas, in particular, are associated with low educational outcomes. Socioeconomic status or family background typically explains more than half the variation between schools in pupil achievement, and low family income in childhood years makes a significant difference to subsequent educational outcomes. Chudgar and Luschei (2009) provide new support for this well-known finding in their recent analysis of international achievement tests across twenty-five countries.

Part of the reason for the decline in social mobility in many countries is the strong bond between low levels of family income and subsequent educational attainment. Underachievement and levels of deprivation continue to be strongly and powerfully linked. Furthermore, poverty continues to be a chief explanatory factor for the persistent low levels of attainment for certain groups of young people.

Many recent policies aimed at tackling underperforming schools have failed to acknowledge the full extent of the socioeconomic challenges facing many of them. Governments continue to impose standardized models of school intervention and improvement on failing schools in spite of evidence suggesting that this is counterproductive to schools located in the most vulnerable communities (Harris, James, Harris, & Gunraj, 2006). High-stakes testing and tight accountability measures may achieve some instant improvement in student performance, but these improvements often vanish quickly. Most of the strategies that accompany the "no excuses" or "zero tolerance" rhetoric of accountability, whether in the United States or the United Kingdom, for example, can actually harm the very schools they are seeking to improve. Improvement strategies for turning around such schools often are too little, too late, work on only part of the problem, and unwittingly establish conditions that actually guarantee unsustainable student performance, as Mintrop and Trujillo (2004) point out in their nine-state U.S. study.

So where does this take us? To the recognition that achieving sustainable school turnaround requires an in-depth understanding of the factors that powerfully combine to create school failure in the first place. Some of these factors are external to the school, as we have pointed out, and sometimes beyond their control. In their recent synthesis of evidence about external factors contributing to school failure, Murphy and Meyers (2008) highlight urban school settings, minority student populations, the low socioeconomic status of students, and lack of readiness for school (lack of prerequisite knowledge) on the part of many students in many failing schools. Other factors are internal to the school and can be influenced, changed, and realigned more directly. For example, the most common internal factors Murphy and Meyers identified in their review of primarily U.S research are different dimensions of poor teacher quality, such as poor classroom instruction, inadequate teacher knowledge and skills, limited teacher experience, teachers assigned to subjects for which they are not trained, high teacher turnover, and low teacher morale. This review also identifies ineffective leadership and inadequate resources as common causes of school failure.

This chapter describes the most fundamental causes of school failure in the schools in which our research was conducted. Of course, these are among the larger causes others have identified as well.

Fundamental Causes of School Failure

We subscribe to the view that "deadwood didn't kill itself" (Fink & Brayman, 2006)—that is, school failure is not self-inflicted. Instead, our evidence suggests that it can be traced to five powerful interlocking factors.

1. Poverty and diversity create challenges for individual student learning that many schools are ill equipped to address.

It should come as no surprise that a disproportionate number of failing schools are located in contexts of high poverty. We have already started to outline the powerful link between poverty and underachievement, but the contextual factors that affect underperformance are worth further scrutiny. Within the category of "failing" schools, those located in high-poverty or challenging contexts are disproportionately represented. The extent of their overrepresentation means that the labels of "schools in challenging circumstances" or "in high poverty" are often taken as a proxy for underachievement. However, this is both inaccurate and misleading. Although a large proportion of schools in challenging circumstances and high-poverty contexts do underperform, not all do.

A small proportion, but a significant number, of schools in challenging contexts add considerable value to the academic achievements and life chances of young people (Harris et al., 2006). These schools are able to overcome the negative influences of social disadvantage through a variety of strategies, approaches, and interventions, all centrally and persistently aimed at improving teaching and learning (Harris, 2009). It is certainly possible to improve schools in the most disadvantaged contexts, but it is hard and relentless work, as Jacobson, Johnson, Ylimaki, and Giles (2005) make clear in their study of a small number of successfully turned-around schools in Buffalo, New York.

For every school in challenging circumstances that succeeds against the odds, many more find it difficult to get to the starting line of improvement (Maden, 2001). These schools face multiple problems. They are most likely to have higher-than-average numbers of pupils with low literacy levels on entry. They are also likely to have a higher proportion of refugee children or students who have been excluded from other schools because of the challenges they present and the lack of resources in the school to meet them. Incidents of violence, crime, and drugs also tend to be more prevalent in communities where poverty and disadvantage are endemic. These powerful interlocking variables make the daily business of educating young people demanding and often dangerous for teachers.

The "school improvement" literature has often been criticized for ignoring the powerful socioeconomic influences that affect schools and for offering naive and sometimes simplistic solutions to complex social problems (Thrupp, 2001). Consequently, more recently researchers within the school improvement field have concentrated their attention on developing contextually specific approaches to improvement.

2. The negative effects of poverty and diversity on student learning are greatly magnified in schools with homogeneous populations.

Thrupp's (2001) work has shown that the social composition of students—or the social mix—has a big influence on student achievement. Children from families with low or average socioeconomic status (SES) tend to have better educational outcomes if they attend a school whose students come from families with high average SES. But if these students attend a school where the SES mix is predominantly low, they are unlikely to make as much progress. In short, the social composition and the context of the school make significant differences to students' subsequent performance, over and above the effects associated with the child's individual family background. This effect is what Willms (2003) calls the hypothesis of double jeopardy: if children from low-SES families are in low-SES schools, they are doubly disadvantaged by their socioeconomic status and the socioeconomic status of their peers.

The benefits of attending a high-SES school include, on average, higher expectations of school staff and parents, positive peer interaction, and higher parental engagement in learning. Schools where the SES composition of pupils is mainly low often lack the norms, expectations, and values associated with high academic achievement and success. The relative absence of social capital that is in abundance in more affluent schools (Driscoll & Kerchner, 1999) makes it much more difficult for schools in disadvantaged circumstances to convince young people of the merits or benefits of education and achievement. Many young people at schools in high-poverty contexts come from homes where there are several generations of unemployment and schools are viewed as a problem rather than a solution. These schools are not just in inner cities. They can also be found in rural settings and the other communities where unemployment, crime, and drugs are a way of life for young people and their families.

In England, a study that focused on schools in former coal-field areas that had demonstrated improvement over a five-year period identified shifts in local employment patterns as one of the main factors that influenced improved school performance (Harris, Muijs, Chapman, Stoll, & Russ, 2003). Where new employment opportunities became available in the area, particularly white-collar opportunities, the influx of children from families who were relocating to take these opportunities made a difference to school performance. Essentially the development of a more heterogeneous mix of students in terms of background, aspiration, attitude, and ability increased the chances that schools would significantly improve the performance of students who would otherwise be much less likely to succeed.

Especially in England and the United States, neoliberal policies emphasizing the benefits of competition and choice are also responsible for rendering many schools in high-poverty contexts less equipped to improve. The combination of market individualism and control through constant and comparative assessment has relegated certain schools to the lower echelons of performance indefinitely. As Apple (1996) has explained, more affluent parents often have more flexible hours and can visit multiple schools to assess whether they are suitable for their children. They have cars—often more than one—and can afford driving their children across town to attend a "better school." As well, these parents can provide the hidden opportunities and experiences such as camps and after-school programs (dance, music, computer classes, and so on) that give their children an ease or a style that seems natural and acts as a set of cultural resources. Conversely, parents and families in poor and disadvantaged communities are less able to work the system, leaving more and more students in high-poverty areas grouped together in the same school, thus creating the kind of social mix that has been shown to significantly reduce a school's ability to improve its performance. These same negative consequences of greater competition and choice, so popular with right-leaning policymakers, were the primary outcomes of early efforts to create a quasi-market system of education in New Zealand as well (Lauder & Hughes, 1999).

3. Underperforming schools often lack the capacities needed to sustain initial gains made with considerable external assistance.

Schools go through cycles of change and development, a little like businesses do. The idea of year-on-year improvement, with schools continuing ever upward on the trajectory of performance is illusory, as our analysis of Ontario data in the Introduction illustrated. All schools, even the most successful ones, experience periodic dips or downturns in performance to varying degrees. This is sometimes related to shifts in student composition, sometimes because of changes in the external environment and sometimes due to issues like staff turnover. The central point is that schools are in constant flux, but for schools that are underperforming, this flux is much bigger and the net falls and rises are more accentuated because of their starting point.

Gray's (2004) research demonstrated that schools in England in the category of special measures (the most serious category, requiring external intervention) can and do improve performance through intensive intervention, and subsequently, a significant number leave this category. However, Gray's research showed that in a relatively short space of time, many of these schools when reinspected were placed back into special measures. The improvements had been temporary; the increases in student performance had not been sustained. This cycle can be best summarized as crisis, intervention, improvement, destabilization, and crisis. All underperforming schools reach a crisis point when failure is visible above the waterline. At this point, some intervention occurs, usually externally imposed and defined. With the injection of additional resources, expertise, and help, these schools float slowly upward. At this point, the intervention is deemed to be successful, and the added support, resources, and help fall away.

For a while, like a novice swimmer, schools make progress unaided, and their direction of travel looks secure. But without the internal capacity or proficiency to continue unaided, it is only a matter of time before many of these school starts to sink once again. Often some unexpected event will destabilize or undermine progress, and all too quickly, the school is thrown back into crisis mode, and the whole cycle simply starts again. The cycle of decline from crisis to crisis may take several years, during which time many schools are unnoticed by those concerned about turnaround; but inevitably and predictably, most of these schools resurface in need of help once again.

A project that was undertaken with the eight worst performing schools in England illustrates this cycle very nicely. Each of the schools was in extremely challenging circumstances, and all were significantly underperforming. The percentage of students achieving success in external qualifications at sixteen (these are the exams given at age sixteen) was below 10 percent in some of these schools. These examinations at sixteen allow school performance to be compared.

The project, commissioned by England's Department for Education, aimed to raise performance in these eight schools by building professional learning communities within the schools, between the schools, and across the schools and their wider communities (Harris et al., 2006). Student behavior, emotional literacy, and effective pedagogy were the focus of primary attention in the project. Each school was given extra resources, extra teachers, and a range of external supports. After the first year, results in all schools started to creep up, and by the time the project finished in the third year, all schools were well in line with national norms. The project was held up as a great success and the schools rightfully celebrated.

Yet this success was short-lived and improvement was fragile. Within a year, some schools slipped backward quite dramatically, although others kept on course. In less than two years, all but one school had reverted to previous performance, and two faced reconstitution or closure under new government policy. This cycle is by no means unique to the schools in this project, and Chapter Nine in particular, describes and illustrates promising strategies for sustaining improvements once they have been made.

Cyclical decline is not only confined to the education world. It is also a feature of the corporate environment. In *How the Mighty Fall*, Jim Collins (2009) explores the reason for business failure (as do Murphy & Meyer, 2008) and presents a five-stage model of decline:

1. Hubris born of success

2. Undisciplined pursuit of more

3. Denial of risk and peril

4. Grasping for salvation

5. Capitulation to irrelevance or death

Collins's basic argument is that every institution is vulnerable no matter how great, and no law of nature suggests that those who are at the top will remain there. Any organization can fall, and most eventually do. One need look no further than today's newspaper for examples. The point is that decline is a common part of a cycle of change, but successful businesses and successful schools acknowledge and actively avoid this phase— or stave off the decline—before the downward spiral begins. They do this in two ways: by constantly evaluating their position and using data to confirm their evaluation and by acting quickly and appropriately at the first signs of danger.

It is not the case that successful schools or businesses do not hit periods of crisis or destabilization or threat; they do, but the critical difference is how they respond to the threat. Successful businesses and schools actively look for any indications of decline in the organization and are constantly seeking improvement.

Even in successful businesses and schools, bad results or falling share prices can come as a shock as complacency sets in. Collins (2009) makes the point that organizational decline is largely self-inflicted and that decline is often generated through complacency, overreaching, and neglecting the core business. Businesses in the process of meltdown are also often in denial and can be resistant to the idea that anything could be wrong. By the time this realization hits, it is too late. No matter how much they grasp for straws and salvation, the outcome is the same.

The model Collins (2009) proposes in response is powerful, but in terms of school decline or failure, our evidence surfaces some important differences. Failing schools, first of all, know they are underperforming. The data with which they are regularly confronted show this, and it has become the job of all manner of people to constantly remind them of it. They live and breathe their failure. There is no hubris of success; in fact, the opposite tends to be true. Second, failing schools tend to be reluctant to pursue more. They tend to be ground down by the challenges of their day-to-day survival and are chiefly preoccupied with doing what they do much better rather than extending their reach. Third, failing schools are rarely in denial about their performance, but they can be in denial about whether such performance is acceptable, as well as the reasons for such (under)performance. There is a tendency, perhaps justified in some cases, for failing schools to externalize the reasons for their failure and attribute it to such causes as "too many tests, the overpressured curriculum, and too much administration." Attributions such as these prevent some underperforming schools from grappling with the fundamental causes of their underperformance, such as poor classroom instruction. These schools are in denial about the causes of failure and, like businesses, can ignore them.

A fourth difference between failing businesses and schools is that many underperforming schools have "saviors" and solutions imposed on them whether they like them or not; indeed, there is little evidence of schools such as these actively seeking external intervention. And finally, businesses that fail or atrophy into insignificance die outright, hurting only their employees and shareholders. Schools, however, may be reconstituted or, at the very extreme, closed. But unlike businesses, the markets served by such schools are not transient, and the net effect of their failure hits more than the bottom line.

4. Identifying schools as "failing" is highly contingent on a surprisingly large number of circumstances.

Whether a school is identified as underperforming is partly an issue of definition and is contingent on a number of things. It is, first of all, contingent on the policy context. For all politicians, failing schools represent the worst problem and the best solution. They are the worst problem because they represent the inability of policy to influence practice. No matter what intervention, program, or treatment policymakers think up, a group of schools remains immune and continues to underperform no matter what government is in power or what interventions are applied. They represent the best solution because any government that transforms their performance is guaranteed popular support.

Many voters have little choice other than to send their children to underperforming schools and are therefore quick to lay the blame for serial school underperformance on the government of the day. Improving these schools to the level of the best schools would make voters and politicians very happy; hence, whatever government is in power, improving this group of underperforming schools will remain a priority.

Second, the definition of underperformance is contingent on the criteria and benchmarks set for judging adequate performance. For example, in England, at one point all schools in which less than 25 percent of students achieved success in public examinations at age sixteen were considered failing. The 25 percent threshold, an arbitrary line in the sand, categorized schools with 24 percent as failing and those with 26 percent as not failing. In 2008, this threshold was increased to 30 percent. Overnight more than four hundred schools that had not been considered as failing were catapulted into the "failing" category. Indeed a number of schools that had been commended for their performance one week were being vilified the next as failing. In short, the definition of a failing school is relative. There is no absolute measure.

Third, underperformance is contingent on who assesses underperformance. For example, a district supervisor visiting a school may know its community, background, and history very well. The judgment he or she subsequently makes on the progress secured by the school will be heavily influenced by this knowledge and by the quality of social relationships with staff at the school, particularly the principal. He or she may conclude that the distance traveled by the school has been significant and label the school as improving. Another member of district staff less familiar with the school and looking only at annual performance data may conclude that the school is underperforming. But it is the same school. Especially when judgments about success or failure are based only on achieving a fixed target, the chances of mislabeling a high-performing school serving a group of students who have traditionally struggled at school a failure are high.

The important point here is that the notion of underperformance is relative and contestable. It is for many schools a label that is applied, removed, and reapplied as policies change and political imperatives alter. Underperformance is contingent on definition and the criteria on which this definition is applied. Politicians may want to set ambitious, tough targets and underline these as expected minimum performance, but in so doing, they create many more "failing" schools.

5. Weak leadership is a major cause of school decline.
Stories of successful turnaround in high-poverty contexts are not in short supply. (Murphy & Meyers, 2008). Although every

example is unique in some respects, all stories highlight the centrality of a small number of factors or conditions that make improvement less or more possible. The external conditions we have already explored: these are contextual, compositional, cyclical, and contingent. But what about the internal conditions—those factors or elements over which the school has more direct control and influence? One of our recent studies carried out in England (Day et al., 2009) begins to describe the conditions found in more successful schools. But this study, as well as Duke's (2010) U.S. evidence, also shows that such internal conditions (trust, collaboration, innovation, and a relentless focus on teaching and learning) are not randomly allocated or aligned; they are purposefully created and orchestrated by school leaders.

The literature on effective turnarounds points again and again to the importance of effective leadership. This evidence shows that talented leadership is one of the strongest explanations for the success of schools performing beyond expectations in high-poverty settings (Harris & Chapman, 2002a). High-poverty schools can achieve high academic performance, but this is unlikely without effective leadership.

The nature of leadership practices in successful school turnaround schools is a central theme in this book, so a detailed exploration of the exact nature of these practices is left to later chapters. Suffice it to say that compelling evidence now shows that leaders in successful schools actively set directions, develop people, and engage in organizational redesign. They create the organizational conditions that allow improvement to be sustainable. They also match their leadership approach to the needs or phase of the organization, and they are able to develop and adjust their leadership practices to align with the growth state of the organization (Day et al., 2009).

In contrast, evidence about ineffective or failing schools places weak leadership at the top of the list of reasons for underperformance. Lack of vision, poor communication, inattention to teaching quality, and failure to make decisions are cited as some of the characteristics of poor or weak leadership in failing schools. As Stoll and Myers (1998) point out, the correlation between poor leadership and ineffective organizational functioning is strong. The business literature similarly highlights how leadership can make or break a company (Collins, 2009). This is less an issue of charisma and personality and more an issue of what leaders actually do—their core practices and the conditions that they create within an organization that can guarantee its success or seal its fate.

A Perfect Storm with Imperfect Solutions

Many underperforming schools are caught up in a perfect storm with imperfect solutions. Contextual, compositional, cyclical, contingent, and conditional factors all work against them at the same time. One set of influences—for example, being located in a deprived area and having largely low-income students; or having experienced a sequence of failed, externally imposed initiatives; or having weak leadership—would be bad enough, but the aggregate effect of these influences renders many schools unable to cope. While improvement is desirable, these factors in combination make it almost impossible to improve. For every failing school, the mix is different. It varies according to context, and it is this variation that renders so many solutions to the problem of failing schools faulty, naive, and imperfect. Treating all failing schools the same is the cardinal error. So many imperfect solutions discount context and ignore the perfect storm of influences, choosing instead to offer standardized undifferentiated approaches to improvement that make little, if any, difference.

Although schools in high-poverty contexts tend to share certain socioeconomic characteristics and face similar external challenges, this is where the similarity ends. As Hargreaves (2004) notes, these "schools are not all alike and the reasons for their underperformance vary greatly" (p. 30). Unlike "effective" or "improving" schools, which research shows consistently share the same characteristics, the sheer range of complex variables affecting failing schools means that they are very different from one another. Despite sharing similar sets of socioeconomic characteristics or facing similar sets of external challenges, these schools are far from homogeneous. For example, in a study of nineteen first-year U.S. turnaround schools, Duke, Tucker, Salmonowicz, and Levy (2007) found evidence of some fifteen conditions associated with low performance, including lack of clear focus, unaligned curricula, inadequate facilities, and ineffective instructional interventions. Consequently, such schools require highly differentiated approaches to improvement that recognize the many types of failing schools (Chapman & Harris, 2004).

Work on the differentiation of schools and improvement strategies undertaken by Hopkins, Harris, and Jackson (1997) suggested that improvement approaches were needed that matched the growth state of the school. However, within the categorization Hopkins offered, failing or ineffective schools were not highly differentiated. Subsequent research has produced typologies of "failing" schools. For example, Stoll and Fink (1996) identified sinking and struggling schools within their category of ineffective schools, while Chapman and Harris (2004) talk about immobile schools in their typology of schools in difficulty. Hopkins (2007) has recently extended his work on this topic to suggest three types of "failing" schools: underperforming, low attaining, and failing. Although these categories or types of schools are acknowledged to be relatively crude, without some way of diagnosing a school's growth state it is almost impossible to select appropriate improvement strategies that fit the developmental needs of the school.

Conclusion

If we are serious about improving failing schools, we should pay more attention to the causes of their failure in the first place, as well as the factors that contribute to their continuing failure.

Because failure has many causes, successful turnaround strategies need to be suitably differentiated. Accurate diagnoses of the reasons for failure therefore are fundamental starting points for constructing potentially useful interventions. Much of this initial diagnostic work is leaders' work. Through contextually sensitive enactments of the well-documented successful leadership practices described in Chapters Four, Five, Six, Seven, and Eight, schools can engage in improvement efforts that are most appropriate to their needs and are most likely to have the biggest impact on their long term performance.

Key Points

- Poverty and diversity create challenges for individual student learning that many schools are ill equipped to address.

- The negative effects of poverty and diversity on student learning are greatly magnified in schools with homogeneous populations.

- Underperforming schools often lack the capacities needed to sustain initial gains made with considerable external assistance.

- Identifying schools as "failing" is highly contingent on a surprisingly large number of circumstances.

- Weak leadership is a major cause of school decline.

- School failure is rarely caused by only one factor; it is more often a perfect storm with imperfect solutions.

2

THE THREE STAGES OF SCHOOL TURNAROUND

We didn't want this program. We weren't asked whether we wanted this program. We were told, "You are now a turnaround school," because our [provincial achievement] scores were horrendous, so we got chosen. At our first meeting with the diagnostician, we were all saying, "These kids can't learn all that. These kids can't do this, because they don't have breakfast in the morning, because half of them don't have moms and dads, because they don't go anywhere. How can we talk about an ocean when they haven't seen an ocean?" We all had a negative attitude that this isn't going to work. We were being imposed on and we thought we were great teachers.

We had to change—completely change—that mind-set, and say, "You know what? They don't have the experiences that we have, so it's up to us to give them those experiences." After we realized we're stuck with the turnaround program, it's not going away, we hopped onboard and it makes us excited. That's what has made the biggest change. I am a 120 percent better teacher now than I was two years ago, because this isn't just about more resources. We were taught what to do with these the resources.

Now something's happening. [The school's provincial test scores] are up. This school used to be pitied before; now it's making a name for itself. Teachers didn't want to be here. Now teachers are interested in coming here because of the turnaround program and the resources here. We used to go and visit other turnaround schools; now a lot of schools and principals are coming to this school to see what's happening, and learn. This

school is already in the place other schools have to get to. We
are not to be pitied anymore.

Ontario elementary teacher

This chapter examines the idea of turnaround stages as conceptualized in both the corporate turnaround literature and in
schools. We look briefly at different theories of turnaround
in the private and public sector literature and consider how
far they assist our understanding of school turnaround. We
outline how using stages offers considerable leverage for both
understanding and acting on poor school performance with
respect to student learning and identify the most frequently
proposed and used conceptions of stages in turning around an
organization.

Much of the research on private sector turnaround (Burbank,
2005) portrays the turnaround process as encompassing a
minimum of three stages: a declining performance stage, an
early turnaround or crisis stabilization stage, and a late
turnaround or sustaining and improving performance stage.
These stages, some evidence suggests, may be less distinct
in public sector turnaround cases (Paton & Mordaunt,
2004). Although more broadly focused, organizational life
cycle theory and evidence (Hanks, 1990) provides support
for a staged view of turnaround processes, situating turnaround
stages within a much longer process; it begins with organizational birth and extends nondeterministically (Miller &
Friesen, 1984) through stages of early survival, success and
maturity, renewal, and decline (Lester, Parnell, & Carraher,
2003).

Our Ontario study adopted a three-stage conception of turnaround, a unique adaptation of other stage theories described in
the literature and the one used throughout this book:

Stage 1: Stopping the decline and creating conditions for
early improvement

Stage 2: Ensuring survival and realizing early performance improvements

Stage 3: Achieving satisfactory performance and aspiring to much more

The main features of each of these stages are outlined in this chapter, along with a brief synopsis of what we know from previous research in schools (primarily in the United States) and other organizations about productive approaches to each stage. We summarize how schools in our Ontario turnaround study and several studies in England approached each of these stages. Because leadership inevitably lurks within these approaches, we learn some important lessons about it in this chapter, although subsequent chapters drill much deeper. These lessons are typically inferences from our evidence when the potential influence of leadership is extended through the use of relevant theories and evidence from other studies.

One of the interview questions used in our study aimed to elicit information about how the eight successful case study schools in the qualitative portion of that study were progressing through the three turnaround stages. We asked teachers and administrators: "Over the past three or four years, has the school's approach to improvement changed in any way?" Their responses to this question, as well as the others in the interview protocol, revealed stage-specific themes (conditions, attitudes, beliefs, and the like) across all schools, as well as themes distinctly associated with elementary or secondary schools.

Based on what teachers and administrators told us, all schools had implemented a sequence of changes over the past few years, resulting in improved student achievement on provincial tests, but they were largely still engaged in the second stage, ensuring survival and realizing early performance improvements. Many respondents also described conditions in their schools during the first stage in which student performance was declining. However, few people had begun to think about what the next steps would be, or what the next stage (achieving satisfactory performance and aspiring to much more) would look like in their schools. Evidence suggests that the reason for this impasse is that schools have a partial model of change that concentrates on early successes rather than sustainable improvement (Harris, James, Harris, & Gunraj, 2006). Chapter Nine delves into this third turnaround stage.

Stage 1: Stopping the Decline and Creating Conditions for Early Improvement

The first light bulb moment was in the first year that had to do with the data from the Educational Quality and Accountability Office (EQAO) provincial achievement tests for both the junior and primary showing us there's a double-edged sword here. The positive side was that we had been succeeding at EQAO in some areas over the previous two or three years. Obviously to be chosen as a turnaround school, you have to be less than successful, so we felt it's not all bad; we weren't too bad. But the flip side, the double-edged sword, was that we were doing terribly in some areas. What we had been doing well at were very low-level things in the taxonomy of the thinking scale like punctuation and very explicit comprehension questions and answers. We realized we're very good at that because teachers felt confident and they felt supported, and the resources supported that. The EQAO results allowed us to look at where we did not do well, and it's probably not a surprise that they were in the higher-order thinking skills. We realized that we don't feel confident in teaching those. We don't feel supported in teaching those. That really was a good way to start building capacity among staff. We had smaller light bulbs throughout, but nothing like the first one.—Elementary principal

This first stage is not literally about turning around. Rather, it is about bringing a halt to decline in student performance and creating some of the conditions needed to improve the learning of students as they go forward. In his latest book, Collins (2009) underlines the importance of stopping the downward spiral of performance and securing quick wins, an indicator of recovery.

Evidence from private sector research (Slatter, Lovett, & Barlow, 2006) associates declining performance with, for example, one or more sources of failure, which reduce the resources available for change and the openness of key actors to the enactments of change (the Introduction provided a detailed account of these sources of failure in schools). As the situation deteriorates, various vicious cycles take hold, including loss of key staff, eruptions of internal conflict, and increasingly rigid behavior, all of which accentuate the problems, suggesting that any change and renewal processes have to be multidimensional. Also at this point, denial of the situation can set in, and retrenchment is a position adopted in the face of threat (Harris, 2009). It is useful to understand this situation as the first stage in a conception of turnaround stages because it is the focus of the turnaround leader's initial situational analysis (Murphy & Meyers, 2008).

In addition to demonstrating low levels of student performance and lack of annual progress, schools that are potential candidates for turnaround often experience frequent leadership turnover, poor staff morale, staff divisiveness, and low levels of staff collaboration (O'Day & Bitter, 2003), each a potentially useful focus for intervention. This initial stage of turnaround often includes the appointment of a new leader or, in many current school contexts—as was the case in our Ontario study and is certainly the case in England with its program of executive principals—the assignment of external personnel to the school, along with the provision of professional development and school improvement planning resources (Holdzkom, 2001). (Executive principals are brought into schools in difficulty to provide leadership. This role is above the role of the principal and takes ultimate responsibility.)

Evidence from the Ontario Study

In Ontario, the provincial Ministry of Education created the Turnaround Teams Project, an expert assistance approach to school turnaround, which Murphy and Meyers (2008) found often to be productive. The teams were to work with elementary schools that volunteered to be assisted. Typically these were schools in which only a third or fewer students were meeting the province's proficiency standard for literacy (Pervin, 2005).[1] In order to be selected for our study from this large group of schools, student achievement had to have started at a level significantly below the average for its district as well as the province, and after three years increased to the point of being significantly better than the district and provincial averages.

Evidence from this study suggested conditions and approaches to the first turnaround stage that were common across successful elementary and secondary schools, as well as conditions and approaches unique to each group of schools. These stages are largely reinforced in the literature on school turnaround and endorsed by experiences of improving schools in difficulty in the United States, England, and Australia.

Common Conditions. Teachers in both elementary and secondary schools recalled the anxiety of being in a school with publicly declining provincial test scores. As one teacher said, everyone thinks "you're the worst school in the district." Both groups of respondents also spoke about concerns prompted by declining enrollments and the threat that their schools might be closed. In the competition for students, the school's provincial test scores and its reputation were among the factors that could sway parents' and students' choices. This was an especially critical matter for those in small schools. As one secondary teacher explained to us, "Parents are concerned about academic standards. We always fight because we're small. . . . The ministry [of Education] wants big schools . . . and the rumor never goes away that they're going to shut you down." This reflects the feelings of many teachers in schools in England who find themselves in special measures and also teachers in the United States where No Child Left Behind has propelled certain schools toward closure or reconstitution.

Elementary and secondary teachers also recalled that collaborations among staff during the time that student achievement was declining were mostly "short term and task oriented" rather than focused on schoolwide goals. "Before we got the ministry expectations," explained one elementary teacher, "teachers used to work together, but it wasn't for the common good of all students in the school. It wasn't for the same goal."

During this first stage, some respondents claimed that information about the format, administration, and scoring of provincial tests was often unavailable, and even when it was available, it was typically underused. Noted one secondary teacher, "You knew there was this type of question and this type of question, but you didn't know what they were looking for in the evaluation."

Elementary Schools. In response to our question about changes in the past few years, three of the four elementary schools referred to the arrival of the Ministry of Education's turnaround teams. While the fourth elementary school was not involved with teams, the principal and staff had developed goals, acquired resources, and worked through professional development activities similar to those associated with schools participating in turnaround teams and with similar increases in test scores.

During the first turnaround stage, one elementary teacher told us that in spite of their students' low achievement levels, she and her colleagues had considered themselves to be good teachers. In fact, they were quite shocked to find themselves in the turnaround program: "Why were we chosen for this? How awful are we that we would be chosen for this?" Teachers in the elementary schools, furthermore, had low expectations for their students. One teacher explained: "We were stuck in a mode that our kids weren't getting any better. We thought we were trying different ways of teaching . . . [but] . . . the kids just weren't buying into them. So consistently we were at the bottom of the whole region in performance."

Before declining student performance could be stabilized, then, there was a period (usually the first year) when teachers had to work through their discomfort with external intervention. One of our studies in England that was focused on the lowest-performing schools in the country also had to address a range of emotions—anxiety, anger, and resentment—before the real work could commence (Harris, 2006). In the Ontario project, one teacher explained, "We were our own moral support: 'Come on, we can do this! It's not that we're so awful; but it's how can we take it to the next level?'" Staff were not used to consulting with colleagues for help with teaching strategies, noted another teacher: "A lot of the time, teachers are on their own in their classrooms doing their own thing, and sometimes you might feel you don't want to bother someone else with a question, everyone is so busy."

During the first turnaround year, teachers working with turnaround teams found they were being held accountable for taking action by having to report on their efforts and share results with their colleagues: "When you do a book study kind of thing, you have to do it and say what worked, didn't work. There's an expectation that you come [to meetings] prepared to share, and that's forced some people along." Some teachers were clearly uncomfortable with the frequent classroom visits by members of the turnaround teams. "There's this feeling of being watched and being monitored," noted one teacher.

Challenges faced by schools during this stage were not immediately resolved by the literacy-focused interventions of the ministry's turnaround teams, although Duke's (2010) U.S. evidence suggests that poor literacy performance is one of the common issues facing almost all poorly performing schools. Much depended on the configuration of the team, the skill base, and its appreciation of the local context and conditions.

Secondary Schools. Teachers in the Ontario turnaround secondary schools said that their schools had always been focused on students and had "always had a 'Students First' attitude. Our school has always had the philosophy about wanting to serve students, and being open to creative new ideas, but wanting to do it well." For many teachers however, this had not included taking the provincial grade 10 literacy test seriously (this test, which had been administered for about six years at the time of the study, was initially administered in grade 10 but could be retried several times later if not passed the first time). One teacher explained, "At the beginning, the teachers kind of resisted the literacy test. For those of us around for a long time it wasn't something we were used to." But the province's decision to make passing the test a diploma requirement had a significant impact on many teachers' indifference to these test results. "It was here to stay," explained one of our secondary school interviewees, "[so] we needed to work with the kids to improve the scores." This shift in attitude toward the test results seems to have marked the transition to the next turnaround stage.

Lessons About Stopping the Decline and Creating Conditions for Early Improvement

1. Authentically enlisting teachers in stopping the decline in student performance will usually require reductions in teachers' sense of being under threat and at great risk.

Creating the conditions for early improvement essentially necessitates that the basic foundations for improvement are in place (Clarke, 2004). Staffs in both elementary and secondary schools were anxious about their students' performances on provincial tests, especially in light of how publicly available their scores were. Furthermore, some features of those tests remained opaque to them, and this increased their sense of insecurity and uncertainty about how to respond. Public opinion was an especially important issue for smaller schools, since their staffs often felt the threat of imminent closure by districts pursuing a school consolidation agenda in order to save money.

In spite of such insecurity—or more likely because of it—many teachers reported a lack of authentic collaboration with their colleagues on all but the most immediate and short-term tasks. The literature is very clear about the importance of building trust in the initial stages of turnaround, as the Chicago-based evidence reported by Bryk and Schneider (2003) indicates. While rationally counterproductive, this response is predicted by risk-rigidity theory (Staw, Sandelands, & Dutton, 1981), a promising perspective only recently applied to schools. According to this theory, when a group is confronted with a significant threat to its existence, psychological stress reaches dysfunctional levels, and this limits the ability of individuals within the group to think flexibly and innovatively about how they might respond productively to the threat. The outcome of such inflexible thinking is to reduce the flow of information, quality of decisions, and divergent views.

The lesson for leaders facing threat rigidity among their teaching colleagues is to help to reduce their anxiety and uncertainty somehow. Daly's (2009) evidence suggests that this can be done by working hard to build trusting relationships among teachers and between teachers and administrators. Increasing teachers' feelings of empowerment and involving them more in decision making are the most promising avenues for building trust.

2. Stopping the declining performance of many schools, especially secondary schools, often requires external intervention.

Sustainable improvement rarely happens without external intervention. Turnaround processes in Ontario secondary schools, for example, were prompted in large measure by a testing program imposed from outside the school by provincial leadership. This stimulus combines two influences often considered anathema by teachers: standardized or standards-based tests and external imposition. Our evidence suggests that few other stimuli would have been as successful in stopping declining performance and initiating the improvement processes. Certainly the school reform literature has long bemoaned the lack of success of most other strategies that have been used to bring about significant change in secondary schools.

3. One of the most powerful conditions for realizing initial improvement will be the deprivatization of teachers' instructional practices. But successful deprivatization usually depends on the development or recovery of trusting relations among teachers and between teachers and administrators.

The most challenging feature of the early turnaround process for elementary teachers was what Louis, Marks, and Kruse (1996) and others have referred to as the deprivatization of practice. Used to working in the famously isolated cultures of elementary schools, teachers participating in the deprivatization process felt much more vulnerable to other adults within and external to their schools than ever before. Such vulnerability is likely to be functional in environments suffused with trust, but highly threatening to those who are uncertain about how much their colleagues can be trusted to be supportive and helpful rather than critical and competitive. This is further endorsement for the importance of a trust-building agenda for leaders in the early stages of school turnaround.

Stage 2: Ensuring Survival and Realizing Early Performance Improvements

Ensuring survival, a challenge at this second turnaround stage, has always been important to private sector organizations. But recent educational accountability policies now mean that schools in many educational jurisdictions can be put out of business, or at least be placed in receivership, if they do not shape up. In England, schools have been closed or reconstituted as academies (an effort to elevate their reputation) or placed into federations where other schools assist the process of raising standards.

Substages of planning and implementation have been observed in schools (Kowal & Hassel, 2005). For key actors, this stage is characterized by intensity, stress, excitement, and excessive work-load (Burbank, 2005). The diagnosis resulting from situation analyses (Burbank, 2005) undertaken in stage 1 must be used to formulate (at least) a short-term but dramatic improvement plan. Leaders at the beginning of this stage, private sector evidence suggests, often behave quite autocratically, aiming to control most significant decisions. However, the best turnaround leaders gradually move toward much greater delegation and staff involvement (Slatter, Lovett, & Barlow, 2006) so that ownership in the renewed organization begins to develop, and the existing expertise of the organization is put to greater use. This gradual involvement of staff, as much as anything else, stimulates initial performance improvements.

Evidence from the Ontario Study

Common Conditions and Approaches. A key shift in teachers' attitudes marked the beginning of this second stage. This was achieved by a series of quick wins about a year after the Ministry of Education's turnaround interventions began, a strategy endorsed in other studies (Rhim, 2007) because it provides a sense of moving forward. Teachers were now convinced that what they were being asked to do was in their students' best interests. "We've got everybody onboard more in the last two years," noted a secondary teacher. As a result of this shift in attitude and the practices it fostered, both staff and the wider community began to be aware of improvements in students' provincial test results. This small success helped allay some of the apprehension felt about school closure in the smaller schools: "When you see increases in the level of achievement on [the grade 10 literacy test], it becomes a public message—this school is on the rise." Another teacher observed, "One year we had a huge jump in the pass rate, and that was a good selling feature for the school with the competition with other schools around us. That was something we could brag about to the parents of grade 8 students who might be coming here."

The quantity and quality of professional development had improved noticeably by this stage in the process, as one secondary principal explained: "I give credit to [the principals at the local school board]. In the past three years, we've worked on some strategies to create capacity for leadership and learning. This board has really put a great deal of effort and supported us as a school to develop a PLC [professional learning community]." Teachers, generally agreeing with this assessment, spoke about experiencing a satisfying increase in their own expertise as a result of participating in more powerful professional development. Said one elementary teacher, "I am enjoying my teaching so much more because I see how you can. I'm starting over. When I see someone retiring, I feel sorry for them. No one seems to be on the defensive like we were before. We don't want to leave at 3:30." Another claimed, "Attitudes have changed because they've [teachers] gotten the in-service they need and they're more confident."

By this point in the turnaround process, the provincial testing agency, EQAO, had also expanded the amount and accessibility of resources and practice tests, as well as detailed explanations of grading criteria, test questions, and test results. The teachers considered this information quite helpful for their efforts. In the words of one secondary teacher: "We've had more feedback from EQAO about what the questions are like. We can see the questions kids aren't doing well on, and we've been better able to prepare them." At least partly because of the increased usefulness of provincial test data, districts and schools began to place much more emphasis on data-based decision making to meet individual students' instructional needs. "One big change is working with data to make decisions. We review EQAO data and report card data," explained one elementary teacher.

Elementary Schools. When describing the changes in approach to improvement over the previous three or four years, the descriptor many of our elementary respondents used was "increased focus" on literacy-related goals and initiatives: "I think this has helped us focus on exactly what we need to do. How we can improve student learning . . . and we're all on the same page." Structured collaborations among teachers to get this job done, often through the establishment of PLCs, were considered very helpful by most respondents: "PLC is a new initiative in our board—a time to get together, not to chat, but to focus and look at where weaknesses are, then together decide what strategies they're going to try and then have that professional dialogue about how that's going to happen." Duke's (2010) U.S. evidence also argues for knowing what to focus on as a key issue for leaders at this stage.

New resources, including instructional materials for students and teachers, were considered a great improvement over what had been available previously. According to this teacher, "The funding has really helped. The resources are generous, so we aren't so worried about losing a book; we're more worried about losing a child through illiteracy."

Accountability for implementing instructional strategies was new to most teachers: "Our principal makes sure that we are actually using the strategies: 'What works? Can we meet in a few weeks?'" Having the process of change divided into steps was motivating for teachers as well: "When turnaround began, we saw it was going to be a lot of work, and it seemed a bit challenging. Now we see it has been broken down into manageable bits."

Although the ministry's Turnaround Teams Project targeted the primary division grades (K–3), it had benefits for the rest of the school as well. One primary teacher pointed to "spin-offs for junior and intermediate teachers. We help them use the [literacy instruction] materials." Almost all the respondents spoke of positive results from the recent changes. However, one of the downsides of success, the frequent visitors in the school to witness and learn from the success of Turnaround Teams Project, meant that whenever strangers came into classrooms, students were distracted from paying attention to their teachers.

Secondary Schools. Teachers and administrators in secondary schools agreed with their elementary counterparts regarding the increased focus they had noticed in the past three or four years, especially the focus on schoolwide cross-curricular involvement in literacy instruction (primarily reading and writing) and test preparation: "Literacy is a priority in every area. All Department Heads are developing it in their area. Program heads are receiving PD [professional development]." Another important change was the intensification of specific, strategically timed test preparation efforts: "We have a week that's dedicated to literacy for grades 9 and 10. We are focusing in on the testing in terms of preparation . . . so students, when they sit down to do the test, don't have to figure out what the test is asking, as well as demonstrating the skills of reading and writing."

Students with special needs and those considered to be at risk had been targeted with additional programs and accommodations: "A big change has also been through the way the test is administered to the special needs students. We're really, as a staff, trying to reach out for those kids who may not make it through."

Lessons About Ensuring Survival and Realizing Early Performance Improvements

4. *Increases in teachers' individual and collective efficacy or confidence about their ability to improve student learning is a key driver for realizing early improvements in students' performance.*

Across both elementary and secondary schools, our evidence suggests that the uncertainty and initial rigidity of teachers' responses to perceived threats were replaced with feelings of increased self- and collective efficacy or confidence. These were feelings of efficacy about responding to the challenges of significantly improving the achievement of their students. Such efficacy building was a deliberate part of the combined provincial and district commitment to provide the support these schools and their teachers would need to get the job done. This support consisted of restructuring school schedules to allow time for teachers to work together, a dramatic increase in the quality of professional development experienced by teachers (a view the teachers shared), and evidence that new practices resulted in improved student test scores.

The unchallenged guru of efficacy theory, Albert Bandura (1997), points to four sources of teacher efficacy, three of which were an influence on teachers' experiences by this point in the turnaround process. Teachers' *mastery experiences* were enhanced through substantial increases in the quality of professional development provided to teachers. Professional learning communities and the deprivatization of practice also enhanced the chances of teachers' receiving encouragement, or *verbal persuasion*, to try new practices from their colleagues and members of the turnaround teams. Deprivatization of practice also offered chances for teachers to *vicariously experience* the teaching strategies their colleagues believed had been successful.

5. Professional development for teachers at this stage should aim to improve teacher efficacy as much as to improve actual teacher capacity.

There is no denying the importance of focusing professional development directly on improving or refining teachers' instructional practices. This is especially crucial in the early stages of school turnarounds in which situational analysis suggests that one of the main causes of declining student performance is a failure by significant numbers of teachers, for example, to adapt instruction to changing student populations or changing curricular expectations.

In the long term, however, it is unrealistic to expect teachers to be provided with professional development built for whatever instructional challenges they might be facing. In addition, evidence points to the limitations of externally prescribed professional development interventions to secure long-term improvement (Timperley, 2005). More realistically, a school's continuous improvement depends on the persistent instructional problem solving of its teachers. Efficacy leads to such persistence; it fosters an attitude of being able to figure out what to do when one's existing capacities are not up to the job. So creating conditions that foster teachers' professional efficacy empowers teachers, both individually and collectively, to look after their own continuous professional learning. Building internal accountability is a much more powerful lever on organizational performance than any externally imposed accountability system (Elmore, 1999).

Stage 3: Achieving Satisfactory Performance and Aspiring to Much More

This third turnaround stage is a return to a "new normalcy" and entails reaching and sustaining, if not surpassing, satisfactory levels of performance. Organizational conditions that exist at this stage no longer reflect the actions that led to the original decline.

Conditions in high-performing schools have been studied extensively, beginning with the effective schools research movement in the early 1970s, which is still thriving (Reynolds, 1998), and, more recently, research about the nature of high-performing, high-poverty schools (Kannapel & Clements, 2005). According to one recent review of U.S. research, for example, these conditions include a culture of high expectations, a safe and disciplined environment, a principal who is a strong instructional leader, a hard-working and committed staff, and a curriculum that emphasizes basic skills but includes serious attention to higher-order thinking as well (Center for Public Education, 2005).

These conditions provide schools with the capacity to sustain themselves in the face of many unpredictable challenges. But many turnaround schools seem to arrive at the third turnaround stage with few of these conditions firmly in place. This likely accounts for the fragile nature of improved student performance in such schools.

Schools in our study had been involved in turnaround efforts for only two or three years. Although student performance in all of these schools had significantly improved, it was early to be thinking about sustaining that performance or enhancing it much further. Nevertheless, a few people offered comments related to the third turnaround stage. Their remarks largely demonstrate the changes in attitudes and beliefs that had occurred during the turnaround stage and were likely to help schools make the transition to the third stage. These comments demonstrate states of mind or conditions that are likely to foster sustained improvement efforts:

- A willingness to be held responsible for what students learn:

    The days of excuses are over. We really literally did have an attitude of: "What can we do? These are the kids we've got." So that had to be taken right off the table.—Elementary principal

Everything has to be related to student achievement. It's focused instruction. Everything that happens all the time here needs to have a purpose. . . . A little thing, but on inclement days I've asked that movies not be shown unless they're curriculum related.—Elementary principal

- A growing awareness of the long-term nature of the job:

Now we have the mandate of sustainability, which is weighing heavily on my shoulders, because we were able to improve all of our EQAO scores.—Elementary principal

- A new realization about the interdependence of elementary and secondary schools:

We can't discount the progress made at the elementary school. Students are coming much better prepared now than they were four years ago—I think because of the work they're doing at that level. With the extra funding, they've done a tremendous amount of professional development in terms of literacy. —Secondary teacher

- Awareness of the wide array of factors that produce strong student performance in the long run:

One goal is to promote a happy atmosphere because kids need to want to be here. They have a lot of baggage, quite a lot of them. If they don't want to be here, if we don't show them we want them to be here, then what's the point of teaching?—Elementary teacher

We saw increased success in other ways [in addition to improvements in OSSLT (the Ontario Secondary School Literacy Test) scores]. School pride is a big part of what happens. Students start attending more regularly. That's probably our biggest challenge: student attendance and apathy."—Secondary principal

Conclusion

We conceptualized school turnaround as a staged process beginning with stopping the decline and creating conditions for early improvement, followed by ensuring survival and realizing early performance improvements, and then achieving satisfactory performance and aspiring to much more. Evidence from our study of eight successful Ontario turnaround schools revealed most about the second of these stages, the stage in which most schools found themselves at the point of our data collection. Many interviewees, however, could easily recall key conditions that had prevailed in their schools when student performance was still declining, and they were quite clear about what ended such decline and began the improvement of student performance. Much less information was provided about the third stage, largely because schools were just approaching it and had little direct experience to share at that time. Chapter Nine fills in the picture of this stage more fully.

Across both elementary and secondary schools, the first stage in our sample of schools was characterized by teachers' feelings of helplessness, their denial of responsibility for the learning of all students, and their resistance to external intervention. They perceived themselves to be under siege. School staff who were generally aware of the relatively poor performance of their students on provincial tests nonetheless did not see their own efforts as likely to make much difference. Rather, they cited as explanation the conditions that many students experienced in their family and community environments, along with limited learning potential. In such schools, a siege mentality that locates blame everywhere else but the school can dominate.

Based on such an explanatory framework, it was difficult for school staffs to accept overall responsibility for turning around their students' poor performance. This contributed to an attitude that provincial efforts were largely irrelevant or not to be taken especially seriously. With a view of their own expertise unrelated to the performance of many of their students, school staffs at this stage had difficulty seeing much value in complying with external efforts to improve their students' performance.

For elementary schools, the government's commitment to significant improvements in primary language achievement was the key stimulant. Flowing from that commitment was the establishment of the province's Literacy and Numeracy Secretariat (LNS) and the creation of the Turnaround Teams Project. These initiatives together conspired to make it extremely difficult to ignore the need to act on poor student performance. Furthermore, and unlike circumstances faced by low-performing schools in some other contexts (Orr, Byrne-Jimenez, McFarlane, & Brown, 2005), most Ontario district leaders were highly supportive of the Ministry of Education's initiatives and added their support when they felt it would be useful. The quality of professional development and the other work of the turnaround teams were the most significant factors in moving elementary schools from declining performance to crisis stabilization. The turnaround teams in particular expanded enormously the instructional leadership capacity of the schools in which they worked and were widely credited by school staffs with facilitating much of the improvement that occurred in those schools.

For secondary schools, the transition from the first to the second turnaround stage was prompted by the ministry's decision to make passing the grade 10 literacy test a requirement for graduation. This requirement made paying attention to the tests mandatory for teachers and began the process of aligning their efforts with those of the province. Without the intervention from policymakers, the focus and energy directed toward improving the literacy skills of their less successful students demonstrated by staffs in the four secondary schools in this study seems unlikely to have emerged—certainly not in the brief span of several years.

Moving to the stage of beginning to improve student performance, initially prompted by ministry policy initiatives, and also widely supported by districts, was accompanied by important shifts in both attitude and beliefs.

The leadership of formal teacher leaders such as literacy coaches, as well as school administrators, was a key part of the success of these turnaround schools. School-level leaders acted not just as conduits for the influence of the ministry, its turnaround teams, and district staff; they also supported such influence in many ways, ensuring attention to the unique contexts of their schools and often making the efforts of these external resources more meaningful.

Among the many insightful analyses appearing in Malcolm Gladwell's (2008) book *Outliers* is one that accounts for the terrible plane crash record of Korean Airlines over the twenty-year period between 1977 and 1997. Although the story is one of a dramatically different context, what occurred over several years in our sample of successful turnaround schools was very much like the "renorming" that Gladwell describes taking place within Korean Air as it was turned around.

Between 1977 and 1997, Korean Airlines lost eight airplanes. "To put that record into perspective," Gladwell points out, "the 'loss' rate for an airline like the American carrier United Airlines in the period 1988 to 1998 was .27 per million departures which means they lost a plane in an accident about once in every four million flights. The loss rate for Korean Air, in the same period, was 4.79 per million departures— more than *seventeen* times higher" (p. 180). Why such a discrepancy?

Drawing on extensive records accumulated after these crashes and the initiatives that finally turned Korean Air's safety record around, Gladwell traces the sources of the problem to

Korea's culture of deference for authority and age, which was responsible for what linguists refer to as "mitigated language" both in the cockpit and between the flight personnel and air traffic control. Put simply, crew members were reluctant to offer the pilot blunt expressions of what they, often correctly, perceived to be emergency conditions.

Furthermore, and in cases beyond those provided by Korean Air, flight crews from countries with similarly deferential cultures failed to make clear to air traffic controllers unused to such language the critical nature of their situations. In the case of one Colombian airliner attempting to land in New York City, the crew barely mentioned the fact that they were almost out of fuel. This was because they were intimidated by the blunt and aggressive style of the New York air traffic controllers, who, as a consequence, put the airliner in a holding pattern from which it crashed.

Not surprisingly, the primary effort to turn around Korean Air's crash record focused on language. The new approaches to language included not only ensuring that flight crews could speak and understand English, the common language of the airline industry, but also requiring that crews routinely be very clear about their concerns and opinions, regardless of whom they were speaking to. This is what Gladwell refers to as renorming—a situation where culturally determined norms of deference gave way to blunt, straightforward expressions of professional opinion.

In the case of our schools, renorming meant no longer assuming that family background determined a student's success in school. It instead meant that teachers began to view themselves as responsible for students' success, whatever their students' circumstances. And it also meant that teachers began to base judgments about the value of their own teaching practice on the hard evidence of its effects on students' learning.

Key Points

Lessons for Stage 1: Stop the Decline, and Create Conditions for Early Improvement

- Authentically enlisting teachers will require reducing the teachers' sense of being under threat and at great professional risk.

- Stopping the declining performance of many schools, especially secondary schools, often requires external intervention.

- One of the most powerful conditions will be the deprivatization of teachers' instructional practices. But successful deprivatization usually depends on the development or recovery of trusting relations among teachers and between teachers and administrators.

Lessons for Stage 2: Ensure Survival, and Realize Early Performance Improvements

- Increases in teachers' individual and collective efficacy or confidence about their ability to improve student learning is a key driver in this stage.

- Professional development for teachers at this stage should aim to improve teacher efficacy as actual teacher capacity.

Entering Stage 3: Achieve Satisfactory Performance, and Aspire to Much More

- A turnaround leader must foster the following:
  - A willingness to be held responsible for what students learn
  - A growing awareness of the long-term nature of the job
  - A new realization about the interdependence of elementary and secondary schools
  - Awareness of the wide array of factors that produce strong student performance in the long run

3

THE STAGES ILLUSTRATED

A Case Study

Rowlatts Hill Primary School serves a housing development on the eastern side of Leicester in England. The school serves a suburban area that experiences high levels of social and economic disadvantage. The proportion of pupils eligible for free school meals is twice the national average, an indicator of significant disadvantage. Over half of the pupils in the school are from minority ethnic backgrounds, with the largest proportion from families of Indian heritage. Almost half the pupils speak English as an additional language. Many young people who start school are at a very early stage of learning English. The proportion of pupils with learning difficulties or disabilities, or both, is well above the national figure. There is a high level of turbulence among the pupil population, with significant numbers admitted to school at times other than the start of the school year. There is a high mobility of pupils, and the percentage of pupils who join or leave the school each year can have a negative effect on the continuity of their education. One class had a 50 percent change in students over the course of a year.

The academic performance of the school has been highly variable over the past decade. In 2004 it reached national average performance, but in the years that followed, it experienced a significant downturn. By May 2006, inspectors had placed the school in special measures, a category used in England to signal that the school is failing and to highlight the need for urgent improvement. The inspectors noted that levels of pupil attainment were well below national averages and that teaching was inadequate. The inspection report highlighted a litany of problems that the school faced and reinforced that it was severely underperforming. At the time of the inspection, there was widespread underachievement, linked with weaknesses in teaching and ineffective leadership. The legacy of weak teaching meant that standards were low and that the school was adding little value to the young people who came through the school doors.

Eighteen months later, in November 2007, the school was taken out of special measures, and inspectors reinforced that it had made rapid improvement. Performance is once again nearing national norms, and added-value assessment is high. The quality of teaching has strengthened considerably and is now satisfactory overall, with a number of main strengths. Pupils are behaving well and have positive attitudes to learning. Attendance and punctuality have improved significantly. Leadership and management, including governance, have been transformed since the last inspection, and the principal's excellent leadership has galvanized staff and driven the school's development. Leadership responsibilities are sensibly delegated and developed. School development planning engages all staff and is soundly based on accurate self-evaluation. Effective systems are in place to monitor performance and hold staff to account. In summary, the school has been turned around, largely, but not exclusively, because of the efforts of a new principal.

The introduction of special measures led to the resignation of the principal at that time. An interim principal appointed for the next two terms achieved some success and put in place new structures and processes. These helped the school move forward, but it was very clear that his form of leadership was not that of a turnaround leader. The current principal joined the school in April 2007 and has been in place almost two years. Her leadership has been the prime driving force for change and improvement at the school. She reflects:

> I joined April 07, and the school had been in [special] measures two terms and they had an interim principal teacher here. Standards were an issue—poor morale and a huge culture of complaints. Parents just didn't come in. If they came in, it was extremely aggressive. The children used to hit the previous principal teacher; we had knives on the premises. Our community is a very mixed community where we have a lot of deprivation; we've got the drugs, prostitution, and violence, so we have set up a nurture provision—a learning mentor who meets and greets certain children. We had to change the culture of the school from within.

The previous situation was described by staff as "having a black cloud over the place." Neither children nor staff felt safe, and physical attacks on staff by pupils were part of life in the school. The school was volatile, and many staff were absent because of sickness. This meant that on a daily basis, there was a constant flow of substitute teachers in the school, which fueled the instability further. The school was in crisis and free fall. It needed a leader and leadership to halt the decline and turn around its fortunes.

The current principal recognized the need to "get hold of the school" and immediately began the task of stopping the decline and putting in place the foundations for improvement to occur.

Stage 1: Stopping the Decline and Creating Conditions for Early Improvement

Initially there was widespread discomfort and disillusionment among staff because of the "special measures" label. When the notice of special measures was announced, staff morale had been low, with individual self-esteem eroded by criticism of the school. The media had been quick to highlight the school's failures and shortcomings with little concern for the negative impact of such attention on staff, pupils, and the community. Staff resented the label of "special measures" and were strongly resistant to the idea that the school was failing. Some staff viewed socioeconomic factors, not the school itself, as the main problem. Undoubtedly there was, and still is, some truth in this association, as it is more difficult to perform well in contexts of challenge and deprivation.

The principal quickly recognized the danger that such negative emotion could undermine change efforts, so she established regular meetings with all staff to talk through the issues, concerns, and responses to the proposed changes. This regular communication and consistency about the way forward was the first step in halting the decline and overcoming the initial feelings of disquiet and discomfort. Greater self-belief emerged from the conversations, and staff felt more confident about the future. A literacy coordinator said, "We were unsure at the start that there was any option other than to close, but through talking to each other, rehearsing other possibilities, we realized that we were actually in control."

Another step in halting the decline was a very visible one. The physical condition of the school was initially poor, with leaking classrooms, broken windows, graffiti-covered furniture, and littered corridors. Consequently one of the first actions the new principal took was to improve the immediate environment in which students and staff worked. She allocated resources to painting and repair work, new furniture, a new reception area, display boards, and refurbishment of the staff room. Emphasis was placed on litter removal, and students were given the task of eradicating graffiti. This had a symbolic purpose as well as a real one: it demonstrated to staff, students, and parents that the school was changing and improving.

THE STAGES ILLUSTRATED   71

The school also introduced a uniform for children, and once again this was a visible signal of improvement, as it generated a newfound respect for the school:

> They now have pride in the school; before, they just used to turn up in everything, anything. And it's the same with teachers; we have a dress code now. So we all take more pride in the school and ourselves. Everybody looks the same, which is nice. There's not so much bullying now as there was before, as everyone is dressed the same way; no one has designer clothes or anything that others would be resentful about.—Foundation year teacher

Behavior at the school had been very poor. There had been little respect for teachers, and classrooms were often violent and volatile. Exclusion rates were very high, and the culture had been control based—premised on punishment or removal from the school as a last resort. The new principal immediately introduced a zero tolerance policy for behavior, which has proved to be a major factor in halting the decline. This behavior policy is based on a rewards system with the idea of "golden time," defined as time for other activities chosen by the pupils, such as sports, use of electronic technology, creative design, and the like, earned through positive classroom behavior in curriculum subjects. Pupils are now rewarded for good behavior, and punishments have been removed. This behavior policy has substantially reduced the time pupils engage in poor behavior and has allowed a greater focus on teaching and learning, as these comments show:

> There's always been a behavior policy, but there's been more continuity with the new behavior policy. Everybody, you know, is following the same song sheet. That's proved to be very effective.—Teaching assistant

Behavior, I would say, is now particularly good. Children are being much more motivated than they were before. It feels a very different school.—Literacy coordinator

Behavior in this school was a major issue before, and it was almost as if there was a culture of, What do you expect in these children? And that's an appalling way to think, that is, because they live in an area of social deprivation they either don't deserve to behave properly or just don't know how to behave properly. You know, it's really hard to put it into words what has made a difference, but it's that change in expectations of behavior.—Foundation stage teacher

Setting clear expectations around behavior, creating a vision, and sharing this vision with others caused the decline to halt, and the possibility for improvement was significantly enhanced. The principal established a more positive climate for learning within the school by "talking up" the school, setting clear expectations (on such matters as behavior, truancy, and attendance), and encouraging respect for others. She imparted a sense of urgency for maintaining high academic standards and exerted pressure on staff and students to excel. The considerable emphasis placed on raising the expectations of staff and pupils about behavior and achievement was a turning point for the school. Initially, raising the expectations of staff performance meant holding staff to account by putting in place clear monitoring and observation processes. Initially this met with resistance and suspicion, but now staff see this as part of their professional obligation and a way of sharing ideas about teaching and learning.

The principal seized on every opportunity to remind pupils and staff that high achievement was a shared expectation. Emphasis was placed on reward and recognizing achievement, along with encouraging pupils to view the school as a place where they could succeed and that success was a possibility. Through after-school clubs, learning mentors, and incentives such as trips, prizes, and badges, pupils were encouraged to view learning as an entitlement and that enjoying learning was an acceptable thing to do.

Within the school, the conditions for improvement arose from a new climate of trust, openness, and honesty. There was more collaboration around teaching and learning and a general commitment among staff to work together. This climate had resulted from lengthy discussion, development, and dialogue among those working within and outside the school. It was deliberately orchestrated through the provision of opportunities to build social trust. This included opportunities for dialogue between staff and parents. The principal invested a great deal of time in creating opportunities for more positive working relationships to be developed. She secured the services of a consultant to work with her to offer more support, guidance, and advice as the school began the turnaround process.

Staff now had more opportunities to work together both across and within teams. Social events were organized, and staff development activities included the expertise and involvement of those within the school. For pupils, staff-student committees were set up, student councils were established, lunchtime and after-hour clubs were put in place, and trips were organized. For parents, there were evening classes and drop-in sessions. Parents' evenings also included a social component, and more opportunities were created to give parents positive feedback and invite them into the school. An emphasis was placed on breaking down social barriers and creating a climate within school where staff, students, and parents had more opportunities to talk.

Stage 2: Ensuring Survival and Realizing Early Performance Improvements

By the end of 2007, it was evident that the school was starting to move forward. A clear focus on a limited number of goals characterized the next phase, as well as investment in new resources and programs. The positive shift in attitude among staff and students created the real possibility of further improvement. The buy-in from parents also proved to be a major contributor to improvement in this phase of the school's development.

In terms of securing survival and early performance improvements, the principal consistently and vigorously promoted staff development through in-service training, visits to other schools, and peer support. The emphasis she placed on the continuing development of staff was an endorsement that they were the school's most important asset and that, particularly in difficult times, it was important to maintain their own sense of self-worth by valuing them. The principal was highly skilled at using a combination of pressure and support to promote the efforts of teachers, particularly when they were working with the most difficult students. She encouraged teachers to take risks and rewarded innovative thinking. As a result, staff showed increased confidence to try new things, such as philosophy for children or new information and communication technologies packages.

The principal set high standards for teaching and teacher performance and consistently reinforced the focus and emphasis on improving teaching and learning. Time was provided for teachers to meet to discuss teaching approaches, and they began to observe each other's teaching. In addition, teaching performance was monitored and individual assessments made. Poor teaching was not ignored or tolerated. Where it did exist, it was challenged, and strategies were agreed for improvement. Where this did not occur, the principal took the necessary steps to deal with the problem. In the majority of cases, a combination of support, monitoring, and an individual development program addressed the problem of poor-quality teaching. For the principal, effective leadership was about capacity building in others and investing in the school's social capital.

Since entering special measures and then emerging from it, there has been consistent and relentless attention to improving the quality of teaching and learning, which has been identified as the most important factor in the school's subsequent success and improvement. The focus or refocusing on teaching and learning through, for example, assessment for learning, using information and communication technologies, and integrated learning proved to be a turning point for the school as it provided the impetus for much-needed classroom change and development. Teachers were encouraged to engage in professional development activities with an explicit focus on teaching and learning. Training days were used to explore different teaching and learning issues and to engage teachers in dialogue about teaching. As a result of specific training sessions, many teachers incorporated new learning strategies into their teaching:

> It is clear that teaching has changed dramatically across the school—before the introduction of special measures, it was still a very didactic style of teaching. The foundation stage has been very good since the move to special measures; it had been very formal, very didactic. It is now free flow, with parent involvement. The local authority and Ofsted (the Office for Standards in Education) have praised it, and it is often visited by those wanting to recreate the ideas.—Learning coordinator

For the principal, the school's survival was dependent on building the capacity for improved teaching and learning. She was quick to dispel the cultural deficit notion prevalent in many challenging school contexts and was committed to the belief that every child can learn and succeed. She made decisions that motivated both staff and students and emphasized student achievement and learning. The principal talked about creating the conditions that would lead to higher student performance, and she was deeply concerned about the welfare and the educational experiences of minority children. The deputy principal said:

> When we went into special measures, teaching was very controlled—worksheets, didactic-type teaching, very controlled. Children weren't allowed to talk. We've done a lot of question time, philosophy for children, and given them the

opportunity to think about their learning. They are expected to do more talking than the teachers. That's the setup. That's good teaching in my eyes.

The principal set high expectations for students, emphasized consistency in teaching practices, provided clear rules about behavior, and stressed discipline. The developmental focus was on improving the quality of teaching and learning. The principal was a powerful instructional leader because of her emphasis on student attainment and achievement. She created learning opportunities for both students and teachers. She focused strategic attention on the classroom and engaged staff in dialogue about teaching and learning issues, as well as issues of behavior or classroom management. The principal was able to make clear links between the core values of the school and the vision for improved student achievement and learning.

Stage 3: Achieving Satisfactory Performance and Aspiring to Much More

A distinctive feature of schools that are improving is how far they work as a professional learning community. Schools in challenging contexts that are improving usually have a climate of collaboration and a commitment among staff to work together. However, this climate can be created only by lengthy discussion, development, and dialogue among those working within and outside the school. It has to be orchestrated and nurtured through opportunities to build social trust. This includes providing opportunities for dialogue between staff and parents. At Rowlatts, the principal emphasized the need to establish an "interconnectedness of home, school and community." This also meant adopting a multiagency approach to supporting and understanding the wider needs of the community. The implication here is that the school cannot operate in isolation from other agencies or the community it serves.

Research has reinforced the importance of school leaders' connecting with the community and of hearing and taking account of parent and student voices (Chrispeels, Castillo, & Brown, 2000). The principal and teachers at Rowlatts were acutely aware of the need to engage with their community. They visited homes, attended community events, communicated regularly with the parents about successes, and engendered trust by showing genuine caring for young people. They understood the forces within the community that impeded learning, were aware of the negative forces of the subcultures, and listened to parents' views and opinions regularly. The principals tried to create integral relationships with the families in the communities they served. They recognized that "family, school, and community relationships directly affected student outcomes"; hence, the need to connect with the community was of paramount importance to the success of the school.

While staff at Rowlatts do not embrace the prevailing socioeconomic conditions as an excuse for underperformance, they, like other schools facing challenging circumstances, recognize that the disadvantage their pupils face inevitably affect their subsequent aspirations and attainment. They also know that changes in the external environment influence the school's performance both positively or negatively. In short, community can and does affect the school's potential to raise pupil performance and attainment. Therefore, the school has made deliberate and concerted efforts to regain the confidence of parents and improve the reputation of the school in the local community. The principal has been instrumental in engaging with the community: "I have won many families round, and I have worked hard to engage parents in the school. When I started, for the first two terms particularly, parents did not communicate with me; nobody spoke. They wouldn't say good morning to you. Now it's very different."

Although there are no quick fixes for improving schools that face challenging circumstances (Stoll & Myers, 1998), the evidence from Rowlatts suggests that engaging the community is the key to long-term, sustainable improvement.

"Rowlatts had a very bad reputation," noted the deputy principal. "I'd heard about the school even before it had gone into measures. I'd heard about the negativity of the estate [the housing development]. So it's nice now, two years on, to hear good things about it and get good feedback. Last year 93 percent of parents attended Parents' Evening. That's a huge success."

Parents are now engaged with the school; they are supportive and interested in their child's learning. The reputation of the school has improved, its results are steadily rising, and both parents and pupils see the school as part of the solution and not just part of the problem.

Leadership at Rowlatts

The main driver for change at Rowlatts has undoubtedly been the principal. Staff noted that previous principals were "nice people" but did not provide enough leadership. From the outset, the current principal sought to develop a culture of shared understanding, shared responsibility, and shared accountability among all staff at the school. She believed that everyone in the school was a potential leader, and she was committed to distributing leadership widely. There was a recognition that the scale of the improvement task could not be undertaken by the senior leadership team alone, and therefore one of the stated strategic intents was to build leadership depth throughout the school.

For many staff in the school, the new approach to leadership involved a considerable leap of faith. The previous principals had restricted decision making mainly to themselves. Now an extended senior leadership team, plus year (or grade) teams, are all involved in decision making. The principal has invested time and a great deal of support in establishing effective team working among staff. Gradually individuals have taken on more responsibility at the school, and the constant drive for consistency of teaching and learning is having an impact on performance. Teaching assistants are fully involved in supporting the decision-making process, and team spirit at the school is strong:

> We've got a very, very committed principal teacher who has developed her leadership team to feel that . . . they're involved, and then the leadership team are empowering the rest of the staff. We've got a fearless principal teacher, I feel, who believes passionately that these children deserve the best.—Foundation stage coordinator

The principal is very good at developing and maintaining relationships. She is considered fair and is seen as having a genuine joy and vibrancy when talking to students. She generates a high level of commitment in others through her openness, honesty, and the quality of her interpersonal relationships. She has placed a particular emphasis on generating positive relationships with parents and fostering a view of the school as being part of rather than apart from the community. She has put in place the key conditions for the school to survive and thrive: high-quality professional development, new resources and programs, genuine collaboration among staff, and a relentless focus on teaching and learning. The principal is clear that the school can achieve much more.

Looking back on the experience of turnaround, the principal would advise other principals in a turnaround situation first to develop a good team to take developmental work forward and then to have the courage to know that the principal may not always be the best person to lead an initiative. She continues:

> You appoint people or create a team where in a sense, you are an entity and entirety as a team because you all have skills and strengths, and as a principal you have to play to those. At the same time, you have to know when there are people on the team who can do things better that you. But you also know that there

are times when you have to step back, even when you know you would do it differently, and let them do it the way that they want to do it. It's about having courage and humility. I also think you have to have a sense of humor, especially when things go wrong! Finally, you've got to believe in the worth and the value of what you're doing, even on the darkest days.

In summary, the school's turnaround has been orchestrated by a highly effective principal. She and her staff have shown considerable skill and tenacity in addressing the areas for improvement and have also led developments across a wide front. Resources have been used judiciously to transform the school. Classrooms, public areas, and outside spaces have been radically overhauled to create a welcoming and stimulating environment for pupils to learn, and they reflect the school's new vibrancy.

The principal has a clear vision for the school's future and has communicated unequivocally her high expectations to staff, pupils, and parents. She has built a strong team of staff who are committed to improving the outcomes for pupils. All staff feel supported and valued, as well as challenged; morale is good. The school has worked to develop supportive partnerships with parents and outside agencies. Links with parents have improved considerably.

"In the past," said one teacher, "the school contacted parents only when there was a problem with a child, and the parents could be very angry and upset; it wasn't very positive. But now the school says to parents, 'We need your cooperation because we want your child to stay at school to catch up with its course work.' This has proved to be very positively received, and parents have been entirely supportive."

The attendance at after-school and vacation teaching sessions is also very good. The school feels that it is moving in the right direction: the children are in uniforms, their behavior is better, and their attendance is better. Every child is now achieving, and the school provides a safe and secure learning environment.

Conclusion

School improvement is a complex undertaking for any school, but for schools in exceptionally disadvantaged areas, it presents extra challenges. In particular, improvement can be exceptionally fragile, and changes do not always last. Increasingly sustainability is seen as critically important to all improvement efforts, and to achieve this, capacity building is central. Duke (2010) argues that "leadership for sustained improvement is all about building school capacity" (p. 86).

What is noticeable about Rowlatts is that it is a story of building capacity through empowering, involving, and developing teachers to deliver high-quality teaching and through providing systems of learning support, guidance, and assistance to ensure learning is maximized. The principal reinforced the importance of teams working with each other. She built flexible open structures that actively supported staff interaction and development.

The overarching message from this school is that while gains in student outcomes are hard fought and sustainable improvement is particularly difficult to achieve in challenging contexts, both are possible. The resilience, sheer capacity for hard work, and tenacity of the principal and her staff under the most challenging circumstances to provide the best learning opportunities for pupils have made all the difference. By reinforcing the message that individuals matter and by investing in the quality of relationships within and outside the school, the principal has generated high levels of commitment, energy, and effort from pupils, staff, and parents. The school has certainly been turned around; more important, it has the capacity to secure much higher performance in the years to come.

Part Two

WHAT TURNAROUND LEADERS DO, AND HOW THEY DO IT

4

HOW TURNAROUND LEADERS CREATE A SHARED SENSE OF DIRECTION IN THEIR SCHOOLS

> One thing that didn't work quite the way
> I thought—because we didn't structure it right—
> was the PLC [professional learning communities]
> model. We kind of jumped in backward, I would
> say, from my perspective. Because later in the
> year, I was looking at some literature saying we
> should look at what our mission is, and I talked
> to teachers about that too. We need to look at
> some of the basics about what our mission, vision,
> and values are. I want to do that carefully, where
> people have an opportunity to speak to that,
> because it's certainly a gap here at the school.
> Nobody knows what the mission is. I think we
> need to look at that to help shape the PLCs. We
> kind of went backward.
>
> *Elementary principal*

This category of practices for creating a shared direction (including "the vision thing," as one recent American president famously put it) carries the bulk of the effort to motivate leaders' colleagues (Hallinger & Heck, 1998). It is about the establishment of moral purpose (Fullan, 2003; Hargreaves & Fink, 2006) as a basic stimulant for work. Most theories of motivation argue that people are motivated to accomplish personally important goals for themselves. Such goals, for example, are one of four sources of motivation in Bandura's (1986) theory of human motivation.

Practices for Creating a Shared Sense of Direction

Motivating and Inspiring

Four sets of practices are included in this category, all aimed at bringing a focus to the individual and collective work of staff in the school or district: building shared visions, establishing short-term goals, creating high expectations, and communicating directions. Done skillfully, these practices are one of the main sources of motivation and inspiration for the work of staff.

1. Successful turnaround leaders engage their staff in building a shared vision as a key strategy for strengthening staff motivation and commitment.

Building compelling visions of the organization's future is a fundamental task in transformational and charismatic leadership models. Bass's (1985) "inspirational motivation" is encompassed in this practice, a dimension that Podsakoff, MacKenzie, Moorman, and Fetter (1990) define as leadership behavior "aimed at identifying new opportunities for his or her unit . . . and developing, articulating, and inspiring others with his or her vision of the future" (p. 112). Silins and Mulford (2002) found positive and significant effects on students of a shared and monitored mission, while Harris and Chapman's (2002a) qualitative study of effective leadership in schools facing challenging circumstances reported: "Of central importance . . . was the cooperation and alignment of others to [the leader's] set of values and vision. . . . Through a variety of symbolic gestures and actions, they were successful at realigning both staff and pupils to their particular vision" (p. 6).

Locke (2002) argues that formulating a vision for the organization is one of eight core tasks for senior leaders under almost all circumstances. It is also, according to Locke, a key mechanism for achieving integration or alignment of activities within the organization. In agreement with Locke, we include as part of vision building the establishment of core organizational values. These values shape the means by which the vision is to be accomplished.

At least nine studies to date have examined specifically how turnaround school leaders help set directions by developing, articulating, and inspiring others with their vision of the future. These leaders consider a consistent and shared vision to be an inherent part of their approach to leadership (Harris, 2002). In general, they have a clear view of where the school needs to be and how best it can get there (Bell, 2001; Billman, 2004; West, Ainscow, & Stanford, 2005). Regardless of personality or leadership style, turnaround school leaders articulate and model their own vision of the successful school (Bell, 2001). They keep both staff and pupils onboard and communicate the vision to staff, students, and parents, ensuring they all know the current vision, direction, and strategies of the school (Bell, 2001; Harris, 2002; West et al., 2005). These leaders develop the expectation that the main thrust of their leadership is to emphasize teaching and learning and student achievement (Foster & St. Hilaire, 2004; Orr, Byrne-Jimenez, McFarlane, & Brown, 2005). In order to nurture and win people over to this idea, they often identify weekly, monthly, or quarterly goals for tackling low student achievement in the school (Billman, 2004; Foster & St. Hilaire, 2004; Orr et al., 2005).

The Ontario context in which some of our data were collected expands the typical sources of vision building beyond the local school and its leadership to the province. The provincial government had set ambitious targets for student achievement in literacy and math for all schools to follow. These targets served as a long-term vision in all of the elementary turnaround schools in our study. So while this accounts for why none of the respondents in the qualitative portion of the study provided an example of a specific vision of student improvement on provincial tests, school leaders nonetheless expanded on the provincial vision in locally relevant ways. As one elementary principal explained: "It takes a village to raise a child, and I really do believe that we all have to work together, and by working with people at the board, and working with the community and working with the students, I believe that's what helped with our students' achievement. And the parents—we talk about how the parents help with student achievement." In this case, the provincial targets for student performance are a taken-for-granted piece of the school's vision, and the principal's addition is about the collaborative and inclusive nature of the processes for achieving the provincial targets.

In spite of the provincial achievement targets, the principal of a school serving a very needy student population felt the need to build a vision that endorsed a primary focus on students' achievement rather than social goals of one sort or another. Said an elementary vice principal at the school, "We've [administration and staff] been working since my arrival on revisiting mission and vision. Why are we here? What is our focus? Student improvement came out loud and clear."

At the secondary level, three school leaders mentioned the role of vision in direction setting:

I'm very intent on sustaining leadership that goes just beyond me. I rely heavily on the fact that there's a directions team that has ownership—ownership and sustainability across our staff, whether I'm here or not. People have a common vision and a common goal.—Secondary principal

A leader needs to have that sense of direction, some overall sense of direction, and that would be the principal to have some sense of whole school improvement. I think we have that here.—Secondary vice principal

The [department heads] have a vision of where they want the program area to go.—Secondary teacher leader

These comments indicate that our successful turnaround leaders, even in the context of a clear and widely communicated provincial vision, took responsibility for creating with their staffs the most appropriate version of (or addition to) that vision for their school.

Table 4.1 tracks changes across the turnaround stages based on evidence from our interviews with teachers and administrators. In stage 1, teachers did not know what the leader's vision (if it existed) was. In stage 2, principals and department heads had developed (or acquired) a clear vision for literacy improvement which they were able to share with teachers. By stage 3, the articulation of the vision for improvement became an integral aspect of all teaching and learning activities, with adjustments being made as required.

Table 4.1   How Identifying and Communicating a Vision Changed Across the Stages

Stage 1	• If they have a vision for the student improvement process, district and school administrators have not made it clear to teachers.
	• Principals provide little direction for teachers' efforts to improve students' test results.
Stage 2	• Principals have a vision for school improvement and communicate it to others.
	• Department heads have a vision for developing cross-curricular instruction in literacy skills.
Stage 3	• Administrators and staff revisit vision and school mission to ensure they are going in the right direction.
	• Administrators and teacher leaders articulate their belief systems regarding the importance of literacy instruction and improving student achievement.

2. Turnaround school leaders work with their staffs to transform school visions into specific shorter-term goals to guide planning and ensure coherence in both collaborative and autonomous decisions.

While visions can be inspiring, action requires some agreement on the more immediate goals to be accomplished in order to move toward the vision. Building on such theory, this set of practices aims not only to identify important goals for the organization, but to do so in a way that individual members come to include the organization's goals among their own. Unless this happens, the organization's goals have no motivational value. So leaders can productively spend a lot of time on this set of practices. Giving short shrift misses the point entirely. This set of practices includes leader behaviors "aimed at promoting cooperation among [teachers] and getting them to work together toward a common goal" (Podsakoff et al., 1990, p. 112).

In district and school settings, strategic and improvement planning processes are among the more explicit contexts in which these practices are enacted. Planning and organizing, one of the eleven effective managerial behaviors in Yukl's (1989) multiple linkage model, encompasses a portion of these practices. Planning and organizing include "determining long-range objectives and strategies . . . [and] identifying necessary steps to carry out a project or activity" (p. 130).

Evidence from thirteen studies paints a picture of how leaders develop common goals specifically in turnaround school contexts. Moving toward common goals, according to this evidence, is a process of encouraging change (Billman, 2004; Foster & St. Hilaire, 2004; Harris, 2002; Kannapel & Clements, 2005; Ross & Glaze, 2005; West et al., 2005) through communication, consultation (Billman, 2004; Foster & St. Hilaire, 2004; Picucci, Brownson, Kahlert, & Sobel, 1999), and motivation (Harris, 2002; Orr et al., 2005; Ross & Glaze, 2005).

Once school leaders establish a broad direction for their schools, they take actions to align staff and pupils to their particular vision of the school (Harris, 2002). To move the school community forward, successful turnaround leaders allow school staffs substantial autonomy and authority to make needed improvements (Ross & Glaze, 2005), and they energize teachers to take responsibility for change and development (Harris, 2002). They invite those who bought into the school's vision to lead the change (Ross & Glaze, 2005), and they encourage their staff to take risks, try new approaches, and share successes and failures (Foster & St. Hilaire, 2004). Using an enthusiastic and encouraging approach, these turnaround leaders manage to include their faculty as part of the change process (Ross & Glaze, 2005) even in the early stages of the effort, and this involvement helps staff develop coherent approaches toward the accomplishment of school goals (Foster & St. Hilaire, 2004).

A substantial amount of turnaround leaders' work is concerned with how to maintain staff morale and motivation in response to their needs and interests (Harris, 2002; Ross & Glaze, 2005). However, Orr et al. (2005) indicate that given the relatively uniform approach to school improvement now common in most districts and schools (perhaps especially U.S. schools working within the confines of No Child Left Behind), school leaders have limited opportunities and incentives to motivate their staff. They are held accountable for ensuring that teachers are able to realize the school's vision and focus (Lambert, 2006).

Successful leaders in these less autonomous contexts have learned to rely on several strategies that shape how they work with their staff toward school improvement. Orr's (2005) evidence suggests that successful turnaround leaders do the following:

- Explicitly use the school's vision as an instrument for sorting out dilemmas.
- Resist following the implementation of externally imposed reforms blindly, looking instead to multiple ways of accomplishing goals.

- Invest in the lower grades in their schools, not just the grades at which accountability tests are focused.
- Buffer their staffs from district pressures and intrusion.

Evidence from the qualitative portion of our study indicated that goal setting for turning around literacy achievement in Ontario's schools began at the Ministry of Education level. District leaders included ministry goals in their district-wide improvement, or strategic, plans, and school administrators connected their school improvement plans to the districts' initiatives. Teachers, our data suggested, were largely in agreement with these directions and reflected them in their classroom priorities, suggesting a much higher level of alignment among all four levels of the educational organization than the typical "loose coupling" that is often assumed.[1]

The following comments by elementary teachers in a school with a new principal and the arrival of a Ministry of Education turnaround team illustrate the strength of this coupling and the ways in which goal-setting practices were enacted:

All staff are involved in that goal [student improvement]. It's a system goal for everyone in the board.—Elementary teacher leader

With the past administration, the expectations were there, but they weren't announced to staff or talked about a lot.—Elementary teacher leader

I know from last year to this year, it's been a lot more focused. Last year I wasn't really aware of anything specific. This year we have the school growth plan. We have specific numbers, like 50 percent of the students should improve. And the growth plan has been given out to each and every one of us. . . . I guess that's . . . [the principal's] role to tell us and not just tell us. I know she's working with a school achievement team of five or six people, and it's the team that has come up with the goals. —Elementary teacher

I think [the school improvement plan] . . . has gotten to be more intensive. We don't just talk about it. We have to do it. Not just a discussion and writing it down on paper to actually having to do the action, to do the work and not just do it, but we have to show at the end that it's been done. The approach is quite a bit different from the school improvement plans we've had in the past.—Elementary teacher

These comments suggest that teachers generally agreed with their school's official priorities and knew that at least some of their colleagues had been involved in setting them.

Several comments from Ontario principals and teachers illustrate how leaders went about engaging their staffs in the goal-setting process and convincing teachers to commit themselves to cross-curricular literacy initiatives—a particular concern at the secondary level:

I can stand up and preach, and I can stand up and talk and demand. But if we don't bring people onboard, it's not going to happen. So you give people opportunities to buy in. It's really easy to tell people to do something, but the challenge is to get them to believe it's important and to get them to ingrain those tasks.—Secondary vice principal

Starting from the administration down, I think they put the focus on trying to make it an important factor in the school—having kids leaving the school who are very literate, actually being very good at literacy, or trying to be above the average, perhaps. That push, from the top down, goes right through department heads. In general there's a good attitude toward that.—Secondary teacher

There is encouragement now for people to be part of the school improvement plan—not just the principal and vice principal sitting down and making it. Other people are now part of creating it. Then they buy into it more.—Secondary teacher leader

We have a focus on literacy across the curriculum, and we are holding teachers accountable. We want to know exactly what's going on in those classes in terms of literacy, submitting their lesson plans. It's a big challenge keeping that on track. Feedback I get indicates generally departments have accepted the responsibility for providing more literacy experiences for the kids.
—Secondary vice principal

In sum, evidence from our Ontario study suggests that successful turnaround school leaders engaged their staffs in goal setting, believed in the value of staff participation in such decision making about goals, and expected their staffs eventually to all pull in the same direction.

Table 4.2 details how goal-setting processes changed over the three turnaround stages. In stage 1, as far as most teachers were concerned, school goals regarding literacy achievement were unknown, unclear, and unaddressed by administration, and they had been developed without teachers' participation. In stage 2, provincial goals for students' literacy achievement had been clarified and confirmed by leaders at all levels, teachers had been included in the development of school improvement plans, and they were expected to be working toward meeting the school's goals. At stage 3, there was some indication that teachers were hoping to be consulted further in order to provide a reality check when goals for student achievement were being set.

3. Turnaround leaders believe that their teaching colleagues and students are capable of much more than they have been accomplishing and seize every available opportunity to increase their expectations significantly.

Setting high expectations is part of direction setting because it is closely aligned with goals. Although high performance expectations do not define the substance of organizational goals, they demonstrate, as Podsakoff et al. (1990) explain, "the leader's

Table 4.2   How Fostering the Acceptance of Group Goals Changed Across the Stages

Stage 1	• Ministry of Education, district, and school leaders' efforts to get teachers to act on common goals for improving students' achievement on literacy tests show little result. • Administrators are not holding teachers accountable for acting on specific goals related to literacy initiatives. • Elementary and secondary principals show a lack of consistency and follow-through in fostering acceptance of group goals. • Principals and vice principals develop school improvement plans on their own without including teachers.
Stage 2	• The ministry, the district, and principals ensure that provincial goals for students' literacy are clear for all school staff. • Elementary and secondary principals include teachers in the development of school improvement plans. • Secondary principals and teacher leaders get teachers onboard with the ministry's literacy initiatives. • Secondary principals and vice principals check lesson plans to ensure teachers are complying with such ministry goals as cross-curricular literacy instruction. • Elementary principals and turnaround team leaders hold all primary teachers accountable for trying new literacy-focused instructional strategies and reporting on the results.
Stage 3	• Ministry, district, and school leaders agree on common goals for improving students' results and working toward manageable goals for literacy initiatives.

expectations of excellence, quality, and/or high performance" (p. 112) in the achievement of those goals. Demonstrating such expectations is a central behavior associated with virtually all conceptions of transformational and charismatic leadership.

Evidence collected in turnaround schools points to the importance of leaders' "enlarg[ing] the staff's capacity to imagine what might be achieved, and increas[ing] their sense of accountability for bringing this about" (West et al., 2005). The starting point, this research suggests, is to establish a culture of high expectations, high performance, collaboration, and mutual respect. Strong leadership is required to motivate faculty to raise their expectations for the performance of their students (Kannapel & Clements, 2005). At the district level, leaders are expected to be instrumental in setting the tone for shared goals, high standards, and high expectations and to provide supports to staff and students in order to turn high expectations into high performance (Bell, 2001).

Previous research indicates that establishing appropriate, measurable, and agreed-on academic and nonacademic goals and targets is an important means for raising expectations (Bell, 2001; West et al., 2005). School leaders' expectations for high performance from staff are based on a belief, combined with considerable optimism, about the untapped potential of staff and students for growth and development (Harris, 2002).

Our evidence suggests that raising performance expectations in the turnaround schools began at the Ministry of Education level. Once the ministry set specific provincewide performance targets for students on provincial tests and increased their support for the improvement process with additional resources for students and schools that were struggling, districts followed through by introducing higher expectations for students, teachers, and school-level leaders. As an elementary teacher said to us, "We have guidance from the ministry—our turnaround team is excited. We're all on the same page, and the kids are flourishing."

Teachers were able to motivate each other to shift their expectations for themselves and their students, thus enabling the turnaround process to begin. For example, an elementary teacher leader explained: "We had an opportunity to say, 'You know what? We realize it is not just grade 3. How fair is it to the grade 3 teacher? There are kids who maybe we didn't teach well enough before they got to grade 3.' If we approach this properly, we realize it's everybody in this together. If we start as low as kindergarten building blocks, then we're not going to tumble in grade 3."

School leaders took responsibility for communicating high expectations for their teachers with respect to the literacy initiatives and then followed through to make sure the expectations were being met. This responsibility was not enacted in a uniform way, however. One secondary teacher told us, "The school administrators have to encourage you more than anything because really, it's part of the job. But if you [as a teacher] are going to make a difference, you're going to need to go above and beyond the call of duty."

A secondary vice principal described a more specific style of enactment: "We have always taught literacy, but in the performance appraisal [of teachers], it becomes central for our discussion, and I specifically ask teachers what they're doing to promote literacy in their classroom, and I'm looking for evidence of that: evidence in their lesson plans, evidence in student work, evidence in strategies such as word walls, and so forth."

In the turnaround schools, teachers' acceptance of their roles in meeting ministry targets for students' results on literacy tests required unwavering insistence from principals. In all of these schools, some portion of every staff meeting was allocated to raising awareness of literacy issues or providing resources.

Table 4.3 exemplifies how leaders' approaches to increasing expectations changed across the three turnaround stages. In stage 1, school leaders' low or unclear expectations for teachers and students resulted in low performance on provincial literacy tests, accompanied by lack of motivation to improve. School administrators were tolerating, or themselves enacting, relatively low levels of performance in other areas as well, including staffing, student discipline, and instructional leadership. The ministry's decision to make test results public triggered a movement toward greater clarity about performance expectations

Table 4.3   How Creating High Performance Expectations and Motivating Others Changed Across the Stages

Stage 1	• The ministry's and district's expectations for their own, school leaders', teachers', and students' performances are unclear.
	• When the ministry makes provincial test results public and announces improvement targets, expectations start getting clearer.
	• Administrators and teachers have low expectations for their students in inner-city schools.
	• Administrators and teachers are meeting their own (low) expectations for themselves and each other.
	• Although students' results on provincial tests are consistently low, administrators and teachers believe they are acting as effective professionals.
	• Administrators provide little guidance for their teachers about their expectations for literacy instruction.
	• Administrators allow underperforming teachers to stay on staff.
	• Administrators use ineffective approaches to deal with student discipline.
	• Administrators' leadership has resulted in continuing low test scores.
Stage 2	• The ministry sets and enforces high expectations for students' performance on provincial literacy tests.
	• Principals hold teachers accountable for including literacy instruction in all subject areas.
	• Principals motivate staff and students to work on improving results on provincial tests.
	• Teachers motivate each other to raise expectations for themselves and their students.

Stage 3	• Ministry, district, and school administrators continue to give public recognition to positive achievements in literacy instruction and students' results.
	• Administrators continue to hold teachers accountable for improvements in students' literacy results.
	• When students' achievement has improved significantly, administrators feel the burden of maintaining improvements and continuing to improve.
	• The administration and teachers turn their attention and resources to subject areas that have been neglected while literacy has been the prime focus.

for everyone. In stage 2, high expectations had been clarified for administrators, teachers, and students, leading to improvements and increasing motivation. In stage 3, high expectations and motivation were being maintained, and there was some shift in focus to areas of the curriculum that had been overlooked during the time in which literacy improvement held center stage.

4. Turnaround leaders never quit communicating the school's purposes, plans, and expectations to staff, students, parents, and other stakeholders.

To help foster agreement about group goals, turnaround leaders place great emphasis on improving communication with and among school staff (Billman, 2004; Picucci et al., 1999). Such communication aims to pull teachers together around the same set of purposes (Picucci et al., 1999), greatly facilitating the turnaround process. Successful turnaround leaders are able to convince all or most of those within the school and the community that their vision is worth sharing and pursuing (Harris, 2002).

Effective communication among the successful school lead-ers and staff in our study extended to administrators and other leaders who were a visible presence in the school, listened to teachers, and maintained an open-door policy—for example:

> The present principal has really worked to have open dialogue about excellence in teaching and student achievement. She has an open door policy of always discussing classroom issues related to teaching or whole school student achievement and is always willing to talk about it, get feedback or ideas, or suggestions. —Elementary teacher leader

> We have weekly newsletters [from the principal], monthly division meetings, and monthly staff meetings—regularly.—Elementary teacher leader

> [The turnaround team leader] has been down here on a monthly basis for the first two years. She's down-to-earth. Anyone can talk to her. Her personality is helpful. It could be threaten-ing, intimidating, but the key is we feel free to talk to her. —Elementary teacher

> Some administrators make it a great priority to be here and to be seen by the staff and the students.—Secondary teacher

> Open door policy—if he's here, the door is open. You don't have to make an appointment. You can go to the principal or vice principals.—Secondary teacher leader

> The essence is communication—when people understand what's going on, why you have taken a particular approach. Administrators have to set the tone for communication. It can take a variety of forms—sometimes one on one.—Secondary vice principal

The many challenges of working in a turnaround school increased the need for good lines of communication among leaders and staff.

Table 4.4 shows how school leaders at the beginning of stage 1 were often working in isolation from staff and were unavailable

**Table 4.4   How Promoting Effective Communication
Changed Across the Stages**

Stage 1	• Ministry of Education staff work at a great distance from schools.
	• Principals make unilateral decisions.
	• Principals are often away from the school and are unavailable.
	• Principals communicate with staff irregularly.
Stage 2	• Ministry representatives on turnaround teams work directly with primary staff, literacy leaders, and administrators in turnaround schools.
	• Principals are available and accessible to staff.
	• Principals listen to teachers' concerns and ideas.
Stage 3	• Principals continue to listen to staff concerns and help resolve literacy-related instructional issues.

or uncommunicative. In stage 2, the entry of the turnaround teams into elementary schools modeled a more accessible and collaborative approach to leadership, which brought about improvements in the communication between teachers and school administrators. In stage 3, principals were increasingly concerned with communication coming from teachers and were listening more carefully to their concerns.

By the Numbers

To this point in the chapter, our account of direction-setting practices on the part of turnaround leaders has relied on qualitative data from our Ontario study. This study collected survey data from 250 teachers and administrators in turnaround schools as well. And for comparison purposes, such data were collected not only from turnaround schools but from 91 teachers and administrators in schools in the same districts that had shown improvements on student performance over the same period but starting from a much higher level. This section offers a quantitative perspective on direction setting by quantifying the qualitative data (counting the numbers of people providing similar responses to interview questions) and introducing results from the teacher and administrator surveys.

Together these data speak to the relative contributions to the turnaround success of the core leadership practices; differences between elementary and secondary schools in the sources of these leadership practices; specific direction setting practices of unique importance to school turnarounds; and potential differences in the leadership required for turnaround versus more typical improving schools.

5. Direction-setting leadership practices matter most to teachers.

Responses to survey questions asking teachers about the relative importance of the four categories of core leadership practices to the success of their turnaround efforts indicated that direction-setting practices made the greatest contribution (the mean response was 3.21 on a five-point scale) and developing people the least (mean = 2.81). Approximately the same midrange ratings were awarded to redesigning the organization (mean = 3.04) and managing the instructional program (mean = 3.06).

6. Principals are the primary source of direction-setting practices. But there are many more additional sources in secondary, as compared with elementary, schools.

Table 4.5, a quantification of our Ontario interview data, indicates that principals were considered to be the primary source of direction-setting practices in both elementary and secondary schools by just under half of those respondents who spoke about it (48 and 44 percent, respectively). Beyond this similarity, however, there were substantial differences between elementary and secondary schools. In elementary schools, the Ministry of

Table 4.5   Sources of Leadership Practices in Successful Elementary and Secondary Turnaround Schools: Direction Setting

Leadership Sources: Direction Setting	Number (Percentage) of Respondents
Principal	
Elementary	42 (48%)
Secondary	72 (44%)
Vice principal	
Elementary	3 (3%)
Secondary	17 (10%)
Formal teacher	
Elementary	2 (2%)
Secondary	33 (20%)
Informal teacher	
Elementary	6 (7%)
Secondary	18 (11%)
Students	
Elementary	0
Secondary	2 (2%)
Parents	
Elementary	1 (1%)
Secondary	1 (1%)
District	
Elementary	4 (5%)
Secondary	19 (12%)
Ministry	
Elementary	27 (31%)
Secondary	1 (1%)
School teams	
Elementary	3 (3%)
Secondary	2 (1%)
Total	
Elementary	88 (20%)
Secondary	165 (28%)

Note: This table represents four elementary and four secondary schools.

Education (mostly the turnaround teams) was the second most frequently mentioned source (31 percent), while in secondary schools, the ministry was mentioned by 1 percent or fewer of the respondents. Evidence from secondary schools, however, suggests a more distributed pattern of enactment, with formal teacher leaders (20 percent), informal teacher leaders (11 percent), district staff (12 percent), and vice principals (10 percent) all considered to be sources of direction-setting practices.

7. Among the specific practices associated with direction setting, creating high performance expectations was most evident in successful turnaround schools.

Based, once again, on a quantification of our Ontario interview data, Table 4.6 summarizes teachers' and administrators'

Table 4.6 Specific Leadership Practices Most Evident in Elementary and Secondary Turnaround Schools: Direction Setting

Direction Setting	Elementary Schools: Number of Responses (Percentage)	Secondary Schools: Number of Responses (Percentage)
Identifying and articulating a vision	5 (6%)	12 (7%)
Fostering the acceptance of group goals	29 (33%)	49 (30%)
Creating high performance expectations and motivating others	39 (44%)	64 (39%)
Promoting effective communication	15 (17%)	40 (24%)
Aggregate	88 (20%)	165 (28%)

Note: This table represents four elementary and four secondary schools.

responses about which of four specific direction-setting practices were most evident in their schools. Among elementary school respondents, little mention was made of identifying and articulating a vision (6 percent of respondents). Recall that the provincial government had established common achievement targets for elementary students in literacy and math. By far the largest number of respondents spoke about fostering the acceptance of group goals (33 percent) and creating high performance expectations (44 percent); fewer respondents (17 percent) identified effective communication about the school's purposes as part of their turn-around efforts.

Approximately the same pattern of responses was evident from secondary and elementary school interviewees. Primary attention in the turnaround secondary schools was devoted to creating high expectations; 39 percent of respondents spoke about this practice. Less, but still substantial, attention was devoted to establishing agreed-on goals (30 percent) and effectively communicating the school's purposes (24 percent).

In sum, teachers and administrators in the successful turnaround schools did not spend as much time on building a broad or general vision of what the school might become as they did on clarifying what needed to be accomplished in the short term and creating a sense of accountability for those goals through high and widely disseminated performance expectations. These results are likely explained by the province's insistence that all schools work toward a common set of literacy and numeracy targets, effectively establishing a common vision for all schools in the province.

The limited attention devoted to vision building at the local level can be viewed, plausibly, as a testament to the effectiveness with which the province went about its vision-building work. Indeed, some of our qualitative evidence about local vision building, discussed at the beginning of this chapter, had this provincial context as a starting point. So it is reasonable to conclude that local vision-building practices would assume much greater importance, absent the centralized government context in which our Ontario turnaround schools found themselves. Turnaround leadership in England's Rowlatts Hill Primary School, described in Chapter Three, illustrates this point quite nicely.

8. Among the specific leadership practices associated with direction setting, promoting effective communication contributed most to the success of turnaround schools, while creating high performance expectations contributed most to the success of improving schools.

Table 4.7 reports a different type of evidence about broadly the same set of practices. These results are based on teacher survey ratings of the extent to which each of three specific direction-setting practices contributed most to the success of their school's turnaround efforts (1 = very little to 5 = a

Table 4.7   Teachers' Ratings of the Most Important Leadership Practices in Turnaround Versus Improving Schools: Direction Setting

Direction-Setting Practices	Turnaround Respondents: Mean (Rank)	SD	Improving Respondents: Mean (Rank)	SD
Fostering acceptance of group goals	3.18 (2)	1.07	3.20 (3)	1.10
Creating high performance expectations	3.14 (3)	1.32	3.84 (1)	1.06
Promoting effective communication	3.27 (1)	1.06	3.65 (2)	0.96
Aggregate	3.21	.97	3.50	0.87

Note: Response scale: 1 = very little, 5 = a great deal (*n* = 340 teachers from 13 turnaround schools and 228 teachers from 20 improving schools).

great deal). This table also compares the ratings of teachers in turnaround schools with the ratings of teachers in typically "improving" schools.[2]

The three specific leadership practices (omitting vision based on earlier evidence) included in direction setting were rated by turnaround school teachers in the relatively narrow range of 3.14 to 3.27, suggesting their approximately similar value for turning around schools, from the teachers' perspectives. Teachers in the more typical improving schools had a wider range of responses, valuing the creation of high performance expectations most. These two sets of responses are curious on another matter as well: they tended to value all three specific leadership practices more (higher ratings) than did their turnaround teacher colleagues. While the small sample sizes on which these data are based make it hazardous to infer too much about this difference, one might reasonably expect the opposite results: leadership valued most where it is needed most, in the turnaround schools.

Conclusion

Direction-setting functions evolved quite noticeably during the turnaround stages according to our evidence. At the earliest stage (stopping the decline and creating conditions for early improvement), little explicit attention was paid to direction-setting practices at all. Although some leaders had a sense of direction themselves, it was unlikely to be shared with staff, who were thus left to forge their own directions. The next stage (creating conditions for early improvement and realizing initial performance improvements) began with government-imposed targets for all schools. So vision and goal setting at the school level began with the provincial vision distributed by districts and expressed as a set of achievement targets for students in literacy and mathematics.

Principals and, at the secondary level, department heads articulated their visions and goals to staff. Although there was considerable urgency to improve student performance in our eight successful turnaround schools, more specific goal setting was a shared activity, and successful leaders maintained significant staff involvement. High performance expectations flowed from the top down during the second turnaround stage, and effective channels of communication were developed to serve as conduits for these expectations, as well as a means of ensuring agreement on goals. The importance of these leadership practices is hardly unique to the Ontario context in which our data were collected. For example, in their study of three successful turnaround schools in Buffalo, New York, Jacobson, Brooks, Giles, Johnson, and Ylimaki (2007) concluded that "each [principal] in her own way, set a clear course that encouraged a sense of common purpose within their [school communities]" (p. 309).

Evidence described in this chapter confirms the importance of direction-setting practices and of principals as the most important local source of such leadership. But there are other sources, and more of them in secondary than in elementary schools. Direction-setting practices by leaders at higher levels of the education system (the government) have important consequences for the direction-setting practices of local leaders.

Key Points

- Successful turnaround leaders engage their staff in building a shared vision as a key strategy for strengthening staff motivation and commitment.

- Turnaround school leaders work with their staffs to transform school visions into specific shorter-term goals to guide planning and ensure coherence in collaborative and autonomous decisions.

- Turnaround leaders believe that their teaching colleagues and students are capable of much more than they have been accomplishing and seize every opportunity to increase their expectations significantly.

- Turnaround leaders never quit communicating the school's purposes, plans, and expectations to staff, students, parents, and other stakeholders.

- Direction-setting leadership practices matter most to teachers.

- Principals are the primary source of direction-setting practices. But there are many more additional sources in secondary, as compared with elementary, schools.

- Among the specific practices associated with direction setting, creating high performance expectations was most evident in successful turnaround schools.

- Among the specific leadership practices associated with direction setting, promoting effective communication contributed most to the success of turnaround schools, while creating high performance expectations contributed most to the success of improving schools.

5

HOW TURNAROUND LEADERS FOSTER CAPACITY DEVELOPMENT AMONG THEIR TEACHERS

You need the ministry people [involved in the Turnaround Teams Project]. If you had to let something go, I'd say give up some funding, but you need that in-servicing. If there's not someone there providing it, then you're a boat without a keel, without steerage. The ministry people have come in and told the primary teachers: "This is what you're going to be doing. This is how you're going to do it. Go forth and do it." If you're just saying: "Here's the money," that's like saying, "You need to go over to the other side of the world without maps." The ministry is the captain with everything here. You need hands-on, not hands-off. We're at the point of exiting [the program], so the turnaround team leader won't be here as much, so I'll be more responsible. I've put teachers on notice that they're going to be doing more. They're more capable than they think they are. They're going to present on what they've been doing.

Elementary teacher leader

This quotation vividly illustrates the significant role that was played by the Ministry of Education's turnaround teams in the context of our Ontario study. While the provincial government as a whole was the source of the vision for improvement adopted by the turnaround schools, it was the ministry's turnaround teams that came to be viewed as important enactors of the category of leadership practices explored in this chapter: developing people. There can be many sources of such capacity building, of course, and they will be determined by the unique opportunities and resources available to schools.

Holdzkom's (2001) analysis of turnaround approaches in Kentucky, North Carolina, and South Carolina indicates these states relied on the infusion of expertise from educators outside a turnaround school's home district as sources of assistance. Duke (2010) argues that "when there is a need for teachers to acquire new competences quickly, the best course of action may be to retain the services of an expert who can spend time in class demonstrating how to help a struggling student" (p. 92).

The three sets of practices in this category make a significant contribution to staff motivation in almost all organizational contexts, including turnaround schools. Their primary aim is capacity building—building not only the knowledge and skills staff need to accomplish organizational goals, but also the dispositions to persist in applying that knowledge and skill (Harris & Chapman, 2002a). Individual teacher efficacy is arguably the most critical of these dispositions, and it is a third source of motivation in Bandura's (1986) model. People are motivated by what they are good at. And mastery experiences, according to Bandura, are the most powerful sources of efficacy. So building capacity that leads to a sense of mastery is highly motivational as well.

Practices for Building Capacity

This broad category of leadership practices includes more specific initiatives intended to provide both individualized support and intellectual stimulation, as well to model preferred practices and values.

1. Turnaround leaders provide many forms of psychological support for their individual teaching colleagues as they pursue the directions established for the school.

Bass and Avolio (1994) include, as part of this set of leadership practice or behaviors, "knowing your followers' needs and raising them to more mature levels . . . [sometimes through] the use of delegation to provide opportunities for each follower to self-actualize and to attain higher standards of moral development" (p. 64). Podsakoff, MacKenzie, Moorman, and Fetter (1990) claim that these behaviors should communicate leaders' respect for their colleagues, as well as concerns about their personal feelings and needs.

Practices of this sort are common to all of the two-dimensional models of leadership (Ohio State, contingency theory, and situational leadership theory), which include task orientation (one dimension) and consideration for people (a second dimension). Encompassed by this set of practices as well are the "supporting" and the "recognizing and rewarding" managerial behaviors associated with Yukl's (1989) multiple linkage model, Hallinger's (2003) model of instructional leadership, and the "responsibilities" identified in the analysis by Waters, Marzano, and McNulty (2003). As a whole, these leadership behaviors arguably have attracted more leadership research outside schools since the 1960s than any other. Building the confidence, resilience, and persistence of staff to face the challenges of turning around an underperforming school—and all that entails—is the goal here.

At least eight studies conducted in Canada, the United States, and the United Kingdom have described this core practice as it is enacted in school turnaround contexts. Successful turnaround leaders, according to this evidence, provide professional support and encouragement for their staff's personal growth, even when they face the immediate challenges of their classrooms or the accountability-driven demands of state and district mandates (Giles, Johnson, Brooks, & Jacobson, 2005). Successful turnaround leaders monitor their staff on a regular basis, provide them with supports through one-to-one meetings, and give them individual advice for improvement (Ross & Glaze, 2005). They spend significant amounts of time in supporting and encouraging their teaching staff (Billman, 2004), trying to raise their self-esteem and self-image (West, Ainscow, & Stanford, 2005), and influencing their beliefs about their professional ability (Ross & Glaze, 2005). By and large, this research indicates that turnaround school leaders are more facilitators, mentors, guides (Billman, 2004; Giles et al., 2005), and coaches (Lambert, 2006; Ross & Glaze, 2005) than they are administrative managers, much less the ruthless autocrats portrayed in some of the private sector turnaround literature as ideal turnaround leaders.

Evidence from our Ontario study found that individualized support for teachers with questions about literacy instruction was available from district-level literacy consultants, the literacy lead teacher in their schools, and principals. Primary teachers involved with turnaround teams were able to use their collaborative sessions to address each other's individual concerns about instruction and student improvement, as this teacher leader did: "I've been working with the grade 3 teacher supporting what she needs to work with her kids." Secondary teachers could go to their literacy lead or a district consultant for individual help. A secondary vice principal said, "We have an itinerant literacy resource person who will go in and speak to a teacher, provide workshops for teachers."

Often teachers found it more effective to get help from their colleagues with whom they were now collaborating in teams and through regular meetings in their schools where literacy instruction was emphasized than through sources they might have looked to before the turnaround effort began (for example, the district professional development or literacy consultants). When teachers grew more comfortable collaborating

**Table 5.1   How Providing Individualized Support Changed
Across the Stages**

Stage 1	• The district provides consultants, but their availability varies from year to year.
Stage 2	• The ministry and turnaround teams provide help for individual teachers. • The district provides literacy consultants. • Principals who are instructional leaders provide support. • Literacy leaders support colleagues. • Teachers support each other in literacy activities as they develop expertise and confidence.
Stage 3	• Leaders continue to provide some form of individual support regarding literacy instruction and testing when needed.

with colleagues, consultations among peers became a natural approach to solving problems.

As Table 5.1 indicates, in stage 1, district-level consultants were inconsistently available to help individual teachers with improving literacy-related instructional strategies. With the movement to stage 2, district consultants became more consistently available, and there was an influx of support for individual teachers from turnaround teams, literacy leaders, principals familiar with literacy instruction, and teacher colleagues. By stage 3, leaders and experts at both the district and school levels continued to be available to help teachers' individual needs for instructional support.

2. Turnaround leaders use a wide array of formal to informal methods for stimulating the development of their colleagues' professional skills and knowledge.

Behaviors related to this set of practices include encouraging colleagues to take intellectual risks, reexamine assumptions, look at their work from different perspectives, rethink how it can be performed (Avolio, 1994; Podsakoff et al., 1990), and "induc[e] . . . employees to appreciate, dissect, ponder and discover what they would not otherwise discern" (Lowe, Kroeck, & Sivasubramaniam, 1996, pp. 415–416). Waters et al. (2003) include "challenging the status quo" among the practices that contribute to school leaders' effects on students.

Leaders' roles in professional development are part of this set of practices, and they are especially important for leaders of schools in challenging circumstances (Gray, 2000). But such development occurs in many informal as well as formal ways, reflecting current understandings of learning as constructed, social, and situated.

All models of transformational and charismatic leadership include this set of practices. And a considerable amount of the educational literature assumes such practices on the part of school leaders, most notably the literature on instructional leadership. This places school leaders at the center of instructional improvement efforts in their schools (Hallinger, 2003; Stein & Spillane, 2005).

Effective turnaround school leaders, the available research indicates, purposefully build and strengthen their teams by providing appropriate professional development opportunities, in-service training (Chrisman, 2005; Harris, 2002; Kannapel & Clements, 2005), workshops (Giles et al., 2005; Picucci, Brownson, Kahlert, & Sobel, 1999), and peer observation and learning (Harris, 2002; Lambert, 2006; Ross & Glaze, 2005).

Successful turnaround school leaders believe that it is critical to respect teachers' autonomy and support them in their professional development (Foster & St. Hilaire, 2004). These leaders not only maintain funds to help their staff with additional materials and professional development opportunities (Billman, 2004), but they also ensure that their teachers have a reasonable amount of time to participate in professional development (Kimball & Sirotnik, 2000). These leaders often invite into the school a relatively high number of outside expert advisers to deliver in-service training in the school. Moreover, when teachers want to take risks and experiment, these leaders empower their teachers with the freedom and autonomy to find the best ways to teach (Kannapel & Clements, 2005). Effective turnaround leadership is "about capacity building in others and investing in the social capital of the school" (Harris, 2002, p. 15).

Evidence from our study indicated that part of the process of turning a school around was about ensuring that teachers and other leaders had opportunities to acquire the additional instructional strategies they required in order to address their students' literacy needs more effectively. In the turnaround project schools where new reading and writing programs were introduced, along with an individualized approach to meeting children's learning needs, teachers who had been using the same approaches to instruction for many years had much to learn. So professional development was provided to these teachers in their schools by turnaround teams, literacy lead teachers, and district consultants. Workshops were offered through their districts as well.

These different manifestations of intellectual stimulation were evident and valuable to teachers, most likely because they were practical. One elementary teacher leader noted, for example, "The [turnaround team] leaders run in-services on 'What is modeled reading? What does read-alone look like? What does shared reading look like?'" A first-year elementary teacher explained, "The principal exposed us to the [literacy] test. At teachers' college, I'd never even seen a test. So I didn't know what I was preparing the kids for." And another teacher said she was "involved in coaching to help teachers deliver a balanced literacy program." Two other comments, among many others, help illustrate what our

respondents found valuable about the intellectual stimulation
they received:

> The board has been wonderful in providing in-service for lead
> teachers and for administrators around literacy instruction and
> facilitating discussions at the school level.—Secondary principal
>
> I work with teachers to follow up on strategies that work with
> these [at-risk] students. Most teachers still use the Socratic
> method, and these students don't listen well. Their mind wan-
> ders.—Secondary teacher leader

The consequences of this set of leadership practices included distinct improvements in instructional capacity. One
elementary teacher leader noted, "We're more aware as a whole
school of how to teach students better. We have to teach reading strategies for the test—explicitly teach the skills—infer-
ring, questioning, synthesizing so they can understand the
story."

Table 5.2 shows how the approaches to providing intellectual stimulation changed across the turnaround stages. In stage 1,
the Ministry of Education's influence on teachers' professional
development in literacy instruction was indirect. Districts were
providing less-than-helpful workshops and less-than-adequate
numbers of literacy leaders in schools. Many principals were not
yet instructional leaders, and lead teachers with literacy expertise
had been assigned to administrative work rather than instructional leadership.

By stage 2, professional development had become a focused
priority at all levels. In addition to new opportunities provided
by the ministry's turnaround teams and expanding resources,
district professional development offerings improved in scope
and organization. At the school level, principals set aside
time for professional development activities during staff meetings, and with the support of the ministry and districts, school

Table 5.2   How Providing Intellectual Stimulation Changed Across the Stages

Stage 1	• The Ministry of Education is not involved in school-based, literacy-focused professional development (PD) for teachers on how to teach literacy skills.
	• The district provides one-shot workshops or large group training without follow-up to see what worked or did not work.
	• District PD for secondary teachers is directed at academic students, but the instructional methods are ineffective for applied and at-risk students.
	• The district hires a few literacy leaders, but they are spread thinly across schools.
	• Principals are unable to provide necessary PD for teachers until they become instructional leaders in literacy.
	• Lead teachers focus on administrative tasks rather than instructional improvements.
Stage 2	• The ministry provides regular school-embedded PD as part of turnaround teams, including intensive follow-up with primary teachers, literacy leaders, and administrators.
	• The district provides literacy-related PD (often school embedded) with follow-up on how things worked.
	• Teacher leaders and administrators in each school participate in district-level PD on literacy and literacy testing and provide PD for staff.
	• Teachers share their professional learning with colleagues as part of book study (professional learning community activities) or after they have participated in PD activities outside the school
Stage 3	• Ministry, district, school leaders, and teacher leaders continue to provide updated professional development related to literacy initiatives

schedules were rearranged to accommodate other meeting times for teachers to share in professional learning. As our interviewees indicated, by stage 3, the support for appropriate teachers' professional development continued from all levels.

3. Turnaround leaders model desirable practices and values as a means of encouraging their colleagues to reflect on their own practices and become or remain actively engaged in improving them.

This set of practices is about leading by example or walking the talk, an approach associated with models of authentic leadership (Avolio & Gardner, 2005). In addition to focusing on teaching behavior, such modeling often includes demonstrating transparent decision making, confidence, optimism, hope, resiliency, and consistency between words and deeds. The turnaround principals in Jacobson et al.'s (2007) study made themselves visible throughout the day in the halls, classrooms, gyms, and school yards to ensure a safe environment in what had been chaotic circumstances ("a frontier culture") and send "the clear message that a new sheriff was in town" (p. 11).

Locke (2002) claims that leaders' core values are established by modeling them in their own practices. Both Hallinger (2003) and Waters et al. (2003) note the influence that leaders can have when they are highly visible in their schools and this visibility is associated with high-quality interactions with both staff and students. Harris and Chapman (2002a) also found that their successful heads "modeled behavior that they considered desirable to achieve the school goals" (p. 6).

Also encompassed by modeling is Bass's (1998) idealized influence, a partial replacement for his original charisma dimension. Avolio (1994) claims that leaders exercise idealized influence when they serve as role models, exhibiting the behaviors and attitudes required to build trust and respect in followers. Such modeling on the part of leaders "sets an example for employees to follow that is consistent with the values the leader espouses" (Podsakoff et al., 1990, p. 112).

Elementary teachers in our study told us that when they felt uncertain about how to teach literacy skills, literacy lead teachers modeled specific strategies in their classrooms so students' reactions were part of the learning experience. Noted one teacher, "[The primary literacy lead] . . . uses her classroom as a model for differentiated instruction. We visited her class to see how she dealt with the lessons and then applied it in our classes." Principals also viewed themselves as role models for what it means to be a professional, as these comments from a principal and several teachers testify:

> I set high expectations. I work hard. I try to model it.—Secondary principal

> I think you [the principal] have to model what you want the staff to do.—Teacher

> When you see the principal practicing what he preaches, or the admin team, and most people on staff as well, they become role models for others. The bottom line is they see success, they see results. I can't stress this enough. Nothing succeeds like success.—Teacher

> [The former principal] . . . had a soft spot for the kids no one else really wanted to put a lot of attention into, and I think because of her attention to them, we've all kind of picked up on her lead and kind of run with it. She modeled it very well—as much as some staff members just wanted to give up on most kids (myself included).—Secondary teacher

Table 5.3 shows how such modeling changed from leaders being general "role models" in stage 1, to much more conscious and literacy-focused embodiments of qualities and skills related

Table 5.3　How Modeling Appropriate Values and Practices Changed Across the Stages

Stage 1	• Principals and teacher leaders act as role models.
Stage 2	• Districts support literacy and instruction-related model classrooms to serve all elementary teachers.
	• Principals and teacher leaders model values and practices with a focus on literacy improvement for all students.
	• Literacy leaders in elementary schools use their classrooms to demonstrate literacy strategies for colleagues.
Stage 3	• Districts support literacy and instruction-related model classrooms to serve all secondary teachers.

to effective literacy instruction. In elementary schools, teachers had opportunities to observe literacy coaches in their classrooms modeling a particular literacy strategy. In some districts, demonstration classrooms were set up where teachers from many elementary schools could see an expert model instructional strategies. Secondary teachers were hoping for a similar demonstration classroom to become available to them as well.

By the Numbers

As in the previous chapter, this section reflects our quantification of interview data as well as the results of teacher and principal surveys. Sources of the leadership practices aimed at developing people in turnaround schools (see Table 5.4) are more varied than was the case with direction-setting practices.

4. Leadership aimed at developing people is provided by people in many roles in turnaround schools.

While principals were considered a major source of the practices associated with developing people in both elementary

Table 5.4   Sources of Leadership Practices in Successful Elementary and Secondary Turnaround Schools: Developing People

Leadership Sources: Developing People	Number (Percentage) of Respondents
Principal	
Elementary	22 (19%)
Secondary	23 (29%)
Vice principal	
Elementary	5 (4%)
Secondary	8 (10%)
Formal teacher	
Elementary	26 (23%)
Secondary	12 (15%)
Informal teacher	
Elementary	11 (10%)
Secondary	7 (9%)
Students	
Elementary	0
Secondary	2 (3%)
Parents	
Elementary	0
Secondary	0
District	
Elementary	21 (18%)
Secondary	21 (26%)
Ministry	
Elementary	28 (25%)
Secondary	1 (1%)
School teams	
Elementary	1 (1%)
Secondary	4 (1%)
Total	
Elementary	114 (25%)
Secondary	80 (13%)

Note: This table represents a sample of four elementary and four secondary turnaround schools.

Table 5.5   Specific Leadership Practices Most Evident in Elementary and Secondary Turnaround Schools: Developing People

Developing People	Elementary	Secondary
2.1 Providing individualized support	9 (8%)	10 (13%)
2.2 Modeling appropriate values and practices	16 (14%)	23 (29%)
2.3 Intellectual stimulation	87 (76%)	47 (59%)
Aggregate	114 (25%)	80 (13%)

Note: This table represents a sample of four elementary and four secondary turnaround schools. Number and percentage of respondents appear in each cell.

(19 percent) and secondary (29 percent) schools, others are identified about as frequently: formal teacher leaders (23 and 15 percent), district staff (18 and 26 percent), and in elementary schools, the Ministry of Education (25 percent).

5. Teachers perceived intellectual stimulation to be the most prevalent leadership practice associated with developing people in their schools.

As Table 5.5 indicates, of the interview respondents identifying specific practices in this category, intellectual stimulation was mentioned as part of the turnaround effort by more than 76 percent of respondents in elementary schools and 59 percent in secondary schools, with many fewer respondents identifying modeling (14 and 29 percent) or individualized support (8 and 13 percent).

6. Leadership practices aimed at developing people are considered to be moderately useful by teachers in turnaround schools and slightly more useful to teachers in improving

Table 5.6   Teachers' Ratings of the Most Important Leadership Practices in Turnaround Versus Improving Schools: Developing People

Developing People	Turnaround Schools: Mean (Rank)	SD	Improving Schools: Mean (Rank)	SD
Providing individualized support	2.70 (3)	1.14	3.01 (4)	1.03
Modeling appropriate values and practices	2.97 (1)	1.28	3.28 (2)	1.24
Providing intellectual stimulation	2.92 (2)	1.20	3.38 (1)	1.08
Aggregate	2.81	1.09	3.19	0.95

Note: Response scale: 1 = very little, 5 = a great deal. The reliability for this scale (Cronbach's alpha) was .91.

schools. Among those specific leadership practices associated with developing people, modeling appropriate practices and values contributed most to the success of turnaround schools, while providing intellectual stimulation contributed most to improving schools.

Table 5.6 summarizes teachers' survey responses rating the extent to which the practices associated with developing people contributed to the success (1 = very little, 5 = a great deal) of their school's turnaround (first two columns of data) or improvement (last two columns of data) efforts. Responses from turnaround school teachers were in a narrow range (2.97 to 2.70), so no practice stood out in a significant way, although modeling ranked first. Responses from the improving school teachers were in a similarly narrow range, with first rank awarded to providing intellectual stimulation.

Conclusion

Successful turnaround leaders change how they go about developing people across the turnaround stages. From the first stage (declining performance) to the second (creating conditions for early improvement and realizing early performance gains), the successful turnaround schools experienced something of a dramatic change in both the nature and quality of the capacity development efforts of which they were a part. Teachers began to assume much more ownership for their own capacity development, looked to their immediate colleagues much more as sources of insight, and valued their access to highly specialized and focused outside professional development resources, especially from the province's turnaround teams.

In many cases, teacher leaders began the second turnaround stage with a strongly felt need to change and improve their own classroom practices. This felt need gave considerable meaning to the capacity-building efforts in which they participated, as did the new culture of accountability for implementing new practices and improving student performance that had emerged in the turnaround schools.

Key Points

- Turnaround leaders provide many forms of psychological support for their individual teaching colleagues as they pursue the directions established for the school.

- Turnaround leaders use a wide array of formal to informal methods for stimulating the development of their colleagues' professional skills and knowledge.

- Turnaround leaders model desirable practices and values as a means of encouraging their colleagues to reflect on their own practices and become or remain actively engaged in improving them.

- Leadership aimed at developing people is provided by people in many roles in turnaround schools.

- Teachers perceived intellectual stimulation to be the most prevalent leadership practice associated with developing people in their schools.

- Leadership practices aimed at developing people are considered to be moderately useful by teachers in turnaround schools and slightly more useful to teachers in improving schools. Among those specific leadership practices associated with developing people, modeling appropriate practices and values contributed most to the success of turnaround schools, while providing intellectual stimulation contributed most to improving schools.

6

HOW TURNAROUND LEADERS REDESIGN THEIR SCHOOLS

I think it starts with leadership. The schools you've visited certainly have strong leadership. They have in those schools as well a collaborative culture. They work together, and I think they have a strong focus on the students, and try to meet the needs of their students. At the end of the day we know that teacher effectiveness is the single most important thing; it trumps everything else. So if we can have great teachers in front of every classroom, then the chances of us being successful are that much greater. I think that certainly has a huge role to play.

What happens, though, is you have the leadership of the school that creates those kinds of conditions where they're constantly learning and challenging one another and they have a focus on doing whatever it takes to help those students be successful. There's strong leadership at the school level and the system level. It kind of flows down to the school level to create the kind of conditions and opportunities in which teachers can thrive.

I think the most important thing school leaders can do is really articulate a vision that is student focused and supports their teachers. That comes from a perspective that the most important thing with the instructional relationship is between the student and the teacher, and school leaders have to really create that kind of culture and provide support and resources and opportunities for staff to meet, to learn, to grow together on a regular basis. I think if you do that, then people will understand where you want to go.

Superintendent

There is little to be gained by increasing people's motivation and capacity if the setting or conditions in which they work will not allow effective use of those capacities. In Bandura's (1986) model of motivation, beliefs about the setting or situation in which people find themselves is one of four sources of motivation. Motivations are enhanced when people believe the circumstances in which they find themselves are conducive to accomplishing the goals they hold to be personally important.

Practices for Redesigning Schools

The four specific leadership practices for redesigning the organization are about creating conditions of work that allow staff to make the most of their motivations and capacities. These practices aim to build collaborative work cultures, create supportive structures, build productive relationships with families, and connect the school to its wider environment.

1. Successful turnaround leaders nurture the development of norms and values that encourage staffs to work together collaboratively on the improvement of their instructional practices.

> It is hard to imagine sustaining a turnaround initiative in a school where the culture does not undergo fundamental changes. Dysfunctional school cultures are characterized by isolation, privacy, resistance to new ideas, devotion to routines, and low expectations [Duke, 2010, p. 94].

A large body of evidence has accumulated, since Little's (1982) early research, which unambiguously supports the importance of collaborative cultures for schools in most circumstances. Such cultures, this evidence suggests, are central to school improvement, the development of professional learning communities, and the improvement of student learning (Louis & Kruse,

1998; Rosenholtz, 1989). Additional evidence indicates that leaders are able to build more collaborative cultures, and identifies
leadership practices that accomplish this goal (Leithwood, Jantzi, &
Dart, 1990; Waters, Marzano, & McNulty, 2003).

Connolly and James (2006) claim that the success of collaborative activity is determined by the capacity and motivation of
the collaborators, along with opportunities for them to collaborate.
Success also depends on prior conditions. For example, a history of
working together will sometimes build trust, making further collaboration easier. Trust is emerging as a key element in encouraging
collaboration; individuals are more likely to trust those with whom
they have established good relationships (Bryk & Schneider, 2002;
Louis & Kruse, 1995). Participative leadership theory and leader-
member exchange theory are concerned with the nature and
quality of collaboration in organizations and the productive management of collaborative activities.[1]

Leaders contribute to productive collaborative activity in their
schools by being skilled conveners of that work. They nurture
mutual respect and trust among those involved in collaborating,
ensure the shared determination of group processes and outcomes,
help develop clarity about goals and roles for collaboration,
encourage a willingness to compromise among collaborators, foster
open and fluent communication among collaborators, and provide
adequate and consistent resources in support of collaborative work
(Connolly & James, 2006; Mattessich & Monsey, 1992).

Evidence from at least thirteen studies points to the
importance of developing collaborative cultures as part of the
school turnaround process. Creating more positive, collaborative, and achievement-oriented cultures is a key task for turnaround leaders argue West, Ainscow, and Stanford (2005).
Indeed, evidence suggests that turnaround school leaders
are more likely to focus on cultural rather than structural
changes within schools. They consider it critical to generate
a culture that can improve and strengthen teaching practices

(Orr, Byrne-Jimenez, MacFarlane, & Brown, 2005), encompass the divergent perspectives of communities (Barker, 2005), and motivate all students to succeed (Harris, 2002). Based on their Ontario study, Ross and Glaze (2005) claim that "collaboration in the school [is] the prime means to support the development of the school as learning community" (p. 15).

To create strong collaborative cultures requires a collaborative and inclusive style of turnaround leadership (Billman, 2004; Lambert, 2006; Ross & Glaze, 2005). In terms of teacher-administrator collaboration, successful leaders are more likely to build a trusting relationship by reducing the distinction between personal and professional roles. They constructively challenge teachers through collaborative processes (Ross & Glaze, 2005) and keep the school on course with continuous improvement for all students (Lambert, 2006). These leaders, some evidence indicates, view themselves as a force for creating a safe, comfortable, predictable, and orderly environment conducive to adult and student learning (Bell, 2001; Picucci, Brownson, Kahlert, & Sobel, 1999). Harris (2002) found that effective turnaround leaders are able to develop "professional and intellectual capital by encouraging their schools to become inquiring communities" (p. 21). Through their efforts, these leaders are able to change the ethos of a community (West et al., 2005) and make collegiality, collaboration, inclusion, and a sense of community an integral part of the school (Bell, 2001).

In the elementary turnaround schools in our study, development of a more collaborative culture was met with some resistance at first. But teachers changed their minds about working together as they experienced their students' positive responses to the new instructional approaches introduced as a result of that collaboration. Looking back on the process during our interviews, teachers talked about how important leadership and support from the Ministry of Education's turnaround teams, the district, principals, and literacy leads had been in developing the collaborative work culture many of them had grown to value:

> When the turnaround team first came, the staff was reluctant. Teachers weren't working collaboratively together. They were frightened to see how it would work and function. The turnaround team started talking with staff about the goal [being] student success and getting them to do better, to learn with each other. Working together with the ministry leader and our principal guiding them, it just works.—Elementary teacher

> It wasn't that someone came and said, "We're changing everything you're doing. This is what we want you to do." [The turnaround team leader] . . . came and said, "Let's work together to figure out how we can help improve student achievement." —Elementary teacher

> There has been a stress put on [by the district] that it's a schoolwide responsibility. This is a learning community, and so we're all responsible for student achievement and student success. We need to come at the problem together.—Elementary teacher leader

> There's a strong professionalism in the school. The way that we speak to each other, we didn't have the modeling with the previous principal. It wasn't even divisions; just on your own, do your own thing. Some people enjoyed that independence. But I see benefits of working with other teachers.—Elementary teacher

> We do quite a bit of sharing, teachers talking to each other, and that comes from that kind of leadership that allows that kind of climate to work together.—Elementary teacher

Secondary school leaders and teachers were also clear about the benefits of a more collaborative culture:

I think everyone needs to feel valued, part of the community, feel like their voice is heard and so on. I believe strongly that school climate contributes to school success. If teachers feel demoralized, "Nothing's good. No one listens to me," it carries over into the classroom. If they have a good attitude about what they're coming to the school to do every day, I think that really contributes to success. I believe we have a very collaborative school culture.—Secondary principal

Before the big changes, we were sitting at (or achieving) about 48 percent. When teachers were developing their curriculum-related literacy instruction on their own, there wasn't much impact. Lack of collaboration and discussion affected results. —Secondary principal

The leaders we've had have been very good. The principals—it's not a dictating thing: "This is what you do." It's more of a collaboration that everybody buys into—that we need to do this. That works the best. We're all in the same boat, so I think that has worked a lot.—Secondary teacher

Table 6.1 shows the process of developing a collaborative work culture beginning at stage 1, where there were no formal arrangements for staff to collaborate about improving their literacy instruction. By stage 2, various Ministry of Education initiatives and in-school activities got teachers involved in group consultations and decision making about literacy strategies. Anticipating stage 3, teachers and administrators (particularly at the elementary level) spoke about the importance of being able to continue working together and getting more parents involved for the benefit of their students.

2. Turnaround leaders restructure their schools so that teacher collaboration is both possible and likely. The opportunities these new structures provide for teachers to work

Table 6.1   How Building a Collaborative Work Culture Changed Across the Stages

Stage 1	• Principals allow teachers to work in isolation and do not set out expectations for a collaborative work culture.
Stage 2	• Ministry and district- and school-based leaders develop and shape a collaborative culture through modeling and clarifying expectations that teachers will work together.
Stage 3	• Ministry, district, principals, and teacher leaders continually reinforce and refresh their expectation that schools are most effective when the culture of collaboration involves all stakeholders at all levels of the organization.

together also act as symbols of the value attached to such work by the school.

Restructuring to support the work of staff is a function common to virtually all conceptions of management and leadership practice. Organizational culture and structure are two sides of the same coin. Developing and sustaining collaborative cultures depends on complementary structures, typically something requiring leadership initiative—for example, creating common planning times for teachers, establishing team and group structures for problem solving (Hadfield, 2003), distributing leadership for selected tasks, and increasing teacher involvement in decision making (Reeves, 2000). Evidence that Hallinger and Heck (1998) reviewed points to the creation of enabling structures as a key mediator of leaders' effects on students.

At least twelve empirical studies have identified the importance of restructuring on the part of successful school turnaround leaders in particular. These leaders provide extra planning time for teachers, in some cases by changing the format of staff meetings (Billman, 2004; Chrisman, 2005; Kimball & Sirotnik, 2000), forming coordinated teaching teams, and increasing teachers' participation in decision making (Billman, 2004; Giles, Johnson, Brooks, & Jacobson, 2005; Lambert, 2006; Ross & Glaze, 2005; West et al., 2005).

Turnaround leaders, this evidence also indicates, establish teacher teams as structures for helping to manage change and for encouraging the use of new learnings toward the improvement of classroom instruction (Billman, 2004; Harris, 2002). These leaders make sure that their staff feel authentically involved in the school's decisions and activities and are given challenging responsibilities (West et al., 2005), such as sharing the provision of staff development in their schools (Lambert, 2006). On the whole, support for a democratic committee structure, a strong emphasis on teamwork, innovative scheduling of time to facilitate collaboration, and opportunities for shared decision making and teacher leadership characterize the restructuring leadership practices found in successful turnaround schools (Giles et al., 2005).

Our study indicated that the collaborative processes associated with literacy initiatives often took place in divisional teams (in elementary schools), grade teams, literacy teams, school improvement teams, directions teams, and literacy-focused professional learning communities in both elementary and secondary schools. Membership on these teams included teachers, teacher leaders such as the literacy coach, and administrators.

Teachers indicated support from leadership at all levels for getting meeting time for teacher teams embedded in the school schedule, making it possible for them to come together for professional learning and decision making:[2]

The principal really worked hard to bring divisions together through PLCs [professional learning communities].—Elementary teacher leader

This board has really put a great deal of effort and supported us as a school to develop a PLC.—Secondary principal

Our principal provides common time for meeting and looking at [provincial test scores] to see what to improve on.—Elementary teacher

We have a small learning community. We meet once a month. We read, discuss books, go to conferences together, and talk about what we've tried. It's philosophically based discussions. We got started in special ed. We would start our meetings with a bit of learning. We'd talk about a reading or an article. It started last year.—Secondary teacher leader

Both elementary and secondary teachers valued the time that had been made available to engage in professional dialogue with their colleagues:

When you have that time . . . you don't have other things to worry about—not trying to get the next day planned or thinking about talking to parents. You're there and talking about literacy—bouncing ideas that other people have done and what you could do better.—Elementary teacher

What has helped the most is having once-a-month meetings to discuss what we're doing in the classroom. One whole day—supported by the ministry—and we'll continue next year. —Elementary teacher

Admin team and student success lead have worked out a schedule to give teachers in departments and in learning teams opportunities to be released, sometimes going off site or working in a quiet place in the building on a regular basis. We've done this for the last two or three years. It's been excellent. People enjoy the experience and get a lot of work done. The opportunity for planning and discussion: you can't put a price on that.—Secondary vice principal

An important aspect of restructuring that reinforced collaboration began with the ministry's removing sole responsibility for literacy from the testing grade teachers (grades 3 and 6 teachers in elementary and grade 10 English teachers in secondary), and shifting accountability for literacy instruction and students' results to all teachers in all grades. This process evolved quite differently in elementary and secondary schools.

In elementary schools, the focus of the turnaround teams was the entire primary division of the school, and all teachers from kindergarten to grade 3 were considered equally responsible for effective literacy instruction and for students' test results. After some initial resistance to the intervention from turnaround teams, teachers in nontesting grades were able to articulate how they made sense of their expanded roles and responsibilities regarding literacy:

> The staff understands it is not all on the shoulders of the grade 3 teacher. We are working on the same strategies beginning in kindergarten, getting students ready for the grade 3 test. —Elementary teacher

> We are coplanning in grades for consistency, and we are looking at expectations in all grades so everyone knows what's happening in all grades. We all own the kids.—Elementary teacher

> You know what? We realize it is not just grade 3. How fair is it to the grade 3 teacher? How fair is it to think that our students now taking [the provincial] primary literacy test, saying everything is about now, not before? If we are a team, then we're all responsible for those grades. There are kids who maybe we didn't teach well enough before they got to grade 3. If we approach this properly, we realize it's everybody in this together. If we start as low as kindergarten at building blocks, then we're not going to tumble in grade 3.—Elementary teacher leader

In secondary schools, the ministry's new initiatives required the inclusion of literacy instruction in all subject areas, which meant that teachers had to develop more collaborative relationships with their departmental colleagues in order to work out issues such as course assignments and student evaluation. Furthermore, administering, planning for, and preparing students for the grade 10 literacy tests were now intended to be collaborative efforts shared throughout the school. For many teachers, implementing literacy projects in math or science courses presented significant challenges, and although there was a formal literacy lead in each school collaborating with departments and individuals to help with literacy integration, more than a few teachers avoided getting involved in changing curriculum and in collaborations.

Whereas elementary teachers had overcome their resistance to new collaborative structures in a relatively short time, secondary school leaders, even three or four years after the initiatives were introduced, were convinced that some of their teachers were still testing the ministry's resolve:

> Sometimes there's the perception that this is something that's just another initiative that's going to go by the board, so teachers think, "I'm not putting resources into that. I'm just going to do my thing."—Secondary literacy lead

> I don't know exactly how much all teachers are doing to comply with teaching literacy. All I can do is encourage and make the information available, and when a staff member has a question and wants some resources or information, I provide that. —Secondary literacy lead

> Literacy across the curriculum has probably not worked in every department. Some are not taking sense of ownership that they have to do it too, for example, phys ed. Or they say, "I don't have time. I have my own curriculum to deal with." Some signs of that.—Secondary vice principal

Another kind of collaborative structure developed within the elementary turnaround schools when the success of primary teachers' work with the ministry's turnaround teams created a growing interest among teachers in junior and intermediate grades in learning more about new instructional strategies, as this elementary teacher commented: "There're opportunities where we can actually go into someone else's room while they're doing shared reading and see how it's done from a primary [K–3], because the primaries have had the focus on the process and how to do it. It is open to us to go to the primaries to see how to do it."

Table 6.2 summarizes the evidence from our interviews that represents the stages of initiation and development of organizational structures to support teacher collaboration. At stage 1, no structures were in place to facilitate teachers working together on literacy projects. By stage 2, educational leaders at all levels were creating structures for collaboration and affirming their importance for improving teachers' instructional skills and students' test results; there was still some resistance among some teachers in secondary schools. In stage 3, the expectation for collaboration was as entrenched among teachers as working in isolation had been in stage 1.

3. Turnaround leaders understand the enormous effect that family environments have on students' potential for academic learning. They focus considerable energy on building productive educational cultures within families and between families and their schools. They also encourage connections with other schools and stakeholders.

Shifting the attention of school staffs from an exclusively inside-the-school focus to one that embraces a meaningful role for parents and a close relationship with the larger community was identified during the 1990s as the biggest change in expectations facing those in formal school leadership roles (Goldring & Rallis, 1993). More recently, Muijs, Harris,

Table 6.2   How Creating Supportive Structures Changed Across the Stages

Stage 1	• Principals support a culture of isolation through school structures that encourage teachers to work alone.
	• Principals support some teacher teams, but they do not put enough emphasis on teams working toward specific literacy-related goals.
	• Only teachers whose students take the provincial tests (grades 3, 6, and 10) are held responsible for test preparation, administering tests, and students' results.
Stage 2	• In Turnaround Team Project schools, the Ministry of Education initiates collaborative processes related to improving literacy instruction, including PLCs for primary teachers.
	• Districts and principals extend support for PLCs for literacy-based activities to teachers in all grades.
	• Ministry, district, and school administration expectations for cross-grade and cross-curricular collaborations make all staff members in all grades responsible for test preparation, administering tests, and students' results, with varying levels of compliance among secondary teachers.
Stage 3	• Ministry, district, and school administration continue to support and reinforce teacher collaboration and schedule meeting times during the school day.

Chapman, Stoll, and Russ (2004) have identified this core practice as important for improving schools in challenging circumstances.

Attention to this focus has been encouraged by evidence of the contribution of family educational cultures to student achievement in schools (Coleman, 1966; Finn, 1989), the increase in public accountability of schools to their communities through the widespread implementation of school-based management (Murphy & Beck, 1995), and the growing need for schools to actively manage public perceptions of their legitimacy (Mintrop, 2004).

Nine studies carried out in turnaround school contexts provide evidence about the importance of having parents on committees or otherwise involved in school improvement planning. However, these studies present limited evidence about how leaders engage parents in these ways. Billman (2004) indicates that the majority of school leaders attempt to establish strong, enduring ties to the parents and community, and they pursue ways to better involve parents with schools. Maximizing parent and community involvement and including them in school management plans are strategies that turnaround school leaders employ in their leadership practices (Billman, 2004). Successful school leaders not only get parents and other community members involved in goal setting for schools (Foster & St. Hilaire, 2004; Lambert, 2006), they also endeavor to "consciously match their cultural experiences and behaviours and lead community members in solving the deep problems that besiege the school" (Lambert, 2006, p. 238). These leaders place particular emphasis on establishing connections among home, school, and community so as to foster "a view of the school as being part of, rather than apart from, the community" (Harris, 2002, p. 15):

> The school is a partnership between staff and school, between staff and the parents and students you work with. You need to build that up in the best ways you can.—Elementary principal

> I would like to see more parental involvement in the process. That could only have a positive impact. I think we continually try to bring our parents in and the community into the learning process.—Elementary principal

> It takes a village to raise a child, and I really do believe that we all have to work together, and by working with people at the board, and working with the community, and working with

the students, I believe that's what helped with our student achievement.—Elementary principal

I'd also want the school board to come up with some nice flyer for volunteering and the benefits of volunteering. Personally, my benefit is since I've been volunteering, all my children have improved in school. Because I'm involved, I know what's going on. My kids are getting higher grades because I'm here. —Elementary parent

We held a wildly successful community barbecue in the fall. We have trouble with attendance. We have trouble convincing parents that their child has to come to school every day. By getting them in and feeding them, we got parents who had never come to school for parent-teacher night, or called the office to ask about what was happening, to even get them into the schools so they'd see it's not such a scary place. For some parents, they've had really bad high school experiences. For them to follow up is scary even as parents. Socializing helps them realize, "I'm in a community building, and I'm part of that community." It seems to have worked, so they're more able to call the office, or come in and follow up on a student's assignment. Just to make us more visible in the community. This came out of the district's focus on community—outreach, etc., and there was funding provided for some kind of social event.—Secondary vice principal

Teachers and administrators often live outside their school's community and have a superficial understanding of their students' world. At one secondary school, teachers participated in a collaborative activity where teams were given cameras and a list of things to look for (such as For Sale signs and the interior of the coffee shops) in the school neighborhood. One teacher reflected on this experience: "We really understood where our kids were coming from and where they live, and the conditions that they find themselves in that they bring into the building with them."

Another development in relationships outside the school (supported by the ministry and the district) was the establishment of connections between elementary and secondary schools so teachers and administrators could familiarize each other about what happens with literacy instruction and assessment in their buildings during the transition years (grades 7 to 10 when students move gradually from an elementary to a secondary school setting). One of the results was improved and expanded programs for students considered at risk:

> Our admin and our feeder schools' admin meet monthly. They do a lot of work in the literacy area, prepping students.—Secondary teacher leader

> I've also worked with the elementary feeder schools, seeing what preparation they're doing there, how they're helping the students. I think that's made a big difference in what they've been doing over the last several years. I think that's one reason we're seeing improvement.—Secondary teacher leader

Our study indicated that in the early stages of turnaround, elementary teachers had visited other schools that were further along in the process. Now their success had attracted a steady flow of observers to their own classes to see how they were implementing literacy instruction strategies. One of these teachers said, "Now something's happening [as a result of turnaround teams intervention]. [Provincial test] scores are up. Teachers are interested in coming here [to work] and the resources are here. A lot of schools and principals are coming to this school to see what's happening and learn."

Table 6.3 summarizes how teacher and leaders at both school and district levels began from modest and scattered efforts to engage parental participation in school in stage 1. In stage 2, more focused activities were planned and implemented that were intended to increase parents' interest in and confidence

Table 6.3   How Building Productive Relationships with Families Changed Across the Stages

Stage 1	• Administration and staff inspire some parents to work with their children on school-based literacy initiatives.
Stage 2	• School leaders and staff run events aimed at getting more parents to come to the school and get involved.
	• The district and leaders encourage and support meaningful interactions between parents and teachers.
	• Leaders and teachers spend time in the school community and invite parents into the school.
Stage 3	• The district continues to support events that bring parents, teachers, and students together.

regarding the development of relationships with teachers and administrators. Stage 3 would be characterized by continued attention to parents' needs and support from the district so meaningful activities could be developed and delivered.

4. While most successful leaders connect their schools to the wider environment, leaders of turnaround schools in challenging circumstances aim to ensure that their families and students have access to other social service agencies.

School leaders in the Ontario study spent significant amounts of time in contact with people outside their schools seeking information and advice, staying in tune with policy changes, anticipating new pressures and trends likely to have an influence on their schools, and the like. Meetings, informal conversations, phone calls, e-mail exchanges, and Internet searches are examples of opportunities for accomplishing these purposes.

The large number of network learning projects facilitated by the National College for School Leadership in England provides especially powerful opportunities for connecting one's school to at least its wider educational environment (Jackson, 2002). Bringing in external support may also be a productive response to schools engaged in significant school improvement projects (Reynolds, Hopkins, Potter, & Chapman, 2001).

In spite of the considerable time school leaders spent on this function, we are unaware of any research to date that has inquired about its contribution to improving pupil learning or the quality of the school organization. However, research has been conducted about the effects of this practice in nonschool organizations. Referring to it as "networking," Yukl (1994) includes it in his multiple linkage model of leadership as one of eleven critical managerial practices. He describes this practice as "socializing informally, developing contacts with people who are a source of information and support, and maintaining contacts through periodic interaction, including visits, telephone calls, correspondence, and attendance at meetings and social events" (p. 69).

Teachers and administrators in elementary turnaround schools in the Ontario study did not seem to have concerns about their relations with the wider community, but at the secondary level, some administrators and teachers provided examples of how the school operated as a link between students and their families and their community:

> We have a partnership with a group that provides funds to provide nutrition break during the test [the grade 10 literacy test] to reduce anxiety to ensure they are operating under the best conditions possible that we can look after.—Secondary teacher

> This is a strong community. Our students don't much go outside for services. We have lots of community support and a large co-op program.—Secondary vice principal

Stage 1 in Table 6.4 describes schools operating in relative isolation from each other and from the surrounding community. In stage 2, schools developed increasingly meaningful connections

Table 6.4 How Connecting Schools to the Wider Environment Changed Across the Stages

Stage 1	• Elementary and secondary administrators and teachers work on literacy initiatives in isolation with no collaborative relations with other schools.
	• Most school administrators and teachers live outside their school's community and spend little time in the neighborhood.
Stage 2	• The district and Ministry of Education support collaborative relationships between elementary and secondary teachers and administrators to improve literacy programming and support for students as they move through grades 7 to 10.
	• The administration arranges visits to other Turnaround Team Project schools and brings visitors in as conditions improve.
	• The administration and staff engage the wider community in school-level activities that benefit students and their families.
Stage 3	• The district continues to support relations between secondary schools and their elementary feeder schools to enable better continuity of literacy instruction and correct placement of students in secondary school.

with other schools in their communities. Elementary teachers had opportunities to observe literacy instruction at other schools, and elementary and secondary teachers were working together to support students' literacy development between grades 7 and 10. Teachers and administrators at one secondary school had made themselves more aware of their students' home community. Although the people involved in our study showed little indication of planning for the next stage, we could anticipate that connections to the wider communities would become increasingly important for the sake of their school's survival.

By the Numbers

Tables 6.5 and 6.6 summarize evidence from interviews about which of the specific leadership practices aimed at redesigning the organization (Table 6.5), and the more specific practices associated with each (Table 6.6), as described in our framework, were perceived to be most evident to respondents in the successful turnaround schools. These results combine the responses of administrators and teachers but distinguish responses of elementary and secondary school respondents.

5. Sources of leadership to redesign the organization are much more distributed in secondary than elementary schools.

Table 6.5, quantifying interview evidence from both teachers and administrators, indicates that in the eight turnaround schools, sources of leadership aimed at redesigning the organization differed substantially between elementary and secondary schools. Elementary school respondents strongly associated principals (42 percent) with redesigning the organization, awarding only the Ministry of Education a significant minority role (25 percent). In contrast, secondary school respondents were less likely to view principals as a source of these practices (28 percent) and more inclined to identify formal and informal teacher leaders (19 and 17 percent) and district staff (18 percent).

6. Teachers perceived the provision of adequate resources to be the most prevalent leadership practice associated with managing the instructional program in their schools.

Among the four specific practices in this category (Table 6.6), an overwhelming number of respondents mentioned efforts to create more collaborative cultures or to build a learning community in their schools. Ninety (85 percent) elementary respondents and eighty-one (65 percent) secondary respondents mentioned enacting or experiencing this specific practice as part

Table 6.5   Sources of Leadership Practices in Successful Elementary and Secondary Turnaround Schools: Redesigning the Organization

Leadership Sources: Redesigning the Organization	Number (Percentage) of Respondents
Principal	
Elementary	44 (42%)
Secondary	35 (28%)
Vice principal	
Elementary	3 (3%)
Secondary	12 (10%)
Formal teacher	
Elementary	11 (10%)
Secondary	23 (19%)
Informal teacher	
Elementary	14 (13%)
Secondary	21 (17%)
Students	
Elementary	0
Secondary	2 (2%)
Parents	
Elementary	0
Secondary	4 (3%)
District	
Elementary	7 (6%)
Secondary	22 (18%)
Ministry	
Elementary	27 (25%)
Secondary	0
School teams	
Elementary	0
Secondary	3 (2%)
Total	
Elementary	106 (24%)
Secondary	124 (21%)

Note: This table represents a sample of four elementary and four secondary turnaround schools.

Table 6.6   Specific Leadership Practices Most Evident in Elementary and Secondary Turnaround Schools: Redesigning the Organization

Redesigning the Organization	Elementary Schools: Number of Responses (Percentage)	Secondary Schools: Number of Responses (Percentage)
Strengthening school culture	1 (1%)	9 (7%)
Modifying organizational structures	7 (7%)	5 (4%)
Building collaborative process and a learning community	90 (85%)	81 (65%)
Getting involved in community outside the school, and building productive relations with community	8 (8%)	29 (23%)
Aggregate	106 (24%)	124 (20%)

Note: This table represents a sample of four elementary and four secondary turnaround schools.

of the turnaround efforts in their schools. Little mention was made of strengthening the school culture, modifying organizational structures, or building productive working relations with the wider community.

Six items on our survey of teachers in both turnaround and improving schools measured two specific practices within this dimension of leadership: modifying organizational structures and building collaborative processes. In aggregate, principals and vice principals were considered to carry most of the responsibility for enacting this set of practices (71.7 percent). This pattern was most pronounced with modifying organizational structures (86.1 percent), but still substantial with building collaborative processes (57.3 percent). District leaders were assumed by some to be responsible for building collaborative processes as well (13.9 percent).

**Table 6.7   Teachers' Ratings of the Most Important Leadership
Practices in Turnaround Versus Improving Schools:
Redesigning the Organization**

Redesigning the Organization[a]	Turnaround Schools: Mean (Rank) (n = 4)	SD	Improving Schools: Mean (Rank) (n = 20)	SD
Strengthening the school's culture	3.05 (3)	1.18	3.63 (1)	1.16
Modifying organizational structures	3.40 (1)	1.10	3.40 (3)	1.06
Building collaborative processes and a learning community	2.6 (4)	1.08	2.91 (4)	1.15
Building productive relations with parents and the community	3.11 (2)	1.10	3.48 (2)	1.01
Aggregate	3.04	.91	3.31	0.94

Note: Response scale: 1 = very little, 5 = a great deal
[a]The reliability of this scale (Cronbach's alpha) was .82.

**7. Among the specific leadership practices associated with
redesigning the organization, modifying organizational structures contributed most to the success of turnaround schools,
while strengthening school culture contributed most to the
success of improving schools.**

Table 6.7 summarizes survey responses of teachers' rating
the extent to which specific practices associated with redesigning the organization were valuable to their efforts (1 = very
little, 5 = a great deal). Two columns report the mean ratings
(and standard deviations of those ratings) of teachers in turnaround schools, and two columns report the mean ratings (and
standard deviation of those ratings) of teachers in improving
schools.

Considering the turnaround teachers' responses first, ratings ranged from 2.64 for building collaborative processes to 3.40 for modifying organizational structures (typically this meant providing time for teachers to meet). Ratings of improving schools' teachers ranged from 3.63 for strengthening school culture to 2.91 for building collaborative processes and a learning community. The range of responses by the two groups of teachers, as indicated by the standard deviations, is very similar.

Conclusion

This chapter has provided examples of how the successful turnaround leaders in our study modified their approaches to organizational redesign and how their schools evolved. At the beginning of the first turnaround stage, school cultures encouraged individual work on the part of teachers, and structures in their schools mostly reinforced that isolation. But as this stage progressed, these cultures, and the structures that supported them, underwent considerable modification. Collaboration was clearly valued, and teams, committees, and working groups were formed in order to allow and encourage it. Changes in structures were also made to accommodate different approaches to literacy instruction. Connections to the wider community began to acknowledge the contributions of all levels of schooling to the success of students on provincial tests.

Key Points

- Successful turnaround leaders nurture the development of norms and values that encourage staffs to work together collaboratively on the improvement of their instructional practices.

- Turnaround leaders restructure their schools so that teacher collaboration is both possible and likely. The opportunities these new structures provide for teachers to work together also act as symbols of the value attached to such work by the school.

- Turnaround leaders understand the enormous effect that family environments have on students' potential for academic learning. They focus considerable energy on building productive educational cultures within families and between families and their children's schools. They also encourage connections with other schools and stakeholders.

- While most successful leaders connect their schools to the wider environment, leaders of turnaround schools in challenging circumstances aim, in particular, to ensure that their families and students have access to other social service agencies.

- Sources of leadership to redesign the organization are much more distributed in secondary than elementary schools.

- Teachers perceived the provision of adequate resources to be the most prevalent leadership practice associated with managing the instructional program in their schools.

- Among the specific leadership practices associated with redesigning the organization, modifying organizational structures contributed most to the success of turnaround schools, while strengthening school culture contributed most to the success of improving schools.

7

HOW TURNAROUND LEADERS IMPROVE THEIR SCHOOL'S INSTRUCTIONAL PROGRAM

> When we look at attendance and school pride, we really believe that every member of our staff is a part of that effort. We made the decision to make our learning teams comprised of five or six teachers and educational assistants and also to include caretaking and secretarial staff. We're all in one way or another responsible for the success rate of our students and the overall tone in our school.
>
> *Secondary principal*

Core leadership practices classified as managing the instructional program acknowledge the importance of school leaders' attending directly to teaching and learning in their schools. Such practices would seem to lie at the heart of what most writers advocate as instructional leadership. Robinson, Lloyd, and Rowe's (2008) recent meta-analysis of school leadership practices associated with increased student achievement offers some justification for such advocacy. Leadership behaviors most closely associated with classroom practice made the strongest contribution to achievement. Hallinger's (2003) review of those practices included in his own model of instructional leadership offered conflicting evidence, however. This evidence suggested that leadership practices that involve close association with the classroom and supervision of what happens in the classroom had the least effect on students. Such ambivalence in the evidence may reflect inattention to the contexts in which leaders find themselves.

Practices for Instructional Leadership

Our evidence indicates, at least in turnaround school contexts, that close-to-the-classroom leadership practices are essential. These are practices concerned with staffing the instructional program, monitoring school activity (including student learning), buffering staff from distractions to their classroom work, and providing material and psychological support for that work.

1. Both district and school leaders take special care to recruit and assign, to turnaround classrooms and schools, teachers and administrators who have the capacities and dispositions required to solve the challenges those schools face.

Although staff selection is not touched on by most formal models of instructional leadership (Hallinger, 2003; Waters, Marzano, & McNulty, 2003), this is a key function for leaders engaged in both school improvement and the more dramatic turning around of underperforming schools (Gray, 2000). This function involves recruiting, selecting, and retaining teachers with the capacity to further the school's efforts.

At least ten studies about leadership in turnaround or challenging schools point specifically to the crucial importance of recruiting and retaining staff who have these qualities:

- The instructional capacity to help at-risk students learn
- An unshakable belief in the potential of these students to learn given the right opportunities
- The persistence, patience, and optimism needed to create productive learning experiences for children in response to initial failure

The priority for turnaround school leaders, these studies suggest, is to ensure they are able to recruit and appoint teachers with as many of the required qualities as possible. Because this is a difficult and time-consuming process (Orr, Byrne-Jimenez, McFarlane,

& Brown, 2005; West, Ainscow, & Stanford, 2005), it is important for leaders to have much more flexibility than is typical in hiring teachers for their schools (Bell, 2001; Billman, 2004).

Three studies (Kannapel & Clements, 2005; Picucci, Brownson, Kahlert, & Sobel, 1999) demonstrate turnaround leaders' emphasis on staff capacity building and the careful matching of staff capacities to the needs of students (Kannapel & Clements, 2005). These leaders also nurtured the collective efficacy beliefs of their staff (Ross & Glaze, 2005) and ensured both training and mentoring of new teachers (Kannapel & Clements, 2005; Lambert, 2006).

According to the evidence from our Ontario study, staffing decisions had a considerable impact on the success of turnaround initiatives. Hiring staff with the specific skills and attitudes needed for turning around student performance loomed large in the minds of those leaders who commented on it—or example:

> My goal for year two was to get the appropriate teacher in the appropriate classroom.—Elementary principal

> At this school, the success of the whole [literacy] program has come from the entire staff buying in, and that's from hiring the people who have the interest and expertise in the area, and then their enthusiasm carries to the rest of the staff and then having everyone involved. I think that's what turned it around here. —Secondary principal

Over the years, several teachers in turnaround schools who were not prepared to work with the literacy initiatives had moved to other schools.

As the summary in Table 7.1 indicates, the staffing of instructional programs changed across the three turnaround stages in our study schools. At the beginning of stage 1, some district leaders were actually destabilizing or undermining the impact of school leaders through frequent relocation of principals. One consequence of such destabilization was that

Table 7.1 How Staffing the Program Changed Across the Stages

Stage 1	• District leaders move principals around frequently, causing disruptions in the school and a culture of resistance to administrators' initiatives.
	• Principals lead schools in which some staff resist getting involved in literacy initiatives.
Stage 2	• The Ministry of Education hires appropriate people for turnaround teams.
	• Districts assign appropriate principals, vice principals, and literacy leaders to turnaround schools.
	• Principals and district leaders hire and place suitably capable teachers in turnaround schools.
Stage 3	• District leaders and principals hire newer or younger teachers, assuming they are more likely to be in agreement with new literacy initiatives.
	• District leaders and principals place teachers in schools to match their strategic priorities and current challenges.

significant numbers of teachers in these schools initially resisted efforts by their principals, districts, and the province to target improvements in literacy, a provincewide priority.

By the second turnaround stage, however, the Ministry of Education was supplementing staff in elementary turnaround schools with turnaround teams, and many districts had begun to match the capacities of school administrators to specific school needs. These same districts had now opened up to principals the decision-making process about hiring and allocating teachers. These staffing decisions became even more strategic by stage 3. On the assumption that they were more likely to begin with a commitment (rather than resistance) to the provincewide literacy initiative, relatively new and often young teachers became a hiring priority, and these teachers were placed in schools that most needed their particular skills.

2. School and district leaders constantly monitor evidence about the learning of students and the efforts of staff to improve such learning, continuously adjusting their own decisions and actions in response to this evidence.

This practice is enacted by successful leaders in most contexts. For example, Waters et al. (2003) analyze effective leadership practices in many different school contexts with monitoring and evaluating functions, especially those focused on student progress. As another example, Hallinger's (2003) instructional leadership model includes a set of practices labeled "monitoring student progress." Based on evidence collected in nonschool contexts, Yukl (1989) claims that "monitoring operations and environment" is one of eleven effective managerial practices.

Evidence from research conducted in challenging and turnaround school contexts indicates that tracking student progress is a key task for leaders of these schools (Gray, 2000). The majority of leaders in these contexts, this evidence indicates, consider use of data "a key factor in the improvement of teaching and learning, the curriculum, and the culture and image of the school" (West et al., 2005, p. 77; also see Reynolds, Stringfield, & Muijs, forthcoming). Through reviews of achievement data, school leaders identify areas of the curriculum in which student performance is below expectations, as well as areas that need additional instruction for individual students (Billman, 2004; Chrisman, 2005; Picucci et al., 1999).

Reviewing data is part of the school improvement planning process for these leaders (Billman, 2004). They consider data not only as a means by which they are able to demonstrate and celebrate achievements (West et al., 2005), but also as indicators of how far students will likely progress with additional instruction (Kannapel & Clements, 2005) and how student achievement can be improved. Orr et al. (2005) found that turnaround school leaders not only took into account the academic needs of their students but also viewed students' emotional needs as critical factors in the school's improvement efforts.

Evidence from our Ontario study points to a new emphasis throughout the province, advocated by the Ministry of
Education, on data-based decision making about instruction. This
new emphasis gave rise to increased vigilance at both district and
school levels about the progress of individual students on provincial achievement measures administered by the province's testing
agency, The Educational Quality and Accountability Office or
EQAO. In the words of several of those we interviewed:

We've had staff meetings, divisional meetings analyzing EQAO
results to see trends and types of questions where our students
excel in as well as the ones they don't. Looking at results over the
last few years. All grades in the school look at it.—Elementary
teacher

At every meeting we look at the data board to figure out how
to get students to move to the next level.—Elementary teacher
leader

The Student Success initiative has done interesting things: identify kids, monitor their progress . . . getting them in the right
classes.—Secondary vice principal

We seem to have more stats and data to show we're doing better.
Because we see more data, we talk about it outside staff meetings.
We get data at staff meetings about comparing girls and boys and
comparisons to other schools in the board.—Secondary teacher

My role is to find gaps and improve student test scores.—Secondary
teacher leader

Teachers and administrators worked together to ensure that
teaching strategies were selected to address specific literacy
learning challenges that students faced.

Table 7.2 summarizes how the enactment of monitoring
practices in the Ontario schools changed as the turnaround

Table 7.2   How Monitoring School Activity Changed Across the Stages

Stage 1	• The Ministry of Education monitors and publishes students' results on provincial tests.
	• District and school leaders track results by school but not by individual student.
	• Principals become aware of low achievement scores among their students.
Stage 2	• The ministry (through its turnaround teams) train teachers to interpret provincial test data to inform instructional practices.
	• Principals and staff work together regularly on monitoring individual students' progress in school and tracking results on provincial tests.
Stage 3	• School leaders and teachers become increasingly concerned about students who continue to receive low scores in spite of everyone's best efforts.
	• School leaders and teachers are aware that some secondary students are immature and do not understand the importance for their futures of passing the provincial grade 10 literacy test.
	• Administrators and teachers are aware that scores on this test vary with each year's cohort of students.
	• School leaders see that improvements in students' test scores affect other areas (for example, attendance, school spirit) and see that nothing succeeds like success.

process evolved. These changes occurred throughout the system, a reminder that turning around a school involves the aligned work of many people outside, as well as inside, the school. Initially the ministry confined its contributions to testing students and reporting results to districts. These results were examined by both districts and schools, but at the school level, particular attention was given to students with low scores.

This initial monitoring pattern was replaced in stage 2 by a more supportive and interventionist role by the ministry. Now turnaround team members were available to school staffs to provide training in how to interpret test scores for purposes of instructional improvement. Principals and teachers began to examine these data at the individual student level.

By stage 3, school staffs were examining change over time and identifying especially students who continued to score poorly in spite of targeted interventions. School staffs had developed a more nuanced understanding of the causes of poor student performance. They had also begun to appreciate the broader effects on their school's morale overall and individual students' attitudes that had resulted from improved achievement on provincial tests.

3. School leaders buffer staff from distractions to their work with students, especially their classroom work.

A long line of research has reported the value to organizational productivity of leaders' protecting or buffering staff from being pulled in directions incompatible with agreed-on organizational goals. This buffering function acknowledges the open nature of schools and the constant bombardment of staff with expectations from parents, the media, special interest groups, and the government. Internal buffering is also helpful, especially buffering teachers from the considerable distraction of dealing with excessive challenges with pupil discipline.

At least three studies (Bell, 2001; Orr et al., 2005; Picucci et al., 1999) have inquired about how successful turnaround leaders buffer their staff from external demands that are unrelated to school priorities. Leaders in these studies reduced requirements and distractions that might take teachers' energies away from teaching and learning. They encouraged teachers instead to keep their energies focused on their school's academic excellence, instructional improvement, and parents' participation in school functions (Bell, 2001; Orr et al., 2005).

Administrators and teachers identified several strategies for protecting teachers from distractions. One was to respond effectively and consistently to student misbehavior, thereby reducing classroom disruptions for teachers. This was a particular concern for elementary principals:

I worked with the vice principal who knew the families and how much support there would be at home. Last year the suspension rate was really high—well over a hundred kids. It was pretty shocking.

I use consistent assertive discipline throughout the school to deal with the behavior issues.

Principals in the elementary turnaround schools were also expected, by some of their teachers, to buffer them from too many visitors, a function not all principals were deemed to be doing very well. As one elementary teacher explained, "They have to include more people on the decision making about whether we let the principal from this school come in instead of maybe just saying, 'They're coming.' So it's one thing to want to look great to other schools looking in on us, but sometimes you have to think about what's best for the staff in the school." As Table 7.3 indicates, the needs for buffering were different in elementary and secondary school contexts. Buffering elementary teachers from the disruptions caused by students' misbehavior in the classroom (not addressed adequately in stage 1) and from the distractions created by observers hovering in doorways (a result of improving test scores) became part of the principals' priorities in stage 2. In secondary schools, visits from observers were not mentioned, and the potential disruptions from at-risk students had been prevented through the ministry's transition years, which supported collaboration with grade 7 and 8 teachers and resulted in early

Table 7.3   How Buffering Staff Changed Across the Stages

Stage 1	• Principals and vice principals work ineffectively to maintain calm and order in the school.
Stage 2	• Elementary principals and vice principals buffer school staff from disruptive behaviors through consistent assertive discipline policies and practices. • Some elementary principals buffer staff from disruptions of visitors related to the school's turnaround efforts.
Stage 3	• School leaders and teachers in secondary schools placed at-risk students in programs in grades 9 and 10 that help prevent disruptive behavior problems by addressing these students' needs.

placement of struggling students in programs developed to meet their needs:

It's kind hard for the kids to have a man in a suit watching them. You try to prepare them.—Elementary teacher

Turnaround has not just brought those individuals to look around, but other principals from other schools have come and visited, and we have our doors open, so principals can walk in whenever they want. The first little while, it is stressful, because even though we're professionals and you think it doesn't bother you, it does. We have to explain to the kids that this is going to happen, and the majority of them are good, but there're always some who lose their focus on me and turn to whoever walks in. When the principals come in, they don't just come into the primary rooms; they come into everybody. They look around at everybody, so it is a little bit stressful because the junior and intermediate rooms might not look exactly like the primary rooms do. We haven't had all the information that they have had. Sometimes it feels like we don't know why they have to look at our rooms. By no means are we caught up to where the primaries are.—Elementary teacher

4. School and district leaders provide significant amounts and multiple types of support to teachers for their instructional work, in addition to formal professional development opportunities.

This general set of leadership practices is included in most formal models of instructional leadership. Typically these practices include supervising and evaluating instruction; coordinating the curriculum; and providing resources in support of curriculum development, instructional practices, and student assessment. Such a direct focus by school leaders on instruction is advocated in most school circumstances. But it seems especially crucial in challenging or turnaround schools (West et al., 2005), where teachers' conventional approaches to instruction often have not been very successful with struggling students.

Previous evidence suggests that instructional support in turnaround schools also encompasses helping teachers control student misbehavior, boosting teacher self-esteem, and encouraging teachers to talk with and listen to pupils. This evidence indicates as well that school leaders' instructional support is likely to include urging pupils and teachers to put a much stronger emphasis on student achievement, even when students are confronted with remarkable social and economic challenges. "The academic press," or extent of focus on and priority devoted to the academic work of students resulting from such an emphasis makes a powerful contribution to student achievement (De Maeyer, Rymenans, Van Petegem, van der Bergh, & Rijlaarsdam, 2006; Willms & Ma, 2004).

Successful turnaround leaders also nurture an academic press in their schools by focusing their efforts on improving academic instruction in the school (Picucci et al., 1999). They do all that is necessary to help teachers "translate the expectations

of the district curriculum or state standardized tests into effective classroom practice" (Giles, Johnson, Brooks, & Jacobson,
2005, p. 519). Several studies of turnaround schools (Bell, 2001;
Billman, 2004; Orr et al., 2005) point to the importance of turnaround school leaders' seeking out additional funding, providing
fiscal support to their teaching staffs, and having flexibility to
set their budgets. These leaders, in sum, place great emphasis
on "obtaining and making available the financial, material or
human resources to ensure that children and faculty would continue to experience success" (Bell, 2001, p. 8).

Evidence from our study points to the importance of providing resources to school staffs, managing programs and people,
and sharing information with staff.

Providing Resources. Teachers and administrators in the
turnaround schools agreed that the most helpful resource of
all was time to meet during the school day to discuss students'
achievement and improving instruction:

> The biggest change with turnaround itself has been opportunities
> for staff to meet. We have money not only for material resources,
> but also human resources. We can free teachers for two days each
> month to reflect, set out an agenda of study, share ideas that are
> successful, and focus on students who need more help. Providing
> time for teachers is mandatory.—Elementary principal

> We've talked about this. You can see our book room—it's fab-
> ulous. But we've decided, if we had to choose between those
> resources and the human resources and time, we now, in ret-
> rospect, find the time and human resources are in the end per-
> haps more valuable than the material resources, although of
> course you need the material resources as well. The time to sit
> and reflect and talk, and not feel rushed or hurried, and to really
> reflect on kids and our practice has been the most important
> thing, we've decided.—Elementary principal

The turnaround leaders also worked at staying knowledgeable about resources outside the school of potential value to the school—for example:

> The principal hears about current resources at board offices, through participation in workshops. She's very knowledgeable. —Elementary vice principal

> When the literacy coach came, there was practically nothing that was new, current, usable. She was knowledgeable about the resources we needed.—Elementary teacher leader

> The literacy lead is . . . up on literacy. He's always really good with passing on literacy documents and what's happening at the board.—Secondary teacher

> Our admin team and communications program head are very knowledgeable. They read articles on literacy and are in tune with what's going on, what's worked in the [United] States and what has failed.—Secondary teacher leader

The substantial increase in support from the ministry had succeeded in bringing resources to the teachers and students with the greatest needs. "I don't think I mentioned," said one secondary teacher, "the resource room where students can go down to get one-on-one help, and it's available all day long. The head of resource and his crew have worked with kids who were potentially at risk of failing the [literacy] test."

Managing Programs and People. All of the literacy improvement programs at the elementary and secondary levels were related to the Ministry of Education's literacy priority management of these programs and flowed through districts to schools. In three of the four elementary turnaround schools that we studied in depth, principals and teachers worked with ministry turnaround teams without much explicit reference to their districts. In one elementary school, the principal and teachers worked without the intervention of turnaround teams, but through the principal's persistence, they maximized their access to resources available through their district. "In spite of constraints in the budget," according to a teacher leader, "our principal is really good at getting things we need. That's really helped me as a teacher."

A large proportion of the instructional support activities of school leaders in our study was stimulated initially by changes in the policies and practices of the provincial testing agency, EQAO. During the period of our study and a bit before, EQAO had created new tests, altered procedures for scoring tests, and speeded up its annual reporting of results. Elementary schools were responsible for managing everything required to administer the tests. Secondary schools were charged with managing test preparation programs as well, a time-consuming set of activities that engaged many people at all levels for several weeks each year before the test was administered. A flavor of what this involved is evident in these remarks:

> I am chair of the literacy team, coming up with initiatives [in response to provincial test scores for the school], running them by the leadership team, and making up projects.—Secondary teacher leader

> I think it's a board-wide initiative. All will be doing some sort of practice for the literacy test. . . . Yesterday the package was handed out.—Secondary teacher leader

> I think a big change has also been in the delivery of the test to students with special needs. We have improved how we prepare students to use the [specialized] technology on a daily basis and for the test.—Secondary principal

I've been on the literacy committee for six years. I'm chair this year, responsible for running the show. Making the list of who writes [the provincial literacy test], coordinating the classrooms and teachers to supervise, providing accommodations, IEPs [individual education plans] for students considered to be at risk. —Secondary teacher leader

Sharing Information. Sharing literacy-related news was mentioned by a few elementary and secondary teachers in the turnaround schools as a function they believed was important for leaders in their schools:

[At staff meetings] there were flyers or information for us to share and talk about what was good and what would help our students, and how it would align us with our goals—success for the students. There's lots of opportunity to chat.—Elementary teacher leader

The teacher librarian receives extra money. He tells staff what he's purchased. Puts it on the table at staff meetings.—Secondary teacher

[The literacy lead] gives regular updates at staff meetings. He passes it on to departments, and I pass it on to my group.—Secondary teacher leader

All of these new responsibilities served to sharpen the school's focus on student achievement results.

As with the other turnaround leadership functions, enactment of the instructional support function also changed as the turnaround process unfolded (the nature of this evolution is summarized in Table 7.4). Increasing leadership from the ministry was a prominent feature of this evolution. Indeed, without the actions of provincial leaders, the success of most of the turnaround schools we studied seems unlikely.

**Table 7.4   How Providing Instructional Support Changed
Across the Stages**

Stage 1

Providing
resources

- Ministry resources support district-level literacy consultants.
- Support provided by timely and sufficient ministry resources helps convince school staff that turnaround and other literacy-based initiatives have a chance of succeeding.

Managing
programs
and people

- The ministry, some claim, makes tests easier some years than others.
- The district focuses on the literacy test to the detriment of overall literacy.
- District and school leaders rely on teachers' volunteering to participate in literacy initiatives.
- School leaders administer and organize test days according to ministry expectations.
- Administrators limit literacy awareness activities close to test time.

Sharing
information

- Principals and literacy leads share information about literacy-related issues and updates about tests.

Stage 2

Providing
resources

- The ministry and districts provide resources for school turnaround initiatives.
- Turnaround teams provide material and human resources and time for primary teachers to meet.
- Districts extend the collaborative supports available to primary teachers to junior and intermediate teachers.
- Districts and principals allocate resources for helping at-risk students pass the literacy test.
- The ministry and EQAO continue to upgrade test-related resources available for elementary and secondary teachers on their Web site.
- Ministry, district, administration, teacher leaders, and teacher librarians continue to provide effective material and human resources for all teachers to support literacy instruction

Managing
programs
and people

- The ministry and EQAO manage the provincial tests: they create, organize, score, and share results.

- Ministry initiatives include turnaround teams (elementary-school-level interventions to improve literacy in low-achieving schools) and secondary-school-level interventions (to improve educational outcomes for students who are at risk, with an emphasis on literacy).
- District, schools, and literacy teams manage administration of the test in the school, preparation programs for all students who will be taking the test, and accommodations on the test-taking day for students who are eligible

Sharing information

- Principals and literacy leads and teams take information from district-level meetings back to teachers.
- The librarian lets staff know about new resources.

Stage 3
Providing resources

- The ministry and EQAO continue to upgrade test-related resources available for elementary and secondary teachers on their Web site.
- The ministry, district, administration, and teacher leaders continue to provide effective material and human resources for all teachers to support literacy instruction.

Managing programs and people

- The ministry and district continue to support collaborative meetings among secondary staff and administrators to set up school-based programs for at-risk students.
- The district moves professional development from a central location closer to or into the schools that need the most support to improve literacy results.
- Administration and staff in elementary and secondary schools create conditions that make students want to attend and achieve.
- Elementary administrators and staff express concern about what happens after the Turnaround Teams Project is over.
- Secondary administration concedes that for at-risk students, it is not just the literacy test that is important, but how these young people will function in society.
- Secondary administration brings students' attention to consideration of life after the diploma: course selection, work, and careers, for example.

Sharing information

- Principals share information in ways that minimize staff resistance and maximize positive affect and productive activity for majority of staff.

By the Numbers

5. Leadership practices related to managing the instructional program were primarily performed by principals. Ministry turnaround teams, in elementary schools, and formal teacher leaders, in secondary schools, were also significant sources of these practices.

Table 7.5 reports the results of quantifying interview data from turnaround school administrators and teachers (combined), about the most prominent source of leadership practices classified as managing the instructional program. As with the three other categories of leadership practices, elementary school principals were most frequently (32 percent) viewed as sources of instructional program management. Almost as frequently identified was the Ministry of Education (28 percent), even though the specific practices associated with this category (for example, staffing, monitoring progress, buffering staff from distractions) seem most readily carried out by people inside the school. This may be a further indication of just how important the ministry's turnaround teams were for school staff.

Although secondary school respondents still frequently identified the principal as a source of this category of leadership practices (20 percent), other sources were more frequently identified—in particular, formal teacher leaders (36 percent) and district staff (23 percent).

6. Teachers in both elementary and secondary schools believed that the most evident leadership practice associated with managing the instructional program in their schools was provision of adequate resources. Managing meetings and monitoring student and school progress were identified as very evident in secondary schools.

As Table 7.6 indicates, this leadership category was expanded to encompass eight specific practices. Several of these were not part of our original framework (or measured

Table 7.5   Sources of Leadership Practices in Successful Elementary and Secondary Turnaround Schools: Managing the Instructional Program

Leadership Sources: Managing the Instructional Program	Number (Percentage) of Respondents
Principal	
Elementary	45 (32%)
Secondary	47 (20%)
Vice principal	
Elementary	6 (4%)
Secondary	14 (6%)
Formal teacher	
Elementary	19 (13%)
Secondary	85 (36%)
Informal teacher	
Elementary	9 (6%)
Secondary	12 (5%)
Students	
Elementary	0
Secondary	0
Parents	
Elementary	2 (1%)
Secondary	2 (1%)
District	
Elementary	19 (13%)
Secondary	54 (23%)
Ministry	
Elementary	40 (28%)
Secondary	15 (6%)
School teams	
Elementary	2 (1%)
Secondary	5 (2%)
Total	
Elementary	142 (31%)
Secondary	233 (39%)

Note: This table represents a sample of four elementary and four secondary turnaround schools.

Table 7.6   Specific Leadership Practices Most Evident in Elementary and Secondary Turnaround Schools: Managing the Instructional Program

Managing the Instructional Program	Elementary Schools: Number (Percentage) of Responses	Secondary Schools: Number (Percentage) of Responses
Staffing the instructional program	3 (2%)	3 (1%)
Monitoring students' progress and the school's improvement	29 (20%)	47 (20%)
Managing programs, committees, meetings	16 (11%)	69 (30%)
Knowing what's happening and staying up to date	11 (8%)	23 (10%)
Providing resources	66 (46%)	62 (27%)
Sharing information	9 (6%)	22 (9%)
Delegating	2 (1%)	5 (2%)
Buffering	5 (4%)	1 (>1%)
Totals	142 (32%)	233 (39%)

Note: This table represents a sample of four elementary and four secondary turnaround schools.

in the surveys) but emerged as potentially important for turn-around schools from qualitative evidence in our study. Three of the eight practices were mentioned as most in evidence by especially large numbers of interviewees, while the remainder received little attention:

- About 20 percent of both elementary and secondary school respondents mentioned the prevalence of monitoring students' progress in their schools.

- Providing resources was mentioned by almost half (46 percent) of elementary respondents and about a quarter (27 percent) of secondary respondents.

- Reflecting the typically larger size and organizational complexity of secondary schools, 30 percent of respondents mentioned managing programs, committees, and meetings as a dominant leadership activity.

7. Among the specific leadership practices associated with managing the instructional program, staying up to date and monitoring student and school progress contributed most to the success of both turnaround and improving schools.

Table 7.7 summarizes teachers' ratings of the extent to which practices associated with managing the instructional program contributed to the success of their school's turnaround efforts (1 = very little, 5 = a great deal). The table also reports such ratings from teachers in improving schools. Ratings of specific practices associated with managing the instructional program ranged from 2.25 (buffering) to 3.42 (knowing what is happening and staying up to date).

As Table 7.7 also indicates, when the responses of teachers from turnaround and improving schools are compared, turnaround teachers rated lower than improving schools teachers the value of each of the five specific practices measured by the survey. These results are consistent with the overall tendency of teachers in improving schools to provide more positive survey responses than teachers in turnaround schools. However, both groups of teachers ranked the practices almost the same.

Conclusion

This and the previous three chapters have served three purposes. First, they described a sample of the evidence we believe justifies the claim that almost all successful leaders rely on

Table 7.7 Teachers' Ratings of the Most Important Leadership Practices in Turnaround Versus Improving Schools: Managing the Instructional Program

Managing the Instructional Program	Turnaround Respondents: Mean (Rank)	SD	Improving Respondents: Mean (Rank)	SD
Staffing the instructional program	2.90 (3)	1.16	3.03 (4)	1.23
Monitoring student and school progress	3.15 (2)	1.02	3.65 (2)	0.91
Knowing what is happening and staying up-to-date	3.42 (1)	1.03	3.83 (1)	0.87
Providing resources	2.87 (3)	1.16	3.14 (3)	1.25
Buffering	2.25 (5)	1.14	2.45 (5)	1.32
Aggregate	3.06	.92	3.43	0.85

Note: n = 340 teachers from 13 turnaround schools and 228 teachers from 20 improving schools. Response scale: 1 = very little, 5 = a great deal. The reliability of this scale (Cronbach's Alpha) was .88.

the same set of core practices to carry out their work. These are practices that we classified by the short-term aims they are intended to achieve: creating a widely shared sense of direction among members of the school organization; developing the capacities these people need if they are to succeed in pursuing that direction; redesigning school policies, procedures, cultures, and structures in support of organizational members exercising those capacities; and directly managing teaching and learning processes in the school. These core practices capture what successful leaders do across many different organizational and national contexts.

The second purpose served by this and the previous three chapters has been to demonstrate that while the same sets of core practices provide a foundation for successful leadership in many different contexts, how these practices are enacted depends very much on the context in which leaders find themselves. Turnaround schools are a unique context for leaders. To be successful, turnaround school leaders enact the core practices in ways that appropriately acknowledge that context. We invoked evidence from earlier research conducted in the United States and United Kingdom on "failing," "challenging," and turnaround school contexts to illustrate what appropriate enactment of the core practices means in such contexts.

Our third purpose for these four chapters was to describe the results of research carried out in a sample of successful turnaround schools in Ontario. This research tested the proposition that not only do turnaround school contexts require unique enactments of the core leadership practices, but also that each stage in the turnaround process is sufficiently unique to require additional adaptations of the core practices by turnaround leaders, and that each stage may also call for different sources of such leadership enactment. How leadership is enacted, we argue, is a question not only about specific leadership behaviors or practices but also about who exercises those behaviors or practices.

Evidence from our study reported to this point indicates, in sum, that

- The four sets of core leadership practices captured most of the work of leaders in turnaround schools.
- These practices were widely distributed among roles in both elementary and especially secondary schools, and the distribution grew through stages in the turnaround process.
- Even at the first turnaround stage, successful school leaders adopted a much more collaborative approach to their leadership than has been reported to be the case by leaders in private sector or business turnaround contexts.

- Nevertheless, those in formal leadership roles were still identified as the primary sources of most of the core leadership practices. In particular, principals remained key enactors of the core practices in school turnaround contexts, as they are reported to be in most other contexts.

- Provincial-level leaders (the turnaround teams) were significant sources of most of the core leadership practices in the elementary schools. In some cases, they were the most prominent source. The government's vision for improved literacy was not contested by our turnaround schools, and the Ministry of Education's turnaround teams were widely considered to be major sources of instructional leadership in all of the elementary schools in which they worked.

- District-level leaders played background support roles or were largely replaced by provincial leaders in turnaround elementary schools. However, they assumed considerable importance in secondary schools, where the province had chosen a less interventionist role for itself. In addition, formal teacher leaders, often department heads, were a consistent source of leadership in the secondary turnaround schools.

Key Points

- Both district and school leaders take special care to recruit and assign to turnaround classrooms and schools teachers and administrators who have the capacities and dispositions required to solve the challenges those schools face.

- School and district leaders constantly monitor evidence about the learning of students and the efforts of staff to improve such learning, continuously adjusting their own decisions and actions in response to this evidence.

- School leaders buffer staff from distractions to their work with students, especially their classroom work.

- School and district leaders provide significant amounts and multiple types of support to teachers for their instructional work, in addition to formal professional development opportunities.

- Leadership practices related to managing the instructional program were primarily performed by principals. Ministry turnaround teams, in elementary schools, and formal teacher leaders, in secondary schools, were also significant sources of these practices.

- Teachers in both elementary and secondary schools believed that the most evident leadership practice associated with managing the instructional program in their schools was provision of adequate resources. Managing meetings and monitoring student and school progress were identified as very evident in secondary schools.

- Among the specific leadership practices associated with managing the instructional program, staying up to date and monitoring student and school progress contributed most to the success of both turnaround and improving schools.

8

TURNAROUND LEADERSHIP UP CLOSE AND PERSONAL

One of the advantages of examining how multiple turnaround leaders enact a single set of practices, as in Chapters Four to Seven, is that as the practices themselves become clearer, they take distinctive shape apart from the context in which they are normally embedded. This is loosely analogous to repeatedly practicing your tennis forehand or going to the driving range and hitting your nine iron fifty times in a row. Isolating and practicing a single skill does help refine and automatize it. But playing the game itself requires those individual skills, however well refined, to be integrated with many others and under far more varied and unpredictable conditions. Most of this chapter describes how groups of leaders in two schools located in different districts enacted school turnaround. Their efforts illustrate only some of the core turnaround leadership described in earlier chapters, emphasize some of these practices much more than others, and reveal additional aspects of leadership not directly addressed in the previous chapters. The chapter ends with a discussion of some quantitative data that return us to a less context-dependent appreciation of the turnaround leadership practices that seem to matter most.

The two cases are from our Ontario study—one elementary and one secondary school. Descriptions of these cases highlight the activities and approaches described by the people we interviewed in the schools. These were schools that, along with their districts, had demonstrated significant improvements in their students' provincial literacy test results over a period of three or four years. Principals, other leaders, and teachers gave us their impressions of the changes they had made, the forms of leadership that had influenced those changes, and how they had been affected by working together on improving literacy achievement. Differences in size, culture, and organization notwithstanding, these two schools had faced similar challenges with respect to teachers' instructional capacities and students' needs.

In both schools, the stimulus for changes at the school level had been created by the Ministry of Education's policies and resources described in earlier chapters that were aimed at helping to improve students' literacy scores. The two districts in which the schools were located had also played an important role by setting directions and high performance expectations for the schools' efforts and by providing the human and monetary support each school needed to make progress. These districts modeled the importance we attached to differentiated school support in Chapter Two. Much of what accounted for poor student performance in these schools was not under the direct control of the school leaders, but they had a great deal to do with pulling the school staff together around a common set of purposes and establishing a positive and optimistic tone for the schools as a whole.

Both cases are examined using the same set of organizing themes:

- Tracking turnaround results
- Setting directions
- Approaches to improvement
- Leadership distribution
- Positive results
- Sustaining improvement
- Remaining concerns: It is not all perfect

Each section, as far as possible, privileges the perspectives of staffs in the two schools. Although we offer interpretive comments, the voices of the teachers and leaders dominate our narrative description of the turnaround processes. The final section in each case serves to remind us that all schools live in imperfect worlds and that the turnaround process typically unfolds in spite of some factors that are often far less than supportive. School leaders reading these sections should feel comfortable knowing that messiness and friction need not mean failure.

Brookside Elementary School

Brookside Elementary School is located in a midsized city in southern Ontario. The school district has about one hundred elementary and twenty-five secondary schools spread among twelve communities serving approximately twenty-five thousand elementary and fifteen thousand secondary students. District leadership is provided by the director and nine superintendents. The school board consists of the chair and twelve board members.

Brookside's five-year-old two-story building, with its state-of-the-art amenities such as a large library and computer labs, as well as an elevator and other accommodations for children with special needs, was a dramatic replacement for the small, dark, early 1900s schoolhouse that had been outgrown as the neighborhood was transformed. Over the past ten years, the quaint semirural, sparsely spaced streets and houses had become a modern subdivision with narrow lots and curving roadways. The average family income of students attending Brookside Elementary was about sixty-three thousand Canadian dollars.

At the time of our data collection, almost five hundred children were enrolled in kindergarten to grade 8. Several ethnicities were represented in the school, but almost all the children had been born in Canada. Several classes were made up of split grades, and there were two special education classes. Specialists taught French and music/drama for the whole school. In total, there were twenty-five teachers, four of them new to the school. Eleven teachers were assigned to the primary grades (K–3), five taught in the junior division grades (4–6), and three teachers worked with the intermediate grades (7 and 8). A half-time literacy coach worked mostly with teachers and students in the primary and junior divisions. Two of the junior classes were housed in portable classrooms, and the school population was continuing to grow. As one of the teachers explained: "They're moving in more than they're moving out. There's a lot of new development going on."

At the time of data collection, Marlene, a principal with fifteen years of experience in the role, was nearing the end of her second year at the school, and the vice principal, Hal, was completing his first year.

Tracking Turnaround Results

Grade 3 reading results had improved by 28 percent in the span of three years at Brookside. Fifty-one percent of students were successful in meeting the acceptable provincial standard in 2004–05, and 79 percent were successful in 2007–08, well above the district average of 60 percent. In the same time span (2004–08), grade 3 writing results improved from 51 to 70 percent. For students in grade 6, there were similar increases in reading (from 49 to 72 percent) and writing (47 to 72 percent). Grade 3 math showed steady improvement over the years (from 51 to 79 percent), although grade 6 math scores had been erratic (63, 55, 74, 57, and 67 percent).

Setting Directions

Marlene had come to the school with a vision for improving student achievement that had been shaped and reinforced by the new district director's commitment to literacy results. The director's message about student achievement had been circulating in the district for at least a year, and that meant Marlene's priorities and change initiatives were easily accepted by the staff: "I think I had a willing audience, if you will. The director was giving messages, and it was permeating everything the board was about. It wasn't like: 'Where is she getting all these wacky ideas?' It's just very much part of the culture of the district that we must improve these scores."

The district culture was reinforced in senior leaders' conversations with school-level administrators and teachers during school visits. The director had the same question for everyone: "How does that enhance student achievement?" When superintendents (senior district leaders reporting to the district director) came to the school, they would "dispense with the niceties and get to business," asking what was being done to improve student achievement. Marlene knew the strong district leadership helped her staff to focus on literacy: "I think they're fabulous teachers. They've always been fabulous teachers, but what has helped is to focus our priorities more directly on the school's needs."

Approaches to Improvement

Increasing Collaboration. The district's improvement initiatives involved collaborative processes that included teachers in school-level decision making about the new school growth plan. Marlene described developing that plan as a painstaking process that took nineteen days for the divisional leaders and included consultations with classroom teachers along the way. She was grateful to the ministry for providing the resources:

> There was a phenomenal dialogue. As an administrator you can go so deep, but having actual practitioners who are in the trenches all the time to reflect things that needed to be worked on is better. The [extra] time made it possible to take a bottom-up approach. We couldn't have afforded it without the ministry's support. At the end of it, every teacher knew what the school growth plan was, could articulate the goals for the school, and

had developed grade-level classroom strategies they were going to implement for its successful achievement. I've never had nineteen days spent better.

Teachers agreed with this teacher's comments on the benefits of being involved: "This year is the first year I felt that as a school we've codeveloped the direction of the school. We have had more input as a staff about where the school is going to go. I think that's been a real benefit."

Another area where the district required and supported collaboration among teachers was setting up monthly meetings for divisional professional learning communities (PLCs). The district expected that meetings would be embedded in the school schedule for primary and junior teachers. Intermediate teachers were expected to have their PLC meetings before the school day began. Marlene, Hal, and the literacy coach attended all PLC meetings, which they had organized so that on the morning of such meetings, primary and junior teachers covered each other's classes while the others met. Getting the students settled took a few minutes out of the brief time allotment, but there was always an agenda, minutes were taken, and there were plans for follow up. Marlene explained:

> The agenda is usually based on another piece of data [student test results] to examine. It's distributed beforehand. The vice principal graphs it so teachers can get a quick look at how they have done in a particular area. We share the results, talk about strengths. "What did you do?" "What happened here?" "We better really focus on that as a division." "What strategies are we all going to employ to address this gap?" Next month we talk about it again.

Hal was convinced that these meetings were important for the fabric of this school: "PLCs embedded in the timetable are instrumental in developing a sense of community."

Literacy Focus. One of the district's initiatives had been to provide literacy coaches, and both Marlene and the staff appreciated the work of the coach who had been assigned to Brookside. Marlene said, "One thing that made a big difference is that schools were staffed with literacy coaches. Schools where their EQAO [provincial test] scores were stagnant were given a literacy coach, and that was something that was given to Brookside. So when I came . . . a half-time literacy coach had already been assigned. The literacy coach goes into the classrooms, helps identify the areas where teachers would like some help, for example, guided reading or writing activities. Then he models lessons and works together with the teachers."

This teacher identified how the literacy coach had improved and supported their practices: "When he comes into the room, it's not: 'Okay it's my prep.' It's more of a collaborative approach. When he's in the room there's two of us. Which is great."

In addition to practical instructional assistance, one teacher said the literacy coach's collaborative approach had led him to engage in more planning with his grade partner: "Before he was here, I don't think there was that much collaboration, even with my grade partner. We were kind of on the same track, we knew what the other was doing, but we wouldn't sit down and plan."

Another teacher associated the literacy coach with increasing accountability among teachers: "When the literacy coach first came, it was interesting because it was almost like having a literacy coach here started making you more accountable. He's coming in to help you with your program, so you better have a program in place for him to help you with."

Data Use. Marlene described herself as a new principal "keen on understanding use of data to facilitate instructional changes in the classroom." Under her leadership, the staff regularly collected data from standardized tests and then used the results for planning and evaluating instruction. "When we developed the school growth plan," she said, "our goal for last year was to improve EQAO, and we tracked it throughout the year. At the end of the year, it was wonderful to look at where we said we wanted to be and what we actually achieved. That really reinforced to everyone that this is important." Hal noted, "The staff accept the collection and use of student data. They discuss best practices, and they see it as a positive, because they can see the results and then they celebrate successes."

Because they had already seen the benefits of using data to track progress, teachers were aware of how important the information could be for guiding their instruction:

> Having all of that data to look at, there's been a lot more emphasis on accountability and coming up with the data to show what we're doing.—Teacher

> This year the staff has been working at doing things. Let's take CASI [Cognitive Abilities Screening Instrument], for example. You do it three times a year: once as a diagnostic, once as a formative, and once as a summative assessment. I think in the past that even though you were doing the three, there was no real continuation. I did it once, I leave it alone; I did it the second time, I leave it alone. This year the staff is saying, "I'm going to do it once. Now let's look at student responses, let's deconstruct them, work through them, see how we can improve." Then we'll do an example, not the whole CASI. We'll do CASI-style questions. . . . What's happening is we're starting to look at what we did, how we can improve upon it, and work that into day-to-day teaching. It would be tempting to say we're teaching to the test, but I'd disagree. What we're doing is looking at some of the markers that the test indicates and then working at improving.—Teacher leader

Staff Development. Marlene told us that the new director had changed all the principals' meetings to make them about professional development. So she used the same tactic in staff meetings at the school: "During staff meetings I try to dispense with the FYI and have opportunities for professional development. Be it a clip of something that's interesting, a presentation by one of the teachers who had phenomenal success, sharing. Bottom-up leadership."

A teacher gave her side of the experience of professional development in staff meetings and its impact on staff: "Staff meetings used to be [about] in-house things; now they're more of a professional development. And at the end of the day, that may not be what you want to do, but at the same time, it's inspiring, it's invigorating, and sometimes you're given an article to have read for that time and you go, "Oh, man!" But it's so necessary, and even though you're tired, it keeps you fresh and going and learning, and there's always new information, and you end up talking about that in the staff room, just over lunch."

Leadership Distribution

Several teachers noticed that the collaborative structures and culture at Brookside had created a sense they were working with the principal and vice principal as equals. They observed how school leadership was distributed among teacher leaders such as the division heads and the literacy coach, and they appreciated how the principal made all the teachers feel valuable by asking for their input on school matters:

> What we have going on right now seems to be working. Everybody's kind of on the same level. The principal attends all of our meetings, even our junior division meetings, when I'm in charge. She's participating as if we're all at the same level. She has that approach, and I think that really works well with us. And in our whole staff meetings, when she's leading the meeting,

she always asks for input. She makes everyone feel like we are all important here.—Teacher leader

Our administration is probably the driving force behind a lot of the things that are going on. I would say that Hal, our vice principal, has probably been one of the more instrumental people. He has a real hands-on approach to what's going on inside the classrooms. Marlene, though, is really good at disseminating what our school targets are, how we're going about them, and what we need to do to move past that. They provide the initial thrust of discussion, and then from that, the divisional leaders look at how we are going to work with our divisions in order to have that happen. As the divisional leader, I would be responsible for organizing meetings and teacher collaboration.—Teacher leader

Our literacy coach takes a lead role. He's always helping us out with resources. For example, this year we had an opportunity to visit another school and observe guided reading lessons that have been implemented from that school's point of view, and that helps a lot.—Teacher

Our principal's excellent at offering new resources, and often what she will do, if someone has tried a resource, she'll have them present it at a staff meeting to the other staff.—Teacher

That's shared leadership, where you feel like you're working with, not working for. You're a contributing factor to the whole team. Not a top-down approach.—Teacher

Positive Results

A teacher leader illustrated how important all the district's initiatives had been for bringing about improvements in students' EQAO results:

When we got the literacy coach, everything seemed to start at the same time. I can't tell if it's because of the literacy coach, or because of the PLCs, or if it was the divisional meetings—all these things just started happening at once. All of them together made us more accountable, more productive, and increased student achievement is the end result. . . . Over the past three or four years, we've had three to four vice principals, and we've had two different principals. Change in administration is a huge factor. We have the inception of the literacy coach over the past two years. That's made a huge difference. And over the past two years, we've seen a huge improvement already. Also just over the past year has been this embedment of the PLC in the time-table. On top of the PLCs, we also have junior division meetings. So there're divisional meetings once a month. The PLCs focus on literacy. The divisional meetings are for housekeeping—things we need to meet and talk about. Even the change in focus around the SMART (specific, measurable, attainable, realistic, and timely) goals as a board initiative has made a difference, and there's also been a new director in the past three to four years. We were writing smart goals, maybe three or four pages long, and the message came from the director: "Make this a page long." Get more specific goals. I think all these things play an important role in improving student achievement. We can attribute success to any one of these things, but I think it is all of them.

Sustaining Improvement

One of the teacher leaders offered us some insights about the challenges of sustaining the improved results and made some suggestions about continuing changes in staff and administrators in order to keep efforts to improve moving forward. These suggestions reflect the initiatives, outlined in Chapters One and Nine, that successful organizations undertake to stave off longer-term declines in performance after satisfactory performance levels have been achieved:

There's a danger in reaching certain points. I think the staff needs a certain amount of constant self-reevaluation. To maintain where we're at, I think, is going to need a couple of things. First thing is a certain degree of consistency in expectation, not only from administration but from the board [district]. What happens so often, the board focuses changes, and when it changes, it's difficult to maintain results. I think when we start implementing things, it needs to be maintained for a discernible period of time; just because you get results in three or four years doesn't mean that will be maintained. The second thing I think needs to happen, some schools need an influx of new staff. It's very tempting when you're a teacher to think that you're going to stay in a building for a long time, but students respond well to variability, to change and variety. I think that if you bring in staff with new ways of doing things, you're not always getting the same responses to the same problems. I don't know if you need to have a forced change, but I know that's one of the reasons why administrators circulate. We're getting a new vice principal every two years, a new principal every five to six. That helps refocus the staff.

Remaining Concerns: It Is Not All Perfect

Marlene, Hal, and several teachers expressed their concerns about the impact of a new district directive that in September, all schools were to begin their day with a one hundred–minute literacy block. Teachers would be in control of the time but would be asked to submit their plans for the school's focus on guided reading. The principal and vice principal saw it as a vital component of improving literacy learning, but teachers feared the quality of instruction in other subject areas such as math would suffer when their rotary programs (rotating students to different teachers for different subjects) were cut back and people who were not necessarily knowledgeable or comfortable in math would have to teach it to their whole class. Hal explained the situation: "The new timetable means all junior [students] have math at the same time, which means teachers teach their own classes instead of students going to the expert junior math teacher on rotary. There is some dissatisfaction with this, but it is a necessary change to enable the one hundred–minute literacy block."

The junior math teacher gave her perspective: "I'm a math specialist. I'll do the grade 6 math for the other grade 6 as well. The other grade 6 is an art specialist, so it makes sense for her to take my kids for art. So I think we're giving kids the best opportunity to learn something from people who are the most knowledgeable. We're moving away; I'm pretty sure it's coming from the ministry level. But they're trying to get rid of the rotary up to grade 6. Which means the regular classroom teacher is going to be doing math, art, science, up to grade 6. That worries me, because another teacher here has even said to me that they're not comfortable teaching math. That doesn't give me too much confidence in sending the kids to that teacher. The fact that we do that, and we've been doing that over the past few years, I think that is another huge factor in why our levels of achievement have been rising over the past few years."

Another area of concern was raised by one of the three intermediate teachers. She had seen how the primary and junior divisions had been benefiting from increased literacy supports. Her students, however, had been coming through the grades just ahead of the expansion of literacy initiatives, and though the literacy coach provided some support for the grade 7 and 8 teachers, many of her students needed extra help that was not readily available. The strategies teachers shared at staff meetings required adaptations that often took more time than she had. At this point she was doing her best and assuming that her students would be correctly placed in high school programs that would help them prepare for the provincial test in grade 10: "Right now in my own class of thirty-three kids, I have a spread of kids working at a grade 11 level to kids working at a grade 5 level. I have a lot of kids who struggle, and we definitely need learning resource time for these kids as well. How much time do I have to work one-on-one with the kids? Not much. It's another indicator of intermediates being left in the desert."

She pointed to a gap between what students were able to achieve by the end of grade 6 and what was expected of them in grades 7 and 8, which meant she needed to water down what she was teaching: "I'm seeing too many students who don't have the skills they need to go on to high school. . . . They're not fluent writers, they're not fluent readers. They're getting by up to grade 6. They're doing okay. But they hit grades 7 and 8, and the expectations are higher, the reading level is higher, the amount of reading is so much higher, and they're not doing well. So what I have had to do personally is really water down what I'm teaching. So yes, their marks are looking good, but it's not the level of testing that I was doing five, six, or ten years ago."

The good news was that the district was showing an interest in addressing the needs of grade 7 and 8 students. A new approach to literacy instruction in grade 7 was being piloted at Brookside, including providing a teacher from a junior class to mentor the process of learning how to use guided reading strategies adapted from the junior division program. Said the teacher:

> They're finally putting some time and effort into literacy at the intermediate level. We've been basically left out for years, where the primaries [were] in-serviced ad nauseam, but nothing at the intermediate level. Even our literacy coach right now is geared mainly to primary/junior. He will work with us, but the focus again is primary/junior. So we're starting guided reading next year, and we've never done guided reading. It's something the primaries are used to, but not the intermediates. We're looking at taking the lead as a school in the district. We're piloting this in June with grade 7s so that we can do it as well with grade 8s next year.

Central Secondary School

Central Secondary School (CSS) is an inner-city school located in an older part of a large southern Ontario city. The school district, serving students in several towns, has 116 schools (97 elementary and 19 secondary). The district has a student enrollment of over fifty-two thousand and more than seven thousand employees. District leadership consists of the director of education, the associate director, a superintendent of business, and seven superintendents of education with responsibilities for various academic areas. The school board consists of a chair (elected by the trustees) and eleven other publicly elected trustees who are responsible for fifteen "wards" or subregions within the municipality.

Unlike Brookside's up-to-date facilities, CSS was built in the 1960s and is in need of refurbishment. All the windows and a hazardous gym floor need to be replaced, and air-conditioning needs to be installed, at least in the library, auditorium, and computer labs. CSS is a composite high school with programs for applied and academic students, credit recovery support and individualized help for students who are struggling, and an expanding co-op program involving local businesses for students likely to stay in the community after graduation. The school Web site lists thirty sports teams and twenty-five extracurricular activities.

At the time of our data collection, there were seventy-six full-time teachers and seven educational assistants. Eight staff members were considered to be aspiring leaders, and several had been nominated for or had received awards for outstanding teaching. Eleven hundred students were enrolled at CSS at the time of our study. Very few had been born outside Canada, and many students' families had lived in the same neighborhood for generations.

School leadership was provided by Dan, who was in his fourth year at the school, his first principalship after fourteen years working in education. There were two vice principals. We interviewed one of them, Bruce, who had been in education for thirteen years, and in a leadership role for five years, including three at CSS. The challenges facing the school administrators and staff were the same as at many other inner-city schools, and they had been the same for many years: student apathy, lateness and attendance issues, lower success rates for students in applied levels, needy students and inadequate funding to support them, and parents who were uninvolved in their children's education for various reasons. In addition, former students and community youth were causing problems by trespassing, vandalizing the school, and drug trafficking.

Tracking Turnaround Results

In October 2002, the year before Dan began his tenure, only 48 percent of the students who were eligible to take the province's grade 10 literacy test administered by EQAO for the first time were successful. On his arrival in September 2003, the student success rate in the tests was 60 percent. In the following year, the percentage of students who were successful had climbed to 74 percent. The next tests were conducted in March 2005, and there has been an increase of 1 percent in each succeeding year, rising to 76 percent by March 2007, the year of our study. In recent years, graduation rates had also improved, showing a 10 percent increase, from 50 percent to 60 percent of all eligible students.

Setting Directions

Dan's goals for improving the school went beyond the students' results on the provincial tests. Everyone we spoke to used the same words: the vision was for CSS to be "on the map" athletically and academically. One teacher said this about Dan:

He's the initiator as well; also a fire-starter that gets things going. He has a way of getting people to want to put forth the effort and want to help the kids succeed. That's his goal—to bring CSS on the map. That's his line: "We're on the map"— whether in athletics or academics or whatever. If he's not in the foreground, he's in the background being supportive, and he'll do whatever it takes to help people do things.

One teacher talked about Dan's vision:

Big factor in a community like this, a school like this, is understanding the kids. Also, having a vision of something larger than the kids and offering that vision in as many different ways as possible. Get them thinking in broader ways than just their street and their community. Open the world up to them. Some of these kids, their families haven't left this city—parents and grandparents have always lived in the same neighborhood. Believe that success is possible. It isn't going to be for everyone at this stage in their lives, but it might be eventually.

Dan's vision took into consideration a wider view of the future for his students and saw them as becoming more productive citizens in the world as a result of their high school experiences.

Approaches to Improvement

Increasing Collaboration. Dan's approach to working with teachers and other leaders in the school involved creating teams. One of these was the team responsible for determining the overall direction or goals for the school. This team, consisted of department heads and other selected teachers, and was based on a district model. "In terms of building leadership," he said, "I was able to put together a directions team, and this is a model that's used throughout the board. It's comprised of a number of what I would call leaders or high flyers in this school: well trusted, have demonstrated their own level of success with students, and they've been really instrumental in facilitating a lot of the activities that we've been dealing with over the last two or three years."

He had also organized learning teams, charged with sharing for students' success: "We made the decision to make our learning teams comprised of five or six teachers and EAs [educational assistants], and also include caretaking and secretarial staff. We're all in one way or another responsible for the success rate of our students, and people who are support staff beyond just teaching do have an impact on our students and on the overall tone in our school."

In addition, teachers said Dan and Bruce could be relied on to listen to teachers' concerns and suggestions. Several teachers said they felt they had been heard, and responses to the problems they were experiencing had been fair and thoughtful:

> He has an open door policy: if he's here, the door is open. You don't have to make an appointment. You can go to the principal or vice principals.

> Specifically in the last three or four years, I feel comfortable if I have an issue, an idea, a thing I want to try. I know if you bring it to the principal, he will listen to it. He might not necessarily agree, or he might see potential pitfalls, but he does listen to what you have to say. That's really important. People have a chance to voice their opinion. Ultimately a decision will be made by the principal and vice principal. That's where the strong leadership comes in. You express the concern [about literacy test preparations compromising class time to cover math curriculum] and the solution comes, and it works for most people.

Teachers said they were comfortable talking to the principal and found him supportive:

> The principal listens to people's ideas, prioritizing ideas, seeing what works. He is supportive of things staff want to do. People are on board.

> There's not any kind of hierarchy of any sort here. You can talk to any person, whether department head, principal, vice principal, the same as you talk to the people you work with.

> Our principal tends to be very humble. You'll notice that he won't take credit. He will rather defer to those people who are doing things, and just says he's part of it.

> I'm happy with the way things get done. As a staff, we're a good team.

Bruce shed more light on how collaborative groups were the result of Dan's leadership:

> He seems to have a knack for getting the right people involved—in terms of capacity building, empowerment. That's his real important leadership skill, because we've got all kinds of people involved to support literacy and they're all really motivated. He's more or less a guiding hand—for example, the learning directions team. Dan and I started throwing around some names about who would be good for that, and we kind of built the team that way of people who are really interested in getting involved and jumping on something and easy to get along with, and it built from there . . . the whole collaboration. You can be an opportunist, you can be a great leader, but the whole capacity thing, you can't do it all. Being able to identify (which is a kind of opportunizing in itself) the people who can move things along and getting them involved. . . . We've had a lot of success at this school in terms of

building this kind of team approach. It's not 100 percent, but it's enough of a size that things are going to happen and initiatives can take shape and things can get going. I guess the goal is to continue to make it bigger—the number of people willing to get involved in stuff.

Literacy Focus. Literacy improvement was central to the district and to school activities, and many professional development programs had been available to help teachers who had not taught literacy before to develop literacy strategies in all subject areas across the curriculum. Dan told us about reactions from the staff and his response: "Are we being asked to add on to our own curriculum? We have only so much time to cover so much in our program." We emphasized the importance of literacy as part of what they were doing in every subject area. Not just English. Not just those subjects that naturally involve more writing and reading. It's a component of our tech subjects. It's a component of our math and science curriculum as well as throughout other parts of our curriculum.

At CSS, every department developed a literacy improvement plan, and teachers' efforts were monitored. Over the past four years, Dan had worked with a literacy committee with representatives from each department:

We emphasize the importance of cross-departmental initiatives and support. The whole reason for our success, I believe, is that we look at literacy as not just success on one particular test, but literacy embedded in our curriculum across all departments. Our literacy committee has been led largely by staff members, and administration has been part of the team. We have a literacy lead. When we first started to recognize some changes, we had a different lead from now. A staff member took on the initiative, and the board has been wonderful in providing in-service for lead teachers and for administrators around literacy instruction and facilitating discussions at the school level.

The district provided literacy resources and considerable help for students. Dan had initiated and supported several types of programs to meet the needs of the students:

- A schoolwide literacy week for all grades just before the provincial test
- A student success teacher to identify at-risk students who needed accommodations to take the test
- An after-school program funded by the district
- Two male teachers who have strong literacy programs to be mentors and role models for male students
- A group of retired teachers from the community to work on reading and writing skills with students one-on-one
- A literacy computer lab for primarily essential or basic-level classes that was set up using grant funding
- Several educational assistants to work with students one-on-one or in groups
- Three learning resource teachers

In addition to the literacy lead, teachers serving on the literacy committee who had expertise in the area shared their successful strategies with colleagues, and the teacher librarian helped develop programs and other supports for teachers.

Data Use. Data-driven planning was one of the main activities of the learning teams. Dan elaborated that this meant "teachers and staff members looking carefully at results and baseline data and what improvement really means. It goes well beyond what they perceive it to be. We've given them data. We've asked them to look at ways to develop their own data to measure success. We are aiming to develop goals that are measurable, attainable, specific. It's a work in progress. We're still continuing to look at effective ways to measure things, but the mind-set is there."

A teacher described how data were becoming more important to their conversations about improvement: "We seem to be talking about it a lot more—like at staff meetings. We seem to have more stats and data to show we're doing better. Because we see more data, we talk about it outside staff meetings. We're getting data at staff meetings about girls' and boys' results and comparing us to other schools in the board."

Staff Development. Dan credited the district with support for a variety of initiatives: "In terms of staff development, give credit to the board. In the past three years, we've worked on some strategies to create capacity for leadership and learning. This board has really put a great deal of effort and supported us as a school to develop a PLC." Furthermore, he told us about his firm belief that teachers needed to work together and discuss what they were doing in their classrooms. Over the past three or four years, he had supported six half-days per year for staff to get together and work on strategies for differentiated instruction and support for at-risk students. He was instrumental in developing a school schedule that provided teachers with release time:

> If you ask any staff member, what they want more than anything else is to gain knowledge and to look at efforts in terms of differentiated instruction. The number one request is time. Give us time. The administrative team and the student success lead have worked out a schedule to give teachers in departments and in learning teams opportunities to be released, sometimes going off site or working in a quiet place in the building on a regular basis. We've done this for the past two or three years. It's been excellent. People enjoy the experience and get a lot of work done. The opportunity for planning and discussion, you can't put a price on that. In the past, there have always been opportunities for staff to go to in-services. Not to say they're not valuable,

but there's never been the time to come back here and share the knowledge and work with that.

A grant Dan had pushed for made it possible to support more release time for six afternoons over the school year to develop teachers' awareness of their students' lives outside school. One teacher described a recent activity organized by a team of teachers in collaboration with Dan that combined teacher collaboration and professional development:

> One of the days was intended for teachers to learn about their school's community. The literacy lead set up an exercise that was interesting and quite powerful, where teachers were in groups and given a sector of the school's catchment area and told to find things, like a treasure hunt, and given cameras. We drove around looking for signs of neglect or poverty, how many houses were up for sale, how many had security system signs, what kind of restaurants, what community services, what languages on signs. What's our community like? Many of us don't live here.
>
> On the following community day, the head of student success did a slide show of our community and what we had found. It was fascinating because then we really understood where our kids were coming from and where they live and the conditions that they find themselves in that they bring into the building with them. It helps us to understand the barriers and also how to reach kids and help them understand what high school can be for them. One of the groups of teachers went to a student's home. He was home and asleep. They woke him up and took a picture of him sitting on his couch. The idea is, we are part of their community. Several people ran into their students on the streets or in the coffee shop. Students asked, "Oh, what are you doing here?" Just connecting with where they live. A big factor in a community like this, a school like this, is understanding the kids.

Leadership Distribution

Distributing leadership was part of the district's directions team model, and it was a good fit for Dan's approach to leadership:

> I'm very intent on sustaining leadership that goes just beyond me. I rely heavily on the fact that there's a directions team who have ownership. That ownership and sustainability across our staff, whether I'm here or not, people have a common vision and a common goal. I rely on the directions team to help me in building teams together. Looking at who the players are, in various departments—that's how it starts. The other huge part is, through the support of the board, we have funding to give teachers release time and opportunities to work together.

Positive Results

According to Dan, improvements in students' literacy scores had wide-reaching results:

> It's been a domino effect. You see increases in level of achievement in [provincial tests]. It becomes a public message: CSS is a school on the rise. We saw increased success in other ways. School pride is a big part of what happens. Students start attending more regularly. That's probably our biggest challenge: student attendance and apathy. When the school is perceived as being a successful school, people tend to want to put more commitment into their time here and their involvement in programs—inside the classroom and outside the classroom. The overall feeling around the school is one of pride and success.
>
> School pride has improved in the last three to four years. There are changes in success rates in athletics and academics. We've had a few city championships that we never saw before. That results in a great deal of pride. It used to be this school was not good at

athletics. When you speak to coaches from outside this building, then they talk about CSS being on the map, being recognized as a team you try to beat.

The enrollment here has changed—some of it due to boundary changes, some of it because the word is out there. We've gone from just under nine hundred to eleven hundred students.

Sustaining Improvement

Specific references to maintaining improvement did not come up in our interviews at CSS, but people did make comments that pointed to what seemed to be a schoolwide ethos: because of these students' lives, it was considered beyond their ability to do well on the provincial tests. Dan understood the situation for students:

> They're struggling, and they're hearing from their parents: "It's not like it used to be. You can't get anywhere with just a high school diploma." Getting them to understand that, really, in grade 7, grade 8, grade 9. It's no longer the case that you can pull it together in grade 12. You have to start building that ethic all the way through. This board, and particularly this school, we've looked at the Pathways program (a program aimed at helping students determine their postsecondary and career trajectories). In our community, many of our students don't leave the community, so we're trying to gear our programs for job opportunities that are available here.

> We've been working lately with our feeder schools. Looking at the student as a whole when they enter middle school in grade 7 and all the way through to high school.

A teacher leader provided her views on the importance of literacy beyond test results and echoed the vision of a larger reality for students:

I think it's the ongoing rather than cramming close to the test. Especially for at-risk students. It's not about how to pass the test; it's about how well are you going to function in society. I have problems with EQAO. It's a snapshot. I'm more interested in what are pass-fails and medians and overall learning that a student has shown rather than a snapshot. A kid could have a bad day. I would say it's the ongoing daily working toward improved literacy, not just literacy but in any course.

Remaining Concerns: It Is Not All Perfect

Dan told us about two ongoing areas of concern the school had been working on, improving parental involvement and student engagement, and shared some of the successes:

We have a large percentage of the student population we would consider at risk, and the reality for an inner-city school is that one of our challenges is to make connections with parents and bring them onboard as one of the partners in ensuring success for our students. There are a lot of barriers: work schedules (they work shifts), a large population of single-parent families (they need child care), parents may not have had a whole lot of success when they were in school (walking in this building has been they're in trouble or their kids are in trouble).

We started a program two and a half years ago driven by the school council, the parent group. This advisory group started with three people and is now fifteen or sixteen regular members. It's pretty amazing. Our school council chair deserves a great deal of credit for recruiting people. It was their brainchild, along with some staff members, to develop a plan to bring parents in and make them feel comfortable.

We had a series of events that address parents' issues with raising their children in today's society: drug and alcohol abuse; how to get my child to attend school; two open house events with no interviews or talk of marks, just come in and meet the staff and free barbecue. One event focused on volunteering opportunities because there's a belief that parents aren't welcome in high schools. We have staff running extracurricular activities who ask parents to help out and be part of the team. We had a healthy living focus event where we brought in community organizations and agencies just to set up a booth and give parents a chance to see what's out there for me in my community. We provided child care and food and made the time flexible enough so people could come at any time from early evening to late evening. That resulted in a 33 percent increase in parents who come to evening meetings with teachers. They were starting to feel more comfortable with being in the building.

One thing we're working on is student engagement. We took a long, hard look at attendance and apathy. Kids who are just striving to get their diploma but not thinking in terms of futures. We have a small population of students who are definitely high flyers, who know where they're going, but many who are just making the grade. Just getting credits and when they finish, they really haven't put thought into future plans, so our next steps are really to focus on careers and career aspirations and goals. We're working toward an ongoing career focus next year. Much like our literacy focus, we're having an ongoing effort throughout every subject area, and we're developing more co-op opportunities and experiential learning opportunities in every classroom. That's where we're headed.

Summary: Across the Cases

Marlene was loyal to the director's vision of school improvement and during her two years at Brookside had earned the respect of her staff, motivated the teachers to focus on shared literacy goals, kept up the improvement trajectory, and gotten teachers more involved in setting directions at the school level.

208 LEADING SCHOOL TURNAROUND

Dan had accepted the challenges that came with leading an inner-city school without blaming the students or their parents for the initial poor performance of students on provincial tests. He shared credit for the school's improvement with everyone involved in the school. These two school leaders devoted considerable effort to developing the capacities of their staffs in a wide variety of ways.

Both districts were instrumental in the development of teacher collaboration and involvement in schoolwide decision making, a key part of redesigning the school organization. Turnaround leadership was clearly shared between the district and school leaders in both cases. Teachers appreciated these opportunities to participate in meaningful ways and saw their whole school working toward the same goals. Data use, an increasingly important part of managing the instructional program, was more central at Brookside because of the principal's focus. But as more data were being provided and discussed at CSS, they were becoming more relevant for those teachers as well. There were still areas of concern at both schools, but foundations had been laid for continuing improvement. The two principals of these schools had made change both a possibility and a reality.

Stepping Back

The Brookside and CSS cases provide an up-close and personal view of successful turnaround leadership at work, one that highlights some of the leadership practices already outlined, along with others, and describes some of the changes that occurred in these schools in response to those practices. Another perspective on how turnaround leadership works more holistically is provided by some of the quantitative evidence collected as part of our Ontario study: survey evidence collected from 167 teachers and 12 principals in twelve turnaround schools in the province in which we also collected qualitative evidence.

The surveys, including slightly different wording but parallel items for both teachers and principals, asked about the extent to which many of the leadership practices outlined in previous chapters and awarded greatest importance in our case study data, were enacted in their schools (a five-point scale of strongly disagree to strongly agree).

Although surprising in light of the Brookside and Central Secondary cases, our case study data as a whole persuaded us not to include items measuring direction-setting practices. By the time of our surveys, the province's targets for literacy and math achievement had been widely adopted by teachers and administrators as the most important direction for their work.

The teacher version of the items used to measure leadership practices most likely to assist in the turnaround process (no items measured direction-setting practices) was as follows:

Developing People

- Increasing the quality and focus of professional development for teachers
- Increasing the quality and focus of professional development for principals

Redesigning the Organization

- Making the school a safer place emotionally and physically
- Creating policies and practices to improve student attendance
- Changing policies and procedures so that teachers spend less time on student discipline
- Adjusting the school schedule to allow more time for teacher collaboration
- Increasing parent involvement in the school and their children's learning

Managing the Instructional Program

- Monitoring students' learning more closely and using results to plan individual instruction
- Aligning instruction with the content of provincial tests
- Increasing resources

The teacher and administrator surveys also asked about the extent to which specific changes, culled from both our qualitative evidence and reviews of relevant research, had been made in respondents' schools (influenced by those leadership practices) to turn around their students' performance (also a five-point scale of strongly disagree to strongly agree). These questions were about changes in teachers' capacities and motivations and the settings in which they worked. Items used to measure these changes (teacher version) included the following:

Teacher Capacity

- My repertoire of instructional strategies has expanded and improved.
- I am more involved in analyzing my students' individual progress.
- I am more involved in meaningful professional development.
- I am more conscious of my contribution to a safe and healthy school environment.

Teacher Motivation

- My belief that all children can learn has increased.
- I find it easier to ask for help with curriculum and instructional issues.
- I am setting higher expectations for my students.
- I am setting higher expectations for myself.

Figure 8.1 Leadership Effects on Student Achievement

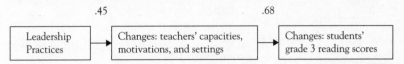

Note: The regression coefficient between leadership practices and changes in teachers was .45. The regression coefficient between changes in teachers and changes in student achievement was .68. The overall model was an acceptable fit to the data according to the usual tests of fit employed in path analysis (for example, RMSEA, RMR, and GFI).

Teachers' Work Settings

- I am collaborating more often with my colleagues about instructional matters.
- I feel like all teachers are sharing responsibility for all students in the school.

We then examined the relationship between responses (elementary and secondary teachers and administrators combined) to these two sets of questions (leadership practices and teacher changes) and changes in grade 3 student reading scores over a three-year period in those schools.[1] Summarized in Figure 8.1, our analysis indicates, in brief, that leadership practices strongly influenced the changes that occurred in the schools, and these changes in turn explained a considerable proportion (46 percent) of the variation across schools of the change in students' grade 3 reading scores.

Conclusion

The two cases summarized in this chapter, in combination with the quantitative evidence collected in our Ontario study, reflect some of the advice arising from three recent syntheses of the school turnaround research conducted primarily in the United States (Duke et al., 2005; Murphy & Meyers, 2008; Rhim et al., 2007). Evidence in this chapter reflects the importance of district leaders who do the following:

- Actively and sensitively help to create circumstances in which turnaround school-level leaders are better able to do their turnaround work
- Actively and visibly support the initiatives of their school-level turnaround leaders
- Signal unambiguously to school-level leaders that significant improvements in student learning are a priority for the district
- Align most district policies and procedures to the goal of improving student achievement

Evidence in this chapter also supports advice emerging from the three syntheses of evidence about the priority of actions on the part of school-level leaders:

- Aligning fiscal and human resources with initiatives aimed at turning around student performance
- Encouraging the systematic uses of good evidence for planning and decision making
- Building their own capacities and the capacities of their staff
- Fostering collaborative work among teachers

Part Three

OUTSTANDING CHALLENGES

9

HOW SCHOOLS MOVE FROM TURNAROUND TO "STAY AROUND"

Chapter Eight described two cases of school turnaround: an elementary and a secondary school in Ontario. In both cases, the turnaround in student performance was dramatic by the time we collected our data in May 2007. A year after collecting those data, we returned to the secondary school, Central Secondary School (CSS), to see what had happened in that short space of time. We learned that in January 2008, the principal, Dan, had started a new job working in the district office, and another principal had been assigned to the school. The provincial literacy results from the March 2008 test showed a 9 percent drop (to 67 percent) in the percentage of students who were successful and stayed at the same level the following year. Apart from small variations in the relative proportions of students involved in academic, applied, and locally developed English programs, the only visible change was in the school's leadership. This observation about CSS provides an appropriate introduction to the theme of this chapter: turnaround schools often do not stay turned around, and much of the explanation can be traced to leadership from different sources.

Much of the evidence concerning the school turnaround process is about the initial stages of the process. The strongest evidence from our study, for example, was about the first and second turnaround stages; evidence about the third stage was more speculative. Similarly, although the wider organizational turnaround literature provides reasonably robust knowledge about the ingredients associated with initial turnaround—for example, crisis stabilization, new leadership, a clear strategic focus, critical process improvements, and organizational change (Slatter, 1984)—it is relatively silent on how turnaround performance can be sustained. Yet only a small percentage of organizations that get into trouble and are turned around achieve long-lasting, sustainable recovery. The foundations for long-term growth and stability need to be properly established, or success quickly dissipates. This chapter considers how schools move from turnaround to "stay around." It considers how sustainable performance is achieved and explores the elements of long-term success. Inevitably we return to the earlier turnaround stages for some of this insight, since the seeds of long-term success are planted there.

There are competing interpretations of the term *sustainability*, so we first clarify its meaning for purposes of this chapter, beginning with what it is not. Sustainability is not about environmental sustainability, it is not about prolonging specific interventions or innovations, and it is not about the durability of an organization to withstand external pressures. Sustainability *is* about establishing the conditions for high student performance over time. As Fullan (2005) points out "You cannot move substantially towards sustainability in the absence of widely shared moral purpose" (p. 87), which, in the case of schools, concerns student learning.

A General Orientation to Sustaining School Turnaround

For a school to go through turnaround and reach a stage of suitable recovery requires fundamental changes to its internal processes and organizational culture. These changes are unlikely to be linear. There are always ebbs and flows, setbacks and successes. The natural course of turnaround to "stay around" may have discrete stages, as we suggest in this book, but the progression between stages is by no means guaranteed, and some backing and forthing among stages is likely. Strong leadership is required to take the organization through the different stages of change to the point of sustainable performance. Indeed, persistence and resilience tend to be the hallmarks of individuals and organizations that demonstrate consistently high performance over time (Fullan & Sharratt, 2007). Evidence also shows that sustained success is dependent on the basic orientation to change-shaping turnaround strategies and leaders.

Although every school is unique, two approaches to change help explain why a school is more or less likely to continue performing at the highest level after the initial turnaround phase. Both theories of change—theory E, which focuses on (E)conomic value, and theory O, which focuses on (O)rganizational capabilities and culture—stem from the literature on organizational turnaround and feature heavily in organizational recovery strategies. Theory E is based on organizational control and compliance, that is, creating economic value, while theory O is based on organizational capability and capacity building. Rowan (1996) means something quite similar by the control and commitment orientations to change.

In both business and education sectors, theory E change strategies make all the headlines. These are the tough, no-nonsense measures for dealing with failing organizations, weak management, inadequate leadership, and poor results. In England, for example, theory E strategies are reflected in a zero tolerance approach to school failure, which combines intense pressure with external intervention to tackle underperformance. Increased accountability, naming and shaming, and, as a last resort, reconstitution or school closure are also features of the No Child Left Behind policy in the United States. Malen, Croninger, Redmond, and Muncey (1999) write, "In recent years . . . state actions have focused attention on holding schools more accountable for students' academic achievement. The state has pressured the district largely through the enactment of mandatory state testing policies, threats of state takeovers, and calls for greater accountability, continuous school improvement, implementation of research-based practices, and development of a teacher corpus that is fully certified" (pp. 5–6).

While there have been some gains in school performance from theory E approaches to organizational change, success has often been short-lived, and the gains in school performance have not proved to be sustainable (Levin, 2009). In addition, the imposition of unrealistic timescales on turnaround, such as a year, is not achievable.

A relatively large body of evidence now argues that sustainable improvement can be achieved only through deeply rooted cultural change that focuses the organization on both individual and collective capacity development. Theory O approaches to change are those aimed at developing such capacity so that performance is self-sustaining. The only sure way that we know of to transform dysfunctional schools into effective schools is to build capacity in them "to provide smart, strong leadership, a mission clearly and intensely focused on children's learning, highly competent committed teachers, clean lines of responsibility, adequate financial resources, and an environment that fosters collaboration, trust, and continuous learning" (Wolk, 1998, p. 7). Sustainable improvement is possible in schools that purposefully create the internal infrastructure to manage any external or internal challenges likely to come their way.

Securing long-term change remains a challenge for both private and public sector organizations. It is clear from organizational theory that successful change is dynamic in orientation and always results in cultural change. The concept of dynamic capabilities is directly linked to issues of organizational change and organizational effectiveness. Teese, Pisano, and Shuen (1998) define *dynamic capabilities* as the organization's ability to integrate, build, and reconfigure internal and external competencies to address rapidly changing environments. Zollo and Winter (2002) further argue that dynamic capabilities are related to the pursuit of improved effectiveness in the long term.

The notion of a cultural dynamic or set of capabilities is important when considering how effective school turnaround and stay around takes place. The culture of a school can either hinder or help organizational growth and change. If culture works against you, there is very little that you can do (Fullan, 2004). So it is imperative that schools develop their internal dynamic capabilities to become self-sustaining. Schools that have sustained turnaround are characterized by a cultural dynamic of trust, positive staff and student relationships, and a willingness to take risks. These features do not arise accidentally. They must be instilled and nurtured, deliberately and painstakingly, by those leading the organization.

Without question, leadership is the central force driving the process of school turnaround and sustainable improvement; all the evidence points toward the importance of leadership in securing sustainable change. But this evidence also suggests that leadership approaches required for the early turnaround stages may not be those needed to secure sustainable high performance (Hargreaves & Fink, 2006).

A Theory O Perspective on Achieving Satisfactory Performance and Aspiring to Much More

Successful school turnaround processes, as previous chapters indicate, incorporate both fixed and flexible components. Among the fixed, nonnegotiable, aspects of improvement are a relentless focus on learning and raising attainment, improving the environment, and improving behavior. Flexible elements of school turnaround include teacher leadership, school collaboration, and school and district partnerships. The particular combination of fixed and flexible components varies by school and will be largely context dependent. But all turnaround schools go through the same stages of recovery and renewal reflected in our three-stage model.

In the third stage of this model, achieving satisfactory performance and aspiring to much more, schools develop processes of constant self-renewal that are generated from inside rather than dictated from the outside They have powerful mechanisms of internal accountability and set high professional standards for themselves. Their feedback mechanisms are sophisticated enough to ensure that innovation is properly evaluated (Harris, 2009). However, this does not mean they are insulated from external influence. Indeed, sustaining high performance is unlikely without some external impetus, drive, and input. According to the U.S. Department of Education (2001), "One of the most important things that states and districts can provide to struggling schools is expertise . . . to provide assistance with the planning, implementation, and evaluation of reform efforts" (p. 37). Evidence from our study, for example, demonstrated just how powerful the provincial government was in prompting serious change in many underperforming schools that would likely have continued to simply drift otherwise. So while some schools are capable of turning themselves around and sustaining high performance without any external help, this is actually very rare. Usually there is external support in the form of other schools or external agencies.

Sustaining improvement depends on continuous innovation and change. Most schools that sustain high performance have an ongoing desire to improve, so they pursue constant innovation. These schools actively seek out new ideas to ensure they are continually moving forward. However, such ongoing innovation asks a great deal of those working in the school. Teachers and other staff are expected to lead innovation and actively try out new ideas. For some, this is energizing, invigorating, and challenging, and it keeps the job interesting and engaging. For others, it can prove to be overwhelming. Achieving satisfactory performance and aspiring to much more is not for everyone, a key understanding for turnaround school leaders when they staff their schools.

Mandated assistance is often provided to failing schools, particularly in the form of expert help and customized assistance. In our study, this assistance was provided by the government's turnaround teams during the first two stages of their efforts but was no longer unavailable to them as they approached the third stage. However, the government continued to provide assistance to districts and schools through its many student achievement officers—typically highly experienced educators with special knowledge about effective literacy and math instruction (Levin, 2009).

In England, the School Improvement Partner (SIP) has played an increasing role in supporting school development and change. The SIP provides professional challenge and support to the school, helping its leadership to evaluate its own performance, identify priorities for improvement, and plan effective change. The partner acts for the district and is the main (but not the only) channel for the district to communicate about school improvement issues with the school. The following principles guide SIP work:

- A focus on pupil progress and attainment across the ability range and the many factors that influence it, including pupil well-being, extended services, and parental involvement
- Respect for the school's autonomy to plan its development, starting from the school's self-evaluation and the needs of the students and other members of the school community
- Professional challenge and support, so that the school's practice and performance are improved
- Evidence-based assessment of the school's performance and its strategies for improving teaching and learning

The next section illustrates many of the elements entailed in sustaining a successful turnaround as outlined to this point. The illustration is provided by a high school in England that has sustained its exceptional performance over the past decade through the application of theory O orientation to change.

Achieving Satisfactory Performance and Aspiring to Much More: A Case Study

Compton School serves children from eleven to sixteen years of age in north London with an enrollment of 752 students serving a mixed social and economic area.[1] Unemployment and other factors are generally favorable, but several selective grammar and faith schools nearby attract a disproportionate share of students from the most advantaged families. The school has 17.2 percent of its students claiming free school meals, slightly above the national average in England. Free school meals are a proxy measure for deprivation, and therefore Compton draws students from significantly disadvantaged families.

Students at Compton School come from many ethnic backgrounds, with about 50 percent from families of white European background and 20 percent from families of Indian heritage. Significant minorities come from a black African background and refugee communities. About three hundred students use English as an additional language, and thirty-one students are at an early stage of English language acquisition. Overall the school's students broadly match the national range in terms of social and economic advantage. About 45 percent of the students have special education needs, twice the national average.

Although the school has many high-achieving students, the performance of its incoming students is below average overall. Forty-two languages are spoken within the school, and its ethnic mix is continually changing. There are an increasing number of West African children and large numbers of Greek Cypriot, Iranian, and eastern Europe students at the school. The school has Leading Edge status, which demonstrates its innovative approach to education, and it has received two outstanding inspection reports over the past five years.[2] Its performance remains consistently good and above district and national averages (see the Appendix).

Compton School was formed from the consolidation of two failing schools. Both schools were closed, and Compton became a "fresh start" school in September 1992. In the early phase of its development, the school was not full, and performance was below average. By 1996 an external inspection found the school to be outstanding, and it has sustained this level of performance for over a decade. It has been included in the national "most improved school" category many times, and its academic performance is consistently high. It is the school of choice for girls because it is perceived to be safe and academically successful. Policymakers and politicians frequently cite it as an example of a high-performing school.

Turnaround Strategies

When the principal took over the school, Compton, she said, was like a "big elementary school." It was very caring and happy. The school was performing reasonably well, but there were things she saw that clearly needed to be done. Recruitment and retention of teachers was an issue, particularly in subjects like math and science. Staff turnover was unusually high as well. There was low-level disruption in lessons, and poor behavior among students was common. The budget was also an initial concern to the newly appointed principal, but this was subsequently improved through additional student numbers and external funding. The principal turned the school around by what she describes, as a process of "reinvention" in which she deliberately employed four key strategies to secure sustainable success.

Find More Money. The school took on additional students and sought external sponsorship, which over time gave them £2.5 million (about U.S. $5 million) to expand. Student numbers have continued to increase year after year at the school, which has meant more resources. There is now funding for a new building.

Build Productive Relationships. The principal focused considerable energy on the quality of relationships. These had been strained and fraught at times, and the principal spent a great deal of time in the initial phase talking to staff about proposed changes and getting their buy-in. Her view was that "if an argument is strong, it will be won." The argument was won, and staff in the school became supportive of the changes made and agreed to try out new ideas.

Create Achievement Targets. The principal and her senior team reinforced a focus on standards and raising achievement. It was clear that significant changes to teaching and learning were needed, along with a general improvement in instructional performance. The school turnaround literature speaks to the necessity of placing teaching and learning at the heart of improvement efforts. Often this improvement requires shifting beliefs and adopting a view that all students can learn; it requires paying attention to the core business of teaching and learning above everything else.

This relentless focus on teaching and learning was at the heart of the reinvention of Compton School. The prime goal was to maximize the potential of all students and reinforce the core message that all students can achieve, regardless of background. Academic excellence for all became the focus, and significant investments were made in new teaching approaches, along with the use of new technologies to make teaching and learning more interesting and exciting. There was a special focus on literacy and proximal learning approaches, with pupils working in pairs in all lessons. Observation of teachers was set up by the senior management team to create a dialogue about pedagogy. Targets were set for improvements in teaching and learning. According to the principal, these targets were an important contributor to sustaining the improvements at Compton, but students are "target aware but not target driven."

Use Data for Decision Making. The use of assessment data has been a key factor in raising achievement at Compton. According to the principal, "Data have just transformed what the school does." Students and parents now use an e-portal to access individual performance and progress data, and clear information is readily available about using the data to support learning in the home. There is a simple system that everyone understands and uses in the school. Departments use their own data to plan ahead, and these data are shared with students. The system is transparent and clear and used to regularly check progress and identify where interventions and support are needed.

The school now routinely uses data to inform teaching and learning developments and assist with the process of raising achievement. It is clear that effective use of data has played a major part in sustaining improvement at Compton; it provided a basis for the scrutiny of performance that did not exist previously, and it allowed the school to monitor the impact and effect of its innovations, particularly those directed at raising performance. In the early stages of turnaround, data helped identify the barriers to learning. "We looked again to the data," said the principal, "and we looked at why students were achieving and why they weren't achieving; we scrutinized whether they still had a potential of getting something." The use of data is unquestionably a powerful tool for assessing where innovation and change efforts are best placed. This targeted approach has proved to be successful and a major contributor to school improvement and raised student performance at Compton.

What Achieving Satisfactory Performance and Aspiring to Much More Amounts to in Compton School

In summary, the principal established norms and a way of working at the school that have been conducive to long-term, continuous high performance. Teachers at the school now see themselves as successful but not complacent. Clear core values are continually reinforced. For example, the school takes pride in being a local school and an inclusive school. Relationships with the local community are important, and the school positions itself as a resource for the community. It has strong links with parents and community groups, which are reinforced through its many activities involving parents.

The culture of making a difference runs through everything Compton School does. Recruitment of staff is no longer a problem. Its reputation has grown locally and nationally, as the principal notes: "We are very good here at growing our own." Internal promotions are encouraged, and talent, wherever it is found, is retained and rewarded. An extended leadership team of ten people shares in decision making. This distributed leadership comes with clear targets and accountability processes.

The sustained success of Compton School is largely due to the strong foundations established by the principal and her leadership team. These foundations support effective teaching and learning and are strong enough to stimulate the school to regularly reinvent itself. The school is a restless organization, actively seeking new ideas, opportunities, and challenges. This innovation orientation is a large part of its success. It is always seeking new ways to do things differently or better. It is not afraid of failure and is a high-trust organization that thrives on challenge.

The Compton School is now working with other schools, as a Leading Edge school, to engender the same passion for change and continuous improvement. It epitomizes school-led, systemwide change in action. It has not only improved and sustained its own performance but is now sharing its knowledge, advice, and expertise with other schools. This ability to learn while innovating is the main characteristic of schools that sustain high performance.

Implications for Leadership

Effective leadership is a key factor in successful school turnaround, including the final, sustaining stage. While leadership styles and approaches vary across schools that sustain turnaround, the vision and core values of the principal are key to positive change and development. Evidence shows that effective leadership is integral to the change process and essential to sustaining successful turnarounds (Fullan, 2006; Hargreaves & Fink, 2006; Murphy & Meyers, 2008).

Murphy and Meyers (2008) suggest that successful turnaround leaders have the characteristics of transformational leadership; they have "entrepreneurial instinct" and are "leaders of change" (p. 151). They are optimistic, enthusiastic and confident, achievement oriented, capable of challenging work, tough-minded, hands-on, courageous and persistent, and flexible, and they lead by example. Compton's principal certainly possesses such qualities, and the 2006 Ofsted inspection reports attribute the school's sustained success to "inspirational leadership of the principal, supported by a committed and extremely talented team that underpins this school's exceptional success" (p. 1).

The dominant model of leadership, in Compton School and other schools that have sustained high performance, is not top-down or overly bureaucratic. Instead there has been a purposeful and deliberate effort to distribute leadership widely (Harris, 2008). This has been driven by the principal with the aim of sharing responsibility and accountability more widely. Staff at Compton School highlighted the importance of distributed leadership and generally saw the key features of effective leadership as a focus on instructional improvement; building collaboration and good relationships; having clear aims and objectives; developing collegiality, trust, and effective communications; and extending leadership responsibility.

Some of our recent research (Day et al., 2009) has shown that while distribution of leadership roles and responsibilities is "a feature in schools that had sustained improvement over a five year period" (p. 9), the research also identified that this distributed leadership was "initiated and nurtured" by principals over time. For distributed leadership to be most effective, trust and confidence had to be built initially between the principal and a range of staff. This research shows that in high-performing schools, there is a progressive and selective leadership distribution that occurs over time and that this is determined by four factors: (1) the principal's judgments of what was right for the school at different phases of its development; (2) judgments about the existing readiness and observed and potential abilities of staff to lead; (3) the extent to which individual, relational, and organizational trust had been established; and (4) principals' own training, experience, and capabilities.

Within schools that have sustained high performance, distributed leadership takes various forms. In some cases, senior leadership teams have been extended; in others, new teams had been formed, new structures were put in place in order to spread out leadership practice, or teacher leadership was given priority. By distributing leadership more widely, schools secure greater collective responsibility, decision making, and support for the quality of teaching and learning. Evidence shows that the organizational impact of distributed leadership is generally positive, but the pattern and timing of distributed leadership have to be carefully judged and orchestrated by the principal (Harris, 2009; Leithwood et al., 2009).

At Compton School, formal leaders empower rather than control; they ask the right questions rather than provide the right answers; and they focus on flexibility rather than insist on conformity. All staff are aware that their ideas are welcome and that they can offer innovative ways to improve the quality of teaching and learning even further, thus laying a more solid foundation for their organization's success. "In this school," said the deputy principal, "there are opportunities to innovate and try things out; that's the best bit. The principal encourages you to try things out and ensures you have support. This way of working means it's a positive environment to work in." Schools that sustain high performance after turnaround have a set of cultural dynamics that allow, and indeed promote, risk taking. These schools understand the need for constant renewal and change in order to maintain and sustain higher levels of performance. Establishing a high-innovation, high-trust culture is dependent on having a leader who has a clear vision for the organization but can also set in place the right cultural conditions where innovation and change can be most effective. The principal at Compton school is without question this type of leader, and it is this leadership approach that keeps the school performing at a consistently high level.

Eight Lessons About Achieving Satisfactory Performance and Aspiring to Much More

The Compton School case, in combination with our review of the broader literature about sustaining high performance in schools, points to eight lessons for leaders to ponder.

1. Sustaining satisfactory to high performance depends on continuous efforts to regenerate.

Schools that sustain high performance, like Compton School, continually seek to regenerate and reinvent themselves. These schools have a pervasive innovative quality and thrive on challenge. Schools that sustain turnaround are restless for change and avoid complacency; they act rather than are acted on. Schools that sustain high performance see innovation and change as an integral part of their day-to-day activity.

Schools that sustain improvement are risk-taking cultures where the dominant ethos is one of "can do" and the need to try new ways of working is a commonly shared imperative. They are restless organizations that have cultivated a need for constant innovation and change that is internally owned and directed. The typical model of innovate and evaluate does not apply to these schools; they are learning while innovating and can adjust their interventions accordingly. High-performing schools are not risk averse; they actively seek new challenges and opportunities. This can be achieved only because of a culture of high trust, where the outcomes of experimentation are not expected to be successful. The dominant message is to learn through all innovation, not just that destined to be successful.

2. Continuous efforts to regenerate are rooted in key cultural norms.

Deep cultural change is at the heart of successful and sustainable turnaround; this is how turnaround schools maintain their success, even in the face of considerable challenge (Harris et al., 2006). They have an internal cultural norm about the need for ongoing change that staff and students widely understand and share.

3. School-to-school collaboration and networking is essential for sustaining performance.

Collaboration provides the infrastructure for new approaches to innovation and change. The power of collaboration is centrally important to understanding the gains in achievement made by schools over the last decade.

4. Trust in and among schools is a key strategy for sustaining their high performance.

Sustaining improvement is unlikely without some external impetus, drive, and alignment across the change and innovation process. But the move in many systems from individualism to collectivism indicates an appreciation for work in schools that has created a climate in which there is greater trust in schools' ability to help other schools to improve. Of course, trust within schools, as in other organizations, has long been known as the oil that keeps the machine running smoothly.

5. Only coherent change succeeds.

Evidence about turnaround schools shows, discouragingly, that after initial gains in achievement, many revert to their previous levels of underperformance. Typically this is because the changes made have focused only on short-term gains and quick fixes rather than also on long-term improvement. Schools that sustain improvement take both a short- and a long-term view and, like Compton School, lay the foundations for improvement in the years ahead. Schools that sustain improvement adopt a comprehensive and coherent approach to change. They avoid narrowly attending just to tactical, short-term changes, seeking instead a holistic approach to change that will have benefit in both the short and long terms. Leaders of these schools deploy a range of strategies that, in combination, provide the foundations for achieving satisfactory performance and aspiring to much more.

6. Sustainable performance requires strategic abandonment.

Sustaining school turnaround requires the active and purposeful abandonment of processes and ways of working that no longer meet the school's stage of development. Schools that sustain improvement are highly innovative but also quick to relinquish ways of working that are no longer fit for purpose. These schools also tend to have fluid, dynamic, and malleable cultures that readily adopt and adapt to new challenges and changes. They are essentially risk-taking cultures where the dominant ethos is one of "can do" and the need to try new ways of working is a commonly shared imperative. However, they do not simply add on new initiative after new initiative; they think carefully about what approaches to adapt and adopt. They decide in advance what to abandon in order to make organizational space for any new initiative or development

7. Paying attention to detail is crucial.

While turnaround principals and teachers tend to see the big picture, it is their attention to detail that contributes more to sustained success. Schools that sustain improvement have powerful mechanisms of internal accountability and set high professional standards for themselves. They have sophisticated feedback mechanisms in place that ensure that innovation is properly evaluated. They also use data to give them a clear sense of the impact and effect on certain change and development. Their leaders are simultaneously on the "balcony and the dance floor." They are continually scanning the horizon but also have a firm grip on how their organization is performing. They pay close attention to the monitoring of data and are quick to intervene if there are any early signals of downturn or underperformance.

8. Collaboration is key.

There is evidence that the process of change is more resilient and improvement more sustainable when schools collaborate and learn from other schools. Schools that sustain improvement are usually well networked and have a good infrastructure of internal support. They tend to be schools that reflect the core principles of professional learning communities and engage in meaningful collaboration and mutual learning with other schools. Schools that sustain improvement stay ahead of the game by using other schools as a reference point and a resource to improve their own performance. While such schools may be considered to be leading the way for others to follow, the reciprocal nature of the relationship and the opportunities for schools to innovate together means that there is added value in both directions from these forms of collaboration. Through the networks, there is a collective responsibility for improvement and a shared belief that schools can learn together and support each other in their quest for improvement.

Over the past decade, the rhetoric of school improvement has changed from a language of school reform to one of school transformation. The educational discourse has shifted away from school improvement to a preoccupation with innovation, change, and sustainability. Gains in performance and sustainable high achievement are now being secured as schools work collaboratively with other schools and with their districts rather than as the direct result of any externally imposed mandate or intervention.

School transformation and sustainable high performance are now much more than desirable headlines. They accurately characterize and describe the way in which schools in many countries are supporting each other to reach higher levels of innovation and performance. Through their collective efforts, major system redesign is both possible and realizable. Sustaining the high performance of many more schools has suddenly become a real possibility.

10

HOW TO REACH HIGH PERFORMANCE

Two overriding insights emerge from reflecting on the evidence examined to this point in the book. First, what successful leaders do to turn around and improve underperforming schools, as compared to improving schools already performing adequately, is different. But it is less different or specialized than much previous evidence would suggest (especially evidence collected in the private sector). Indeed, it is possible that the prevalence of the idea that there are specialized or distinctive leadership approaches for turnaround situations may be commercially rather than empirically driven (Slater, 1999). As Chapters Four, Five, Six, and Seven make clear, leaders in both turnaround and other contexts rely on exactly the same repertoire of core leadership practices, although they enact these practices in subtly different ways to fit the growth stage or context of the school. The particular amalgam of leadership strategies and approaches that successful leaders select are those that best meet the particular needs of the school at the time. This ability to discern exactly what a school requires is at the core of highly effective leadership practice. Good leaders intuitively know when to change direction or approach.

Second, although each of the three stages we have used to describe the turnaround process presents unique challenges, there is no single, best prescription that dictates the specific actions of leaders at each stage. There are certainly useful lessons in helping leaders to decide what those actions should be, and these lessons have been sprinkled throughout the chapters as our data warranted. But as Chapter One made clear, the causes of poor performance can vary widely across schools in need of turnaround. For example, outside a school, the influence of disadvantage and poverty can be acute; and within it, problems can include poor or inappropriate leadership, inadequate instruction, isolated professional cultures, dysfunctional organizational structures, and toxic interpersonal relations. Because the mix of causes of underperformance can vary so widely, it follows that the array of approaches selected to tackle the ensuing underperformance should also be highly differentiated (Harris & Chapman, 2002b). This is why an initial, accurate diagnosis of the real rather than perceived influences and causes of underperformance is imperative. An inaccurate diagnosis can lead to the wrong selection of strategies for improvement that at best will do little harm and at worse could distract the school from a direction of travel that would be more productive.

Each of the within-school causes of poor performance is, more precisely, the negative state of a more general and potentially positive condition (leadership, culture, instruction, and relationships, for example). Our account of the task of turnaround leaders in this concluding chapter is one of creating the school conditions where the possibility of turnaround to stay around is maximized and the foundation for exceptional performance is laid. The main task of leaders is to constantly monitor the status of the internal conditions in the school that influence student learning and improve the status of those conditions that are most in need of improvement and most likely to improve student learning.

We argue in this chapter that much more is known about the conditions likely to turn around a school than to assist it in reaching exceptional performance. As we have shown, the literature on failing schools and turnaround solutions is extensive, yet the literature on high-performing schools and their characteristics tends to be more limited. Consequently this chapter outlines what school leaders need to know about creating the

Figure 10.1 Four Sets of School Conditions to Improve in Order to Influence Student Learning

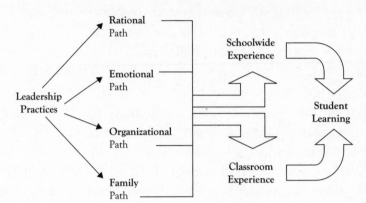

conditions to improve student learning and move the school toward exceptional performance.

Building on and extending evidence about the causes of decline described in Chapter One, this chapter proposes a four-fold classification of school conditions that considerable evidence suggests have important consequences for the learning of students. As Figure 10.1 indicates, this fourfold classification encompasses rational, emotional, organizational, and family conditions. Each category of conditions includes distinctly different sets of variables, each identified as having a direct impact on students' experiences to a greater or lesser degree. These variables could include, for example, those relating to school culture, teachers' practices, teachers' emotional states, or parents' attitudes. These variables can be influenced through the enactment of leadership practices and are the main route to improving student learning outcomes.

The literature suggests that assessments to determine what actions and interventions must be taken to achieve high performance need to consider the individualized needs and conditions of each school and organization in order to determine best how to build capacity (Harris & Chrispeels, 2008;

Hopkins, 2001). High-performing organizations deliberately build capacity and understand the need to develop the internal resources and secure and sustain high performance. They do this through a focus on the conditions within four broad categories: rational, emotional, organizational, and family. Each of the four categories provides leaders with a compass for potential development work, but much depends on the individual school. As we have highlighted, the most effective improvement efforts are always context specific and carefully targeted at individual school needs.

Working on the conditions in each of the four categories can improve the quality of students' school and classroom experiences and can lead to more effective learning plus higher organizational performance. However, exercising leadership in relation to only one category of conditions alone is unlikely to bring a significant return on investment to student learning or secure exceptional performance. The key to demonstrable gains for students is in the alignment of activity to improve and enhance all four sets of conditions over time. It is the interaction of these sets of conditions that can move a school from performing well to performing at the highest level.

The diagnosis, selection, and improvement of each of the four sets of conditions are addressed in the next four sections of this chapter. The chapter concludes by reflecting on the way schools reach exceptional levels of performance by focusing on these four sets of conditions.

Rational School Conditions

Rational and technical conditions relate to a school's routine organization and functioning. Conditions in this category are rooted in the knowledge and skills of school staff about curriculum, instruction, and learning. In general, exercising a positive influence on these variables calls on school leaders to know about the technical core of schooling, extend their problem-solving capacities (Robinson, Lloyd, & Rowe, 2008), and review their knowledge of effective instruction.

Rational and technical conditions are situated in both the classroom and the school. Since a considerable amount of evidence is available about the effects on student learning stemming from such conditions, school leaders can prioritize those known to have the greatest chance of improving their students' learning. Hattie's (2009) synthesis of classroom-level evidence suggests that school leaders would be wise to focus their improvement efforts, for example, on the extent to which teachers are providing students with immediate and informative feedback, teachers' use of reciprocal teaching strategies, teacher-student relations, classroom management practices, and the general quality of teaching in the school.

For turnaround school leaders, simply knowing which conditions in the rational category hold the greatest promise for improving student learning is not enough. It still leaves them with the problem of figuring out how to improve the status of those conditions in their schools. The key question following initial diagnosis and selection of core variables for action is, "What do we do?"

High-performing schools place teaching and learning at the heart of improvement efforts and relentlessly pursue ways of improving the instructional core (Elmore & Fuhrman, 2001). Building instructional capacity requires shifting beliefs and cultures, adopting a view that all students can learn, and a coupling of needs with high expectations. Instructional leaders in high-performing schools are characterized by the ability to outline a clear vision and values relating to high expectations for all students. They understand the definition of quality instruction and pedagogy and are able to strategically implement a plan that addresses capacity building among staff while also building trust. Investment in teachers' continuous professional development can increase student achievement and has been shown to be one of the primary factors in promoting school improvement.

High-performing schools place a premium on teachers' professional development as a route to improving instructional outcomes, and teachers are encouraged to form professional learning communities to support inquiry and investigation into their pedagogical practices.

A small number of studies have identified the leadership practices that are most likely to increase a school's academic expectations or improve its academic press (the degree to which staff, students, and parents consider the academic work of students to be the school's main priority) (Alig-Mielcarek, 2003; Jacob, 2004; Jurewicz, 2004):

- Developing and communicating shared goals
- Establishing high expectations
- Helping to clarify shared goals about academic achievement

Other leadership practices have been identified by the evidence as influencing higher student achievement and higher organizational performance—for example:

- Not burdening teachers with bureaucratic tasks and busywork
- Grouping students using methods that convey academic expectations
- Providing an orderly environment
- Establishing clear homework policies
- Monitoring and providing feedback on the teaching and learning processes
- Monitoring student performance in relation to instructional objectives
- Requiring student progress reports to be sent to parents
- Buffering in order to protecting instructional time
- Basing remediation efforts on a common instructional framework

Elmore (1999) outlines a number of dimensions that contribute to instructional improvement and high performance. First, professional development needs to focus on knowledge and skills that the students need, considering the necessary conditions of how such knowledge will be acquired. Second, educators' knowledge and skills need to be compatible with the requirements of learners, thus leading to a consideration of additional areas of training in order to address student learning. The third dimension focuses on incentives aimed at improving the staff's commitment and collaboration to unified purposes and goals. Fourth, resources and capacity for change must be addressed if the school is going to move to a higher level of performance and operation. Finally, account must be taken of the emotional dynamics within the organization that can make higher performance more or less likely.

Emotional School Conditions

The leadership literature spends a great deal of time on the rational dimensions of practice and less so on the emotional features that can so powerfully affect culture and well-being. Although the idea of rational and emotional conditions may seem oppositional and contradictory, both are more tightly connected than many leaders might believe. Considerable evidence indicates, for example, that emotions affect cognition: emotions can structure perception, direct attention, give preferential access to certain memories, and bias judgment in ways that help individuals respond productively to their environments (Oatley, Keltner, & Jenkins, 2006). The literature on turnaround and high-performing organizations also sends a strong signal about the centrality of trust, positive relationships, and supportive cultures as a prerequisite of improved and, ultimately, exceptional performance (Slater, 1999).

A recent review of more than ninety empirical studies of teacher emotions and their consequences for classroom practice and student learning (Leithwood, 2006; Leithwood &

Beatty, 2007) unambiguously recommends the need for school leaders to pay attention to the emotional conditions in their schools as a means of improving student learning. Harris (2003) shows unequivocally that emotions play a significant part in effective leadership and that the emotional dimension of a leader's work is critically important in moving a dysfunctional culture forward and establishing the belief that high performance is a real possibility.

A small but significant number of teacher emotions have been shown to have significant effects on teaching and learning outcomes: individual and collective teacher efficacy; feelings of job satisfaction; level of organizational commitment; morale, degrees of stress or burnout, or engagement in the school or profession; and trust in colleagues, parents, and students.

Evidence from high-performing schools suggests that teachers accept responsibility for their students' learning and accountability for student outcomes. Learning difficulties are not assumed to be an inevitable by-product of low socioeconomic status, lack of ability, or family background. As we have seen, high-performing schools such as Compton School that have come from a low starting point have high expectations for students as well as for staff. Evidence suggests that high expectations encourage teachers to set challenging benchmarks for themselves, engage in high levels of planning and organization, and devote more classroom time to academic learning.

As our case studies have shown, teachers who hold high expectations of themselves and others are more likely to engage in activity-based learning, student-centered learning, and interactive instruction. A feature of high-performing organizations is the sets of cultural norms that reinforce an expectation that exceptional goals are achievable. High-performing schools believe fundamentally in their ability to outperform their own targets or aspirations. This belief comes from a shared or collective sense of powerful self-efficacy that the school leader orchestrates and nurtures. The evidence shows that highly effective schools are not an accidental by-product of the system; rather, they are carefully created and constructed by the school leader. As we have highlighted, the first stage of turnaround is where leaders create a shared sense of direction in their schools. They can create this shared sense of direction only if they have the emotional buy-in from the people they work with. But having a clear vision is insufficient if no one is actually following. Effective leaders know that the work of turning around a school and taking it to the highest level of performance is predominantly emotional work. The need to win hearts and minds is critical for substantial change to take place. Effective leaders know that people are not their best asset; they are their only asset, so the need to nurture, develop, and strengthen relationships is at the very core of what good leaders do.

High-performing organizations tend to establish high-risk and high-trust cultures. In order to take the risks necessary to secure high performance, they must first have in place the organizational trust that allows them to take collective risks. Previous research has established strong reciprocal empirical associations between school improvement, in terms of pupil outcomes, and relational trust as observed in the interactions between head and teacher, teacher and teacher, and school professionals and parents (Bryk & Schneider, 2002) and has claimed that "trust in leaders both determines organizational performance and is a product of organizational performance" (Louis, 2007, p. 4).

Research by Day et al. (2009) confirms and extends these findings. The high performance of schools was a clear expression of the importance leaders placed on gaining others' trust and extending trust to them. The principals played an active and instrumental role in the planful distribution of leadership (Leithwood et al., 2009), and this increased commitment, self-efficacy, and staff confidence, which were associated with improved pupil outcomes. For principals in

effective schools, sustaining and improving performance further depended on five trust factors:

1. *Values and attitudes:* Beliefs that most people cared for their
   students and would work hard for their benefit if allowed to
   pursue objectives to which they were committed
2. *Disposition to trust:* A history of received and observed benefits derived from previous trusting relationships
3. *Trustworthiness:* The extent to which they were able to
   establish trust by others in them
4. *Repeated acts of trust:* Enabling the increasing distribution
   of leadership roles, responsibilities and accountabilities, and
   broadening of stakeholder participation
5. *Building and reinforcing individual relational and organizational
   trust:* Through interactions, structures, and strategies
   that demonstrated consistency with values and vision
   and resulted in observable and felt successes (Day et al.,
   2009, p. 25)

This form of trust includes a belief or expectation—in this
case, on the part of most teachers—that colleagues, students,
and parents support the school's goals for student learning and
will work toward achieving those goals. Transparency, com-
petence, benevolence, and reliability are among the qualities
persuading others that a person is trustworthy. Teacher trust is
critical to the success of schools, and nurturing trusting relationships with students and parents is a key element in improving
student learning (Bryk & Schneider, 2003; Lee & Croninger,
1994).

Some recent studies show that trust remains a powerful
and strong predictor of student achievement even after the
effects of student background, prior achievement, race, and
gender have been taken into account. Therefore, school leaders need to pay careful attention to the trust they engender in

teachers, students, and parents if they wish to improve organizational performance even further.

Goddard (2003) argues that when teacher-parent and teacher-student relationships are characterized by trust, academically supportive norms and social relations have the potential to move students toward greater academic success. Leaders can engender trust through various behaviors, including these:

- Offering individualized support by showing respect for individual members of the staff, demonstrating concern about their personal feelings and needs, maintaining an open door policy, and valuing staff opinions
- Sponsoring meaningful professional development
- Providing appropriate models of both desired practices and appropriate values
- Encouraging teachers to network with others who are facing similar challenges in order to learn from their experiences
- Structuring the school to allow for collaborative work among staff

The literature on high-performing organizations shows that they are normally characterized by high trust and leaders who develop, nurture, and model trusting and authentic relationships. The evidence on high-performing schools suggests that principals engender trust with and among staff and with both parents and students when their direction-setting practices include setting high standards for students and then following through with support for teachers. Providing individualized support, part of developing people, also builds trust when leaders:

- Recognize and acknowledge the vulnerabilities of their staff
- Listen to the personal needs of staff members and assist as much as possible to reconcile those needs with a clear vision for the school

Trust also develops, according to the evidence, when leaders redesign the organization in ways that create a space for parents in the school and demonstrate to parents that the principal is reliable, open, and scrupulously honest in his or her interactions. Buffering teachers from unreasonable demands from the policy environment or from the parents and the wider community, part of managing the instructional program, has also been shown to be a trust-building practice on the part of school leaders.

Organizational Conditions

The third set of conditions that contributes directly to sustaining school performance, after turnaround and securing high performance, relates to organizational arrangements. Structures, culture, policies, and standard operating procedures are the types of conditions included among the conditions that influence organizational change. Collectively these conditions constitute teachers' working conditions, which have a powerful influence on teachers' emotions and their subsequent working practices (Leithwood & Beatty, 2007). These variables reflect both the school's infrastructure and a large proportion of its collective memory—that is, practices and procedures that are believed to be successful as a result of a staff's hands-on experiences over an extended period of time.

Like the electrical, water, and road systems making up the infrastructure of a neighborhood, conditions in the organizational category are often not given much thought until they malfunction. At minimum, a school's infrastructure should not prevent staff and students from making best use of their capacities. As we highlighted earlier, organizational conditions affect the culture of the school, and if these conditions are not optimum, it is likely that the culture will be less than optimum also. If the culture is less than optimum, the chances of underperformance will be high and the possibility of slow but inevitable decline becomes very real.

At best, school infrastructures should magnify the capacities of staff and make it much easier to engage in productive rather than unproductive practices. Ensuring that conditions in the organizational category are working for, rather than against, the school's improvement efforts and contributing to a positive culture is vital to a school's ability to sustain any improvement or gains made. A new instructional practice, for example, will not be sustained if it requires unusual amounts of effort for an indefinite period of time.

Sustaining improvement depends on generating and supporting an organizational culture that can maintain development and change (Harris, 2009). Organizational learning first occurs in a school at the level of the individual. The challenge for organizations attempting to improve is how to take collective advantage of what its individual members are learning and the way they are learning it (Cohen, 1996). Capturing and sharing what individual members learn creates the potential for that learning to shape the behavior of many others in the organization. So the school leader has a critical role in ensuring that the best learning, expertise, and knowledge are shared and reinforced across the institution. This can be achieved by cross-department groups, working collaborative, or specialist interest networks in schools. Through social networking, implicit knowledge is made explicit, and innovative practices move beyond the domain of the few to the discourse of the many. It is through professional dialogue that professional knowledge is best shared and distributed (Timperley, 2008). The critical question is how to create the internal conditions where professional dialogue and knowledge creation are most possible.

In schools that recognize the importance of how students spend their time, structural changes are made to ensure that the barriers to learning are removed. So, for example, school schedules, timetables, structures, administrative behaviors, instructional practices, and the like are all designed to ensure that students are engaged in meaningful learning for as much of their time in school as possible. Distractions from meaningful learning are minimized. The key to successful leadership, in the case of instructional time, is to help ensure that the day-to-day functioning of the school conspires to focus everyone's efforts on desirable student learning. Indeed, optimizing instructional time, increasing academic press, or the priority given to the academic work of students, and improving the school's disciplinary climate are interdependent leadership initiatives.

In terms of the cultural organizational conditions, which are potentially more difficult to change than structural conditions but are infinitely more important to organizational performance, these tend to converge around issues of involvement, participation, and empowerment. Research has consistently underlined the contribution of strong collegial relationships to school improvement and change. Little (1990) suggested that collegial interaction at least lays the groundwork for developing shared ideas and generating forms of leadership. Rosenholtz (1989) argued even more forcibly for teacher collegiality and collaboration as a means of generating positive change in schools.

Collaboration within the school among different professional groups is at the heart of a positive organization culture. It often requires a power redistribution within the school, moving from hierarchical control to peer control. In organizational models, the power base is diffuse, with authority dispersed within the teaching community. An important dimension of this leadership approach is the emphasis on collegial ways of working. For collaboration to be most effective, it has to encompass mutual trust and support. There has to be a shared understanding and shared purpose at the core collaborative practice. It has to be a reciprocal learning process that leads to collective action and meaningful change.

Creating the conditions for collaboration within the organization requires the leader to create time, resources, and incentives for positive and productive sharing of knowledge. It also requires dismantling certain structural barriers that get in the way and facilitating opportunities for teachers to work together in a meaningful way. There are few examples of school turnaround without some fundamental change in organizational behavior. The main task of leaders therefore is to create the organizational conditions through redefinition and redesign, where a different way of working is not only possible but absolutely required because of the new organizational arrangements and associated set of expectations.

Family and Community Conditions

The fourth set of conditions for leaders to consider is located in the family and wider community. It is often claimed that improving student learning is all about improving instruction (Nelson & Sassi, 2005; Stein & Nelson, 2003). While improving instruction is both important and necessary work in many schools, this claim by itself ignores the powerful relationship between the emotional and organizational conditions already outlined. Just as critical, it is important for leaders to remember that the most powerful lever they have to secure high performance resides outside the school in the family and wider community.

As we saw in Chapter One, external factors account for as much as 50 percent of the variation in student achievement across schools (Kyriakides & Creemers, 2008; Harris, Allen, & Goodall, 2008); these family and community conditions make a significant difference to a school's ability to secure improvement and sustain improvement in the long term. Best estimates suggest that everything schools do within their walls accounts for about 20 percent of the variation in students' achievement (Creemers & Reetzigt, 1996)—the maximum difference a school can make because the external factors are so powerfully stacked for some schools and against others.

While the external factors in other high-performing organizations, such as business corporations, are important, they are not as powerfully influential as in schools. The influence of the family or wider community is a particularly high-leverage option for school leaders. Evidence shows that parents or other caregivers are the most important influence on a child's subsequent educational attainment other than the school (Harris, Allen, & Goodall, 2008). Long after direct learning from parents in a child's early years gives way to formal education, parents continue to play a key role in their child's success and learning, for better or worse. Challenges emerging from aspects of students' family background, especially poverty, are a key cause of poor student performance in many schools in need of being turned around. But through parental engagement and community involvement, schools can significantly reverse their performance and fortunes.

High-performing schools make a strong connection with parents and their learning community. As we saw, Compton School's principal has made great strides to connect with the community and encourage the community to see the school as part of the solution, not part of the problem. Yet the lives parents lead today means that it is more challenging to secure their engagement in their child's learning. Nevertheless, it remains the case that this factor alone can make a significant difference to the fortunes of a school. Parental and community engagement largely determine whether a school will be high performing. Without this external support, even the very best efforts of schools will be less effective.

The good news is that parental and community engagement is not fixed; it can be developed and extended. It is alterable rather than given and was considered to be the new work of leaders more than fifteen years ago (Goldring & Rallis, 1993). Parental and community engagement has also been a central focus for educational policymakers in England (Reay, 2009), Canada (Deslandes, 2009), the United States (Emmons & Commer, 2009), and many other countries for at least the past two decades. There is now considerable evidence about what these family and community conditions might best focus attention on.

Leithwood and Jantzi's (2006) synthesis of forty studies points to the important influence on children's academic success of family work habits, academic guidance and support provided to children, stimulation to think about issues in the larger environment, provision of adequate health and nutritional conditions, and physical settings in the home conducive to academic work. Recent work by Harris, Allen, and Goodall (2008) reinforces the difference between parental engagement in learning and parental involvement in schools, with the former having an effect on student learning and the outcomes and the latter making little difference at all except for social relationships. The implication is that school leaders need to focus attention on parental engagement in learning rather than parental involvement in schooling.

Although parent involvement in school has far less impact on student learning than parent engagement in learning in the home, children benefit from their parents' support in both locations (Epstein, 1995; Harris, Allen, & Goodall, 2008). Evidence from Leithwood and Jantzi's (2005) review indicates that parent engagement in school is nurtured when parents come to understand that such engagement is a key part of what it means to be a responsible parent; when parents believe they have the skills and know-how to make meaningful contributions to the school's efforts and the learning of their own children, improved learning is more likely to occur. Creating productive relationships with parents and the wider community is a specific leadership practice included in redesigning the organization. According to the evidence, the following leadership actions would maximize this practice:

- Issuing invitations for parent participation in learning support activities that are personal and specific rather than general
- Matching parent skills to the activities in which they will participate
- Providing very specific information and feedback to parents about their child's progress and offering explicit support to parents about helping with their child's learning
- Creating opportunities for parents to interact with one another and talk about learning and supporting their child's development

- Designing classroom activities to involve the direct support of parents in the instructional process and communicating effectively with parents about the opportunities for them to contribute and engage in learning activities at home and at school

- Providing a private environment in which to have parent-teacher conferences, soliciting parent views on key matters concerning their children's learning, and engaging in joint problem solving with parents

- Appointing a community liaison link person as a link between the parents and the school in order to build both teacher and parent capacity to communicate effectively and support one another

Parent engagement in their children's learning at home can take many forms, as Hattie's (2009) synthesis suggests. But some families have far more resources than others to be involved in productive ways. Families facing poverty, linguistic and cultural diversity, unemployment, and housing instability typically have considerable difficulty finding those resources or, indeed, the time to offer support. Research shows that targeted programs of support, including parenting skill programs, can have a significant impact on the engagement of parents who are considered hard to reach (Harris, Allen, & Goodall, 2008). But parents need to understand that they are an integral part of the learning process. They need to know they matter.

School leaders play a pivotal role in reinforcing the message that parents matter. In Rowlatts Hill Primary School, the principal played a concerted and active role by inviting the community to be part of the school. She recognized that she had to bring the community into the school to have any chance of raising standards and improving performance. She also recognized that the staff who could work most closely with parents need not be teachers, as many of her support staff came from the local community.

Without doubt, parental engagement in children's learning makes a difference and remains one of the most powerful school improvement levers that school leaders have. But effective parental engagement will not happen without concerted effort, time, and commitment from both parents and schools. It will not happen unless parents know the difference that they make and unless schools actively reinforce their active engagement in learning. For school leaders currently working toward greater parental engagement in learning, there are some important challenges and considerations:

- Parental engagement has to be a priority, not a bolt-on extra. It must be embedded in teaching and learning policies and school improvement policies, so that parents are seen as an integral part of the student learning process.

- Schools have to be clear about the aims of all communication with parents. Is communication in any given case meant to be open or closed? What response, if any, is required from parents, and how will that have an impact on the school and the child's learning?

- Supporting the engagement of parents who are already involved in the learning of their children is as important as reaching parents who are less engaged.

- Investment in training for staff who work most closely with parents is important; these staff members need not be teachers.

- Flexibility is required in face-to-face communication with parents in terms of times of meetings (shift work, child care issues) and, if possible, locations.

- New technologies can be helpful but are only part of the solution. They are not an end in themselves.

To support parental engagement in learning requires the school leader to assist with the design of approaches and programs to help families support their children's learning. This is not easy work, but when it is effectively implemented, it can have a major impact on learning outcomes. Ultimately effective parental engagement is premised on building trust and mutually respectful relationships between the school and the home. As we have seen throughout the examples of turnaround in this book, the school leader is the chief architect and the ambassador of better school and community relationships.

Alignment of Conditions

While the conditions discussed thus far in this chapter are distinct, they are not mutually exclusive. There has to be considerable interaction across all sets of conditions that reflect the reality and complexity of schooling. Typically failure to take the interdependence of these conditions into account severely limits school leaders' ability to sustain improved performance and secure higher performance. All of these conditions are important as they set the platform for better and higher performance.

As this book has shown, there are three phases of school turnaround:

Stage 1: Declining performance

Stage 2: An early turnaround or crisis stabilization

Stage 3: A late turnaround or sustaining and improving performance

Each of these phases is dependent on school leaders' ability to create, nurture, and sustain the rational, emotional, organizational, and community conditions that will support and drive change forward. Many schools have followed slavishly the blueprint for turnaround laid out in so many texts, and many more have adhered to the stepwise "how to improve your school" guides, only to be bitterly disappointed. Without attention to the rational, emotional, organizational, and community conditions that affect every school, any change will be short-lived. Any gains in performance will be temporary, and another false dawn of recovery will demoralize and disappoint those who have worked hard and long to achieve it.

School leaders who wish to turn around their school, sustain its performance, and reach high performance must pay attention to both the conditions and the particular set of strategies that will get them there. The best leaders work on the internal and external school conditions continuously in order to build capacity for further growth and development. These conditions are the main foundations for organizational renewal. They are the catalyst for even higher performance and collectively can take a school from turnaround, to stay around, to exceptional performance.

Conclusion

This book is not intended as a prescription for turning around underperforming schools. If it were, it would be bound to disappoint. Improvement and turnaround are largely in the hands of leaders and teachers themselves and not to be found in any prescription or blueprint. However, we do believe that this book can be used as a conceptual and practical guide to assist leaders in the turnaround process through providing both concepts and practices for

- Clarifying the different demands and requirements facing leaders at each turnaround stage
- Selecting for attention those school conditions with the greatest potential for improving student learning at a given stage
- Identifying which leadership practices are most likely to help improve the selected school conditions and providing guidance about how best to enact those practices
- Sustaining change and development as the school enters subsequent periods of growth

Evidence described throughout this book has demonstrated that leaders skilled in the craft of turning around underperforming schools have engaged with these concepts and practices either implicitly or explicitly to help them in the turnaround process. The task of turning around underperforming schools is not one to be taken lightly: the challenges can be enormous and the pitfalls perilous. Unless there is a broad repertoire of leadership practices, core understandings, and specialist knowledge, the job becomes much harder—and even impossible. We know that leaders are the critical factor in any turnaround in any sector. What they do makes or breaks the possibility of renewal, regeneration, and recovery.

The ideas in this book are intended to help school leaders facing the challenge of school turnaround by outlining different approaches. The evidence, knowledge, and insights here should be useful to those charged with turning around schools. Much of what is reflected in this book is based on the practical reality of getting the job of turnaround done. The book deliberately draws on the experience of school leaders on different sides of the Atlantic and outlines key findings from the international research.

Without question, there is no greater challenge than turning around a failing school And there is also no better reward. Successful school turnaround is not just about improving test scores; it is fundamentally about improving life chances for and opening new opportunities to the young people who learn there. It means the prospect of higher education, better employment prospects, and, for some, a departure from a lifestyle associated with deprivation and poverty. Leaders have a profound responsibility when taking on the challenge of turnaround, because the lives of many young people literally depend on it. These leaders also have a unique opportunity to raise the stakes by their actions and secure success for schools and students most in need of it.

Appendix: Methods Used
for the Studies

The Ontario Study

Design

A mixed-methods design was used over the two phases of this study. Qualitative techniques were used for the first phase to better understand turnaround processes in schools, to generate theory (Strauss & Corbin, 1990), as well as to substantially deepen understandings about contextually appropriate enactments of core leadership practices. The second phase of the study was a quantitative test of some first-phase findings, as well as a more focused analysis of leadership contributions to school improvement initiatives and teacher changes.

Sample

Phase 1. Evidence for phase 1 of the study was collected from one elementary and one secondary school in each of four districts. Within the districts, elementary schools were selected from a list of 105 schools that began participation in the Ontario Ministry of Education's school Turnaround Teams Project in September 2004. Selected elementary schools also had to have been engaged for at least three years in intentional and successful efforts to improve the achievement of their students on the province's grade 3 and grade 6 tests in reading, writing, and mathematics (our primary focus was the grade 3

259

language results). "Success" was defined by average changes in the proportion of students meeting the province's proficiency level from significantly below to significantly above the average for schools in their districts.[1]

Although no government-sponsored turnaround initiative for secondary schools was underway in the province, the same average change in student achievement was required for selection using results from the provincially administered grade 10 literacy test.

The principal and one vice principal most closely associated with the turnaround initiative were selected for interviews in each school. Three teachers identified by the principal as closely involved with the turnaround efforts were also selected. An additional three teachers were chosen randomly from a staff list. Parent focus group participants were usually active members of the school council and knowledgeable about the school's efforts. Students in focus groups were nominated by principals in consultation with teachers.

This sample selection process risks a positive bias in results. However, the goals of the study demanded close knowledge of the turnaround process on the part of those providing data, and schools had been selected as positive outliers to begin using student achievement data.

Phase 2. Schools in the second phase of the study were of two types. The first type included six elementary and three secondary schools located in the four districts where the first phase of the study was conducted, and they conformed to the definition of turnaround schools described above. In addition, four more schools (from two new districts) that were also involved in the Ministry of Education's turnaround project from two more districts agreed to participate in this phase of the study.

A second type of school was added to allow a comparison of leadership practices successful in turnaround versus improving schools. For purposes of selecting this second sample, improvement was defined approximately, after Potter, Reynolds, and

Chapman (2002), "as a sustained upward trend in effectiveness" beginning below the mean performance of other schools in its district and improving to a level above the district average. The province's grade 3 literacy data for a three- to four-year period were used to determine which schools in participating districts fit this definition of improvement.

Twenty schools were included in this second sample (none involved in the ministry project). The average size of the improving schools (372) was somewhat larger than the average size of the turnaround schools (351). Not surprisingly, in light of what is known about family background factors associated with schools in challenging circumstances (Snipes, Doolittle, & Herlihy, 2002), the turnaround schools in this sample had a larger proportion of single-parent households than the improving schools (29 percent versus 23 percent) and lower (although still middle-class) household incomes ($58,057 versus $65,325).

Surveys were distributed to all teachers and administrators in both samples of schools. Responses were received from 340 teachers and 20 principals or vice principals in the turnaround school sample, a 76.1 percent and 80 percent response rate, respectively. From the improving schools, surveys were received from 288 teachers and 24 administrators, a 72 percent and 92.3 percent response rate.

Data Collection and Analysis

Phase 1. Semistructured interviews were conducted with principals, vice principals, teacher leaders, and regular teachers— an average of ten interviews per school. Typically these interviews lasted from thirty to fifty minutes. In addition, focus group interviews were conducted with a group of three to six parents, as well as a group of four to six students in each school. Individual phone interviews were conducted with central office staff in three of the districts, in most cases the director (CEO) and the senior administrator directly responsible for turnaround initiatives. In total, data consisted of seventy-three individual interviews, and focus group interviews with thirty-five parents and forty-seven students.

Interview questions for administrators, teachers, and parent focus groups were essentially the same:

1. To what extent have you been involved in the school's efforts to improve student achievement in the provincial tests?

2. Who has provided leadership for this initiative? What actions have they taken?

3. Who else has been involved? What kinds of actions have they taken?

4. Which activities have contributed most dramatically to positive results?

5. What has been tried and not seemed to help much?

6. Over the past three to four years, has the school's approach to improvement changed in any way?

7. Is there a particular kind of leadership that seems to work best in turnaround circumstances?

8. On a scale of 1 to 5 (1 = lowest; 5 = highest), how would you rate the influence of each of the following on your school's turnaround efforts? Influences included principal, vice principal, formal teacher leaders, informal teacher leaders, parents, students, district level leaders, and people from the Ministry of Education.

9. Is there anything else you'd like to add?

The interview questions for student focus groups were about their perceptions of life at school and were different for elementary and secondary focus groups.

All interviews were digitally recorded, notes were kept during interviews, and these notes were reviewed, completed, and further developed as needed by listening to the recordings within a day of conducting the interviews. We did not develop verbatim transcriptions of the interviews. Rather we listened to all of the interviews several times to develop codes, answer key questions for the study, and recover illustrative quoted material. Working exclusively (or mostly) from verbatim transcriptions misses, in our opinion, much of the nuanced meaning to be captured by unstructured or semistructured interviews. From the outset, our analysis was designed to produce cross-case results. So we used a common framework for coding all interview responses. This framework is used to organize the subsequent description of results.

Phase 2. Two parallel surveys were used to collect data from teachers and principals in this phase. The administrator survey, for example, contained seventy-one items, seven of which requested demographic information. Using a six-point scale, sixty-one of the remaining items asked closed-ended questions about these topics:

- The extent of effort devoted to school improvement initiatives (ten items)
- The extent of changes in teachers over the past several years (eleven items)
- People or groups assuming greatest responsibility for leadership tasks (twenty-nine items)
- Extent of influence by individuals and groups on the school's improvement efforts (eleven items)

Three write-in items were also included. These items asked about "the two or three most important actions taken this year," "the biggest challenges to maintaining progress," and "what is important that we have not asked about."

Means and standard deviations were calculated for all responses to the teacher and administrator surveys. Factor analyses were carried out on all items intended to measure the same variable. The reliability of all scales was calculated using Cronbach's alpha. Correlations and regression analyses were conducted to examine relationships among selected variables.

The U.K. Study

Design

The study adopted a qualitative design and a case study methodology (Harris, Allen, & Goodall, 2008). A stratified sample of twenty schools was selected. All schools had moved from the lowest quartile of added value to the highest level of added value over a five-year period.[2] All schools had significantly improved their academic performance (as measured in external examinations taken by students fifteen and sixteen years old) significantly and consistently over the five-year period.[3] All the schools were considered by a range of external measures (including inspection) to be effective, and all schools had maintained improved performance over a minimum of five years.

The schools in the sample were geographically spread and located in a variety of contexts. The vast majority served areas of high socioeconomic disadvantage where the need for specialist support for young people and their families was considered to be a high priority. Within the sample, a number of schools had been previously identified as failing and had previously been categorized as requiring special measures.[4]

Data

The main objective of the project was to capture and illuminate the process of transformation through reflection and dialogue with key respondents about the process of change and improvement. A case study methodology was used to capture a diverse range of participant and stakeholder perspectives.

Data were collected during two-day visits to each school, and semistructured interviews were undertaken with a cross-section of respondents. A thematic approach was used to identify key components of success and sustainability factors across schools in the sample.

Semistructured interviews were undertaken with a range of stakeholder groups with a particular focus on students and parents. Data were collected from six major participant groups:

1. Young people
2. Governors
3. School leaders and leadership teams
4. Teaching staff
5. Support staff
6. Parents

Documentary evidence from each site was also used to inform the thematic framework.

Analysis

Interview data were analyzed in detail using the NVivo qualitative analysis program. Grounded themes that emerged during this process were also added to the thematic framework.

The research was analyzed inductively, then thematically through individual and cross-case comparison. The emerging thematic framework was informed by the theoretical perspectives derived from the literature plus the preliminary inductive analysis of interview data.

Key themes were also reinforced by using the Wordle tool to create powerful visual images of commonly occurring themes across the interview transcripts. The Wordle images were also used to frame second-round interviews with young people and other respondents. The themes were refined, scrutinized, and validated

Figure A.1 School Graphs

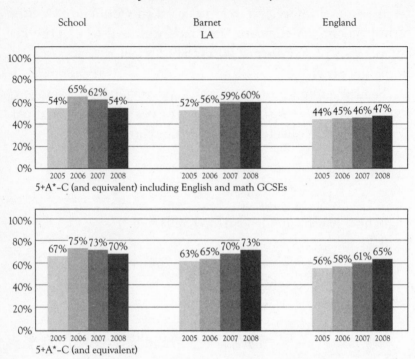

against the original data and the project reference groups comprising young people and other stakeholders.

Overall, one hundred interviews were conducted with a cross-section of respondents, including teachers, parents, students, and governors. The study aimed to capture the process of transformation and identify the features or factors that directly contributed to embedding and sustaining transformation in schools that had previously underperformed.

Notes

Introduction

1. For a comprehensive description of the provincial govern-ment's overall approach to educational reform, see Levin (2009).
2. Writing scores were also examined but are not reported here. They approximately conform to what is reported about read-ing and math.
3. Whether a school had changed from one year to the next was determined by calculating a standard error. This was calculated for each school individually, taking into account the standard deviations and the number of students in each school.
4. Linn (2003) identifies other explanations such as changes in student cohorts, regression to the mean and changes in environmental conditions from one test administration to the next.
5. For a comprehensive account of this policy environment and the change strategies in place, see Levin (2009) and Fullan and Levin (2009).

Chapter Two

1. The Turnaround Teams Project was part of a much larger provincial reform strategy aimed at raising the overall pro-portion of students achieving the province's proficiency level

in language from less than 60 percent to at least 75 percent within a four-year period (2004–2008).

Chapter Four

1. See Cyert and March (1963) for a description of this concept.
2. The reliability (Cronbach's alpha) of the scale measuring direction-setting practices was .89 for turnaround school responses and .84 for improving school respondents.

Chapter Six

1. For descriptions of the theories see Northouse (2007).
2. School staffs often referred to these teams as professional learning communities, reflecting widespread adoption of this concept across the province.

Chapter Eight

1. This examination was carried out using the LISREL path analysis program.

Chapter Nine

1. I am grateful to Teresa Tunnadine, principal of the Compton School, for allowing us to use this case study based on an extensive interview with her and her deputy principal.
2. The High Performing Specialist Schools Programme, launched in 2004, enables high-performing schools to play a central reform role within the system by sharing their expertise and resources with schools locally for the benefit of all young people in the locality. The Leading Edge Partnership program is one of the options open to High Performing Specialist Schools.

Appendix

1. Ontario's Education Quality and Accountability Office reports the results of provincial tests for schools as the proportion of students who achieve each of four levels. Level 3 is considered to be acceptable.
2. *Added value* refers to school residuals based on different pupil outcomes using performance and contextual data sets.
3. The General Certificate of Secondary Education is an academic qualification awarded in a specified subject, generally taken in a number of subjects by students aged fifteen and sixteen in secondary education in England, Wales, and Northern Ireland.
4. *Special measures* is a status applied by school inspection agencies, to schools in England and Wales, respectively, when it considers that they fail to supply an acceptable level of education and appear to lack the leadership capacity necessary to secure improvements. A school subject to special measures will have regular short-notice inspections to monitor its improvement. The senior managers and teaching staff can be dismissed and the school governors replaced by an appointed executive committee. If poor performance continues, the school may be closed.

References

Alig-Mielcarek, J. M. (2003). A model of school success: Instructional leadership, academic press, and student achievement. Unpublished doctoral dissertation, Ohio State University, Columbus, OH.

Anyon, J. (2005). Radical possibilities: Public policy, urban education and a new social movement. New York: Routledge.

Apple, M. (1996). Cultural politics and education. New York: Teachers College Press.

Avolio, B. J. (1994). The alliance of total quality and the full range of leadership. In B. M. Bass & B. J. Avolio (Eds.), Improving organizational effectiveness through transformational leadership (pp. 121–145). Thousand Oaks, CA: Sage.

Avolio, B. J., & Gardner, W. (2005). Authentic leadership development: Getting to the root of positive forms of leadership. Leadership Quarterly, 16(3), 315–338.

Bandura, A. (1986). Social foundations of thought and action. Upper Saddle River, NJ: Prentice Hall.

Bandura, A. (1997). Self-efficacy: The exercise of control. New York: Freeman.

Barker, B. (2005). Transforming schools: Illusion or reality? School Leadership and Management, 25(2), 99–116.

Bass, B. M. (1985). Leadership and performance beyond expectations. New York: Free Press.

Bass, B. M. (1998). Transformational leadership: Industrial, military and educational impact. New York: Routledge.

Bass, B. M., & Avolio, B. J. (1994). Improving organizational effectiveness through transformational leadership. Thousand Oaks, CA: Sage.

Bell, J. (2001). High-performing, poverty schools. Leadership, 31(1), 8–11.

Berliner, D. C. (2006). Our impoverished view of educational research. Teachers College Record, 108(6), 949–995.

Billman, P. (2004). Mission possible: Achieving and maintaining academic improvement. Dekalb: Northern Illinois University. http://www.ilhonorroll.niu.edu/pdf/mission_possible.pdf.

Bryk, A. S., & Schneider, B. (2002). Trust in schools: A core resource for improvement. New York: Russell Sage Foundation.

Bryk, A. S., & Schneider, B. (2003). Trust in schools: A core resource for school reform. *Educational Leadership, 60*(6), 40–44.

Burbank, R. K. (2005). The classic five-step turnaround process: Case study of Prodi-Gene, Inc. *Journal of Private Equity, 8*(2), 53–58.

Calkins, A., Guenther, W., Belfore, G., & Lash, D. (2007). *The turnaround challenge.* Boston: Mass Insight Education and Research Institute.

Center for Public Education. (2005). *Research review: High-performing, high-poverty schools.* Alexandria, VA: Author.

Chapman, C., & Harris, A. (2004). Towards differentiated improvement for schools in challenging circumstances. *British Journal of Educational Studies, 52*(4).

Chrisman, V. (2005). How schools sustain success. *Educational Leadership, 62*(5), 16–20.

Chrispeels, J. H., Castillo, S., & Brown, J. (2000). School leadership teams: A process model of team development. *School Effectiveness and School Improvement, 11*(1), 20–56.

Chudgar, A., & Luschei, T. (2009). National income, income inequality and the importance of schools: A hierarchical cross-national comparison, *American Educational Research Journal, 46*(3), 626–658.

Churchman, C. W. (1967). Guest editorial. *Management Science 14*(4).

Clarke, P. (2004). *Improving schools in challenging circumstances.* London: Continuum.

Cohen, M. D. (1996). Individual learning and organizational routine. In M. D. Cohen & L. S. Sproull (Eds.), *Organizational learning* (pp. 188–202). Thousand Oaks, CA: Sage.

Coleman, J. S. (1966). *Equality of educational opportunity.* Washington, DC: U.S. Government Printing Office.

Collins, J. (2009). *How the mighty fall: And why some companies never give in.* New York: HarperCollins.

Connolly, M., & James, C. (2006). Collaboration for school improvement: A resource dependency and institutional framework of analysis. *Educational Management Administration and Leadership, 34*(1), 69–87.

Corallo, C., & McDonald, D. (2002). *What works with low-performing schools.* Charleston, WV: Advanced Education and Literacy.

Creemers, B.P.M., & Reezigt, G. J. (1996). School level conditions affecting the effectiveness of instruction. *School Effectiveness and School Improvement, 7*(2), 197–228.

Cyert, R., & March, J. (1963). *A behavioral theory of the firm.* Upper Saddle River, NJ: Prentice-Hall.

Daly, A. (2009). Rigid responses in an age of accountability: The potential of leadership and trust. *Educational Administration Quarterly, 45*(2), 168–216.

Day, C., Sammons, P., Hopkins, D., Harris, A., Leithwood, K., Gu, Q., et al. (2009). *The impact of school leadership on pupil outcomes: Final report.* Nottingham, UK: Department for Children, Schools and Families.

De Maeyer, S., Rymenans, R., Van Petegem, P., van der Bergh, H., & Rijlaarsdam, G. (2006). *Educational leadership and pupil achievement: The choice of a valid conceptual model to test effects in school effectiveness research.* Unpublished manuscript, University of Antwerp, Belgium.

Deslandes, R. (2009). Family-school-community partnerships: What have we learned? In R. Deslandes (Ed.), *International perspectives on contexts, communities and evaluated innovated practices* (pp. 162–176). New York: Routledge.

Driscoll, M. E., & Kerchner, C. T. (1999). The implications of social capital for schools, communities and cities. In J. Murphy & K. S. Louis (Eds.), *Handbook of research on educational administration* (2nd ed., pp. 385–404). San Francisco: Jossey-Bass.

Duke, D. (2010). *Differentiating school leadership: Facing the challenges of practice.* Thousand Oaks, CA: Corwin Press.

Duke, D., Tucker, P. D., Belcher, M., Crews, D., Harrison-Coleman, J., Higgins, J., et al. (2005). *Lift-off: Launching the school turnaround process in 10 Virginia schools.* Charlottesville: Darden/Curry Partnership for Leaders in Education, University of Virginia.

Duke, D., Tucker, P. D., Salmonowicz, M., & Levy, M.(2007). How comparable are the perceived challenges facing principals of low-performing schools? *International Studies in Educational Administration, 35*(1), 3–21.

Elmore, R. (1999). *School reform from inside out.* Cambridge, MA: Harvard Education Press.

Elmore, R. F., & Fuhrman, S. H. (2001). Holding schools accountable: Is it working? *Phi Delta Kappan, 83*(1), 67–72.

Emmons, C. L., & Comer, J. P. (2009). Capturing complexity: Evaluation of the Yale Child Study Center School Development Program. In R. Deslandes (Ed.), *International perspectives on contexts, communities and evaluated innovated practices* (pp. 204–219). New York: Routledge.

Epstein, J. (1995). School/family partnerships: Caring for the children we share. *Phi Delta Kappan, 76*(9), 701–712.

Fink, D., & Brayman, C. (2006). School leadership succession and the challenges of change. *Educational Administration Quarterly, 42*(1), 62–89.

Finn, J. D. (1989). Withdrawing from school. *Review of Educational Research, 59*(2), 117–143.

Foster, R., & St. Hilaire, B. (2004). The who, how, why and what of leadership in secondary school improvement: Lessons learned in England. *Alberta Journal of Educational Research, 50*(4), 354–364.

Fredericksen, N. (1984). Implications of cognitive theory for instruction in problem solving. *Review of Educational Research, 54*(3), 363–407.

Fullan, M. (2003). *Change forces with a vengeance.* New York: Routledge Falmer.

Fullan, M. (2004). *Leading in a culture of change: Personal action guide and workbook.* San Francisco: Jossey-Bass.

Fullan, M. (2005). *Leadership and sustainability: System thinkers in action.* Thousand Oaks, CA: Corwin Press.

Fullan, M. (2006). *Turnaround leadership.* San Francisco: Jossey-Bass.

Fullan, M., & Levin, M. (2009). The fundamentals of whole-system reform. *Education Week, 28*(35) 30–31.

Fullan, M., & Sharratt, L. (2007). Sustaining leadership in complex times: An individual and system solution. In B. Davies (Ed.), *Developing sustainable leadership* (pp. 116–136). Thousand Oaks, CA: Sage.

Giles, C., Johnson, L., Brooks, J. S., & Jacobson, S. (2005). Building bridges, building community: Transformational leadership in challenging urban contexts. *Journal of School Leadership, 15*(5), 519–545.

Gladwell, M. (2008). *Outliers: The story of success.* New York: Little, Brown.

Goddard, R. D. (2003). Relational networks, social trust, and norms: A social capital perspective on students' chance of academic success. *Educational Evaluation and Policy Analysis, 25*(1), 59–74.

Goldring, E. B., & Rallis, S. F. (1993). *Principals of dynamic schools: Taking charge of change.* Thousand Oaks, CA: Corwin.

Gray, J. (2000). *Causing concern but improving: A review of schools' experience.* London: Department for Education and Skills.

Gray, J. (2004). Frames of reference and traditions of interpretation: Some issues in the identification of "under-achieving" schools. *British Journal of Educational Studies, 52*(1), 293–309.

Gray, J., Hopkins, D., Reynolds, D., Wilcox, B., Farrell, S., & Jesson, D. (1999). *Improving schools: Performance and potential.* Bristol, PA: Open University Press.

Hadfield, M. (2003). Building capacity versus growing schools. In A. Harris et al. (Eds.), *Effective leadership for school improvement* (pp. 107–120). New York: Routledge Falmer.

Hallinger, P. (2003). Leading educational change: Reflections on the practice of instructional and transformational leadership. *Cambridge Journal of Education, 33*(3), 329–351.

Hallinger, P., & Heck, R. (1998). Exploring the principal's contribution to school effectiveness: 1980–1995. *School Effectiveness and School Improvement, 9*(2), 157–191.

Hanks, S. (1990). *An empirical examination of the organizational life cycle in high technology firms.* Unpublished doctoral dissertation, University of Utah.

Hargreaves, A. (2004). Distinction and disgust: The emotional politics of school failure. *International Journal of Leadership in Education, 7*(1), 27–41.

Hargreaves, A., & Fink, D. (2006). *Sustainable leadership*. San Francisco: Jossey-Bass.

Harris, A. (2002). Effective leadership in schools facing challenging circumstances. *School Leadership and Management, 22*(1), 15–27.

Harris, A. (2003). Successful leadership in schools facing challenging circumstances. In J. H. Chrispeels (Ed.), *Learning to lead together: The promise and challenge of sharing leadership* (pp. 282–304). Thousand Oak, CA: Sage.

Harris, A. (2006). Leading change in schools in difficulty. *Journal of Educational Change, 7*(1/2), 9–18.

Harris, A. (2008). *Distributed leadership*. Thousand Oaks, CA: Sage.

Harris, A. (Ed.). (2009). *Distributed school leadership*. New York: Springer.

Harris, A., Allen, T., & Goodall, J. (2008). *Capturing transformation: How schools sustain transformation*. London: Specialist Schools and Academies Trust.

Harris, A., & Chapman, C. (2002a). *Leadership in schools facing challenging circumstances*. Nottingham, UK: National College for School Leadership.

Harris, A., & Chapman, C. (2002b). Democratic leadership for school improvement in challenging contexts. *International Journal for Leadership in Learning, 6*(9).

Harris, A., & Chrispeels, J. (2008). *International perspectives on school improvement*. Amsterdam: Kluwer.

Harris, A., James, S., Harris, B., & Gunraj, J. (2006). *Improving schools in difficulty*. London: Continuum.

Harris, A., Muijs, D., Chapman, C., Stoll, L., & Russ, J. (2003). *Raising attainment in schools in former coalfield areas*. London: Department for Education and Skills.

Hattie, J. (2009). *Visible learning: A synthesis of over 800 meta-analyses relating to achievement*. New York: Routledge.

Holdzkom, D. (2001, December). Low-performing schools: So you've identified them—now what? *AEL Policy Briefs*, 1–14.

Hopkins, D. (2007). *Every school a great school*. Bristol, PA, and New York: Open University Press/McGraw-Hill.

Hopkins, D. (2001) *School improvement for real*. Milton Keynes, UK: Open University Press.

Hopkins, D., Harris, A., & Jackson, D. (1997). Understanding the school's capacity for development: Growth states and strategies. *School Leadership and Management, 17*(3), 401–411.

Jackson, D. (2002). *The creation of knowledge networks: Collaborative enquiry for school and system improvement*. Paper presented at the CERI/OECD/DfES/QCA ESRC Forum, Knowledge Management in Education and Learning, Oxford, UK.

Jacob, J. A. (2004). *A study of school climate and enabling bureaucracy in select New York City public elementary schools*. Unpublished doctoral dissertation, University of Utah.

Jacobson, S., Brooks, S., Giles, C., Johnson, L., & Ylimaki, R. (2007). Successful leadership in three high-poverty urban elementary schools. *Leadership and Policy in Schools, 6*(4), 291–318.

Jacobson, S., Johnson, L., Ylimaki, R., & Giles, C. (2005). Successful leadership in challenging U.S. schools: Enabling principles, enabling schools. *Journal of Educational Administration, 43*(6), 607–617.

Jurewicz, M. M. (2004). *Organizational citizenship behaviors of middle school teachers: A study of their relationship to school climate and student achievement.* Unpublished doctoral dissertation, College of William and Mary.

Kannapel, P. J., & Clements, S. K. (2005). *Inside the black box of high-performing high-poverty schools.* Lexington, KY: Pritchard Committee for Academic Excellence. www.prichardcommittee.org/Ford%20study/FordReportJE.pdf.

Kanter, R. M. (2003). Leadership and the psychology of turnarounds. *Harvard Business Review, 81*(8). http://sasweb2epnet.com/citation.asp?tb=0&_ug=sid=6FDEDAOF%2DEB51%2D48F7%2.

Kimball, K., & Sirotnik, K. A. (2000, August). The urban principalship: Take this job and . . . ! *Thrust for Educational Leadership, 32*(4), 535–543.

Knapp, M. S. (2001). Policy, poverty and capable teaching. In B. Biddle (Ed.), *Social class, poverty and education.* New York: Routledge Falmer.

Kotter, J. P. (1995). Leading change: Why transformation efforts fail. *Harvard Business Review, 73*(2), 59–67.

Kowal, J. M., & Hassel, E. A. (2005). *Turnarounds with new leaders and staff.* Washington, DC: Center for Comprehensive School Reform and Improvement.

Kyriakides, L., & Creemers, B.P.M. (2008). Using a multidimensional approach to measure the impact of classroom-level factors upon student achievement: A study testing the validity of the dynamic model. *School Effectiveness and School Improvement, 19*(2), 183–205.

Lambert, L. (2006, Spring). Lasting leadership: A study of high leadership capacity schools. *The Educational Forum, 70,* 238–254.

Lauder, H., & Hughes, D. (1999). *Trading in futures: Why markets in education don't work.* Bristol, PA: Open University Press.

Lee, V. E., & Croninger, R. G. (1994). The relative importance of home and school in the development of literacy skills for middle-grade students. *American Journal of Education, 102*(3), 286–329.

Leithwood, K. (2006). *Teacher working conditions that matter: Evidence for change.* Toronto: Elementary Teachers' Federation of Ontario.

Leithwood, K., & Beatty, B. (2007). *Leading with teacher emotions in mind.* Thousand Oaks, CA: Corwin.

Leithwood, K., Day, C., Sammons, P., Harris, A., & Hopkins, D. (2006). *Successful school leadership: What it is and how it influences pupil learning.* London: DfES. http://www.dfes.gov.uk/research/data/uploadfiles/RR800.pdf. Department for Education and Schools.

Leithwood, K., & Jantzi, D. (2005). A review of transformational school leadership research: 1996–2005. *Leadership and Policy in Schools, 4*(3), 177–199.

Leithwood, K., & Jantzi, D. (2006). Transformational school leadership for large-scale reform: Effects on students, teachers, and their classroom practices. *School Effectiveness and School Improvement, 17*(2), 201–227.

Leithwood, K., Jantzi, D., & Dart, B. (1990). Transformational leadership: How principals can help reform school cultures. *School Effectiveness and School Improvement, 1*(4), 249–280.

Leithwood, K., Mascall, B., Strauss, T., Sacks, R., Memon, N., & Yashkina, A. (2009). Distributing leadership to make schools smarter: Taking the ego out of the system. In K. Leithwood, B. Mascall, & T. Strauss (Eds.), *Distributed leadership according to the evidence.* New York: Routledge.

Leithwood, K., & Strauss, T. (2008). *Turnaround school leadership: Final report.* Toronto: Canadian Education Association.

Lester, D. L., Parnell, J. A., & Carraher, S. (2003). Organizational life cycle: A five-stage empirical scale. *International Journal of Organizational Analysis, 11*(4), 339–354.

Levin, B. (2009). *How to change 5000 schools.* Cambridge, MA: Harvard Education Press.

Linn, R. (2003). Accountability: Responsibility and reasonable expectations. *Educational Researcher, 32*(7), 3–13.

Little, J. (1982). Norms of collegiality and experimentation: Workplace conditions of school success. *American Educational Research Journal, 19*, 325–340.

Little, J. W. (1990). The persistence of privacy: Autonomy and initiative in teachers' professional relations. *Teachers College Record, 91*(4), 509–536.

Locke, E. A. (2002). The leaders as integrator: The case of Jack Welch at General Electric. In L. L. Neider & C. Schriesheim (Eds.), *Leadership* (pp. 1–22). Greenwich, CT: Information Age Publishing.

Louis, K. S. (2007). Trust and improvement in schools. *Journal of Educational Change, 6*(1), 1–24.

Louis, K., & Kruse, S. (1995). *Professionalism and community: Perspectives on reforming urban schools.* Thousand Oaks, CA: Corwin.

Louis, K. S., & Kruse, S. D. (1998). Creating community in reform: Images of organizational learning in inner-city schools. In K. Leithwood &

K. S. Louis (Eds.), *Organizational learning in schools* (pp. 17–45). Lisse, NL: Swets & Zeitlinger.

Louis, K. S., Marks, H. M., & Kruse, S. (1996). Teachers' professional community in restructuring schools. *American Educational Research Journal, 33*(4), 757–798.

Lowe, K. B., Kroeck, K. G., & Sivasubramaniam, N. (1996). Effectiveness correlates of transformational and transactional leadership: A meta-analytical review of the MLQ literature. *Leadership Quarterly, 7*(3), 385–425.

Maden, M. (2001). Further lessons in success. In M. Maden (Ed.), *Success against the odds—Five years on* (pp. 307–339). New York: Routledge Falmer.

Malen, B., Croninger, R., Redmond, D., & Muncey, D. (1999, October). *Uncovering the potential contradictions in reconstitution reforms: A working paper.* Paper presented at the annual meeting of the University Council for Educational Administration, Minneapolis, MN.

Mattessich, P. W., & Monsey, B. R. (1992). *Collaboration: What makes it work?* St. Paul, MN: Amherst H. Wilder Foundation.

Mellahi, K., & Wilkinson, A. (2004). Organizational failure: A critique of recent research and a proposed integrative framework. *International Journal of Management Reviews, 5/6*(1), 21–41.

Miller, D., & Friesen, P. H. (1984). A longitudinal study of the corporate life cycle. *Management Science, 30*(10), 1161–1183

Mintrop, H. (2004). *Schools on probation: How accountability works (and doesn't work).* New York: Teachers College Press.

Mintrop, H., & Trujillo, T. (2004). *Corrective action in low performing schools: Lessons for NCLB implementation from state and district strategies in first-generation accountability systems.* Los Angeles: University of Los Angeles, Center for the Study of Evaluation.

Muijs, D., Harris, A., Chapman, C., Stoll, L., & Russ, J. (2004). Improving schools in socioeconomically disadvantaged areas—A review of research evidence. *School Effectiveness and School Improvement, 15*(2), 149–175.

Murphy, J., & Beck, L. (1995). *School-based management as school reform.* Thousand Oaks, CA: Corwin.

Murphy, J., & Meyers, C. V. (2008). *Turning around failing schools: Lessons from the organizational sciences.* Thousand Oaks, CA: Corwin.

Nelson, B., & Sassi, A. (2005). *The effective principal: Instructional leadership for high quality learning.* New York: Teachers College Press.

Northouse, P. (2007). *Leadership: Theory and practice* (4th ed.). Thousand Oaks, CA: Sage.

Oatley, K., Keltner, D., & Jenkins, J. M. (2006). *Understanding emotions* (2nd ed.). Malden, MA: Blackwell.

O'Day, J., & Bitter, C. (June, 2003). *Evaluation study of the immediate Intervention/Underperforming Schools Program and the High Achieving/ Improving Schools Program of the Public Schools Accountability Act of 1999: Final report*. Sacramento, CA: American Institutes for Research.

Ofsted. (2006). Inspection of Compton School, Report. http://www.ofsted .gov.uk/oxedu_reports/display/%28id%29/65579.

Orr, M. T., Byrne-Jimenez, M., McFarlane, P., & Brown, B. (2005). Leading out from low-performing schools: The urban principal experience. *Leadership and Policy in Schools, 4*(1), 23–54.

Paton, R., & Mordaunt, J. (2004). What's different about public and non-profit "turnaround"? *Public Money and Management, 24*(4), 209–216.

Pervin, B. (2005). Turning around student achievement in literacy. *Orbit, 35*(3), 39–41.

Picucci, A., Brownson, A., Kahlert, R., & Sobel, A. (1999). *Driven to succeed*. Austin: Charles A. Dana Center, University of Texas.

Podsakoff, P., MacKenzie, S., Moorman, R., & Fetter, R. (1990). Transformational leader behaviors and their effects on followers' trust in leader satisfaction and organizational citizenship behaviors. *Leadership Quarterly, 1*(2), 107–142.

Potter, D., Reynolds, D., & Chapman, C. (2002). School improvement for schools facing challenging circumstances: A review of research and practice. *School Leadership and Management, 22*(3), 243–256.

Raudenbush, S. W. (2009). The Brown legacy and the O'Connor challenge: Can school improvement reduce racial inequality? *Educational Researcher, 38*(3), 169–180.

Reay, D. (2009). Class acts: Home-school involvement and working class parents in the U.K. In R. Deslandes (Ed.), *International perspectives on contexts, communities and evaluated innovated practices* (pp. 50–63). New York: Routledge.

Reeves, J. (2000). Tracking the links between pupil attainment and development planning. *School Leadership and Management, 20*(3), 315–332.

Reynolds, A. J., Stringfield, S., & Muijs, D. (forthcoming). *Results for the High Reliability Schools Project*. Unpublished manuscript.

Reynolds, D. (1998). The study and remediation of ineffective schools: Some further reflections. In L. Stoll & K. Myers (Eds.), *No quick fixes: Perspectives on schools in difficulties* (pp. 163–174). New York: Routledge Falmer.

Reynolds, D., Hopkins, D., Potter, D., & Chapman, C. (2001). *School improvement for schools facing challenging circumstances: A review of research and practice*. London: Department for Education and Skills.

Rhim, L., Kowal, J., Hassel, B. Hassel, E., & Crittenden, S. (2007). *School turnarounds*. Lincoln, NE: Center on Innovation & Improvement.

Robinson, V. M., Lloyd, C. A., & Rowe, K. J. (2008). The impact of leadership on student outcomes: An analysis of the differential effects of leadership types. *Educational Administration Quarterly, 44*(5), 635–674.

Rogers, T., & Ricker, K. (2006). Establishing performance standards and setting cut scores. *Alberta Journal of Educational Research, 52*(1), 16–24.

Rosenholtz, S. J. (1989). *Teachers' workplace: The social organization of schools.* White Plains, NY: Longman.

Ross, J. A., & Glaze A. (2005). *Creating turn around schools: The effects of project REACH on students, teachers, principals and support staff: Final report.* Toronto: Ontario Principals Council.

Rowan, B. (1996). Standards as incentives for instructional reform. In S. Furman & J. O'Day (Eds.), *Rewards and reform: Creating educational incentives that work.* San Francisco: Jossey-Bass.

Silins, H., & Mulford, W. (2002). Leadership and school results. In K. Leithwood & P. Hallinger (Eds.), *Second international handbook of educational leadership and administration* (pp. 561–612). Norwell, MA: Kluwer.

Slatter, S. (1984). *Corporate recovery: A guide to turnaround management.* Harmondsworth, UK: Penguin Books.

Slater, S. (1999). *Saving big blue: Leadership lessons and turnaround tactics of IBM's Lou Gerstner.* New York: McGraw-Hill.

Slatter, S., Lovett, D., & Barlow, L. (2006). *Leading corporate turnaround: How leaders fix troubled companies.* San Francisco: Jossey-Bass.

Snipes, J., Doolittle, F., & Herlihy, C. (2002). *Foundations for success: Case studies of how urban school systems improve student achievement.* Washington, DC: MDRC (Manpower Demonstration Research Corporation).

Staw, B., Sandelands, L., & Dutton, J. (1981). Threat rigidity effects on organizational behavior: A multi-level analysis. *Administrative Science Quarterly, 26,* 501–524.

Stein, M. K., & Nelson, B. S. (2003). Leadership content knowledge. *Educational Evaluation and Policy Analysis, 25*(4), 423–448.

Stein, M., & Spillane, J. (2005). What can researchers on educational leadership learn from research on teaching? Building a bridge. In W. Firestone & C. Riehl (Eds.), *A new agenda for research in educational leadership* (pp. 28–45). New York: Teachers College Press.

Stoll, L., & Fink, D. (1996). *Changing our schools: Linking school effectiveness and school improvement.* Bristol, PA: Open University Press.

Stoll, L., & Myers, K. (Eds.). (1998). *No quick fixes: Perspectives on schools in difficulty.* New York: Routledge Falmer.

Strauss, A., & Corbin, J. (1990). *Basics of qualitative research: Grounded theory procedures and techniques.* Thousand Oaks, CA: Sage.

Teese, D. J., Pisano, G., & Shuen, A. (1998). Dynamic capabilities and strategic management. *Strategic Management Journal, 18*(7), 509–533.

Thomson, P., & Harris, A. (2004). *Schools that serve neighborhoods and communities in poverty.* Paper presented at the Second International Leadership in Education Research Network Meeting, Boston College, Chestnut Hill, MA.

Thrupp, M. (2001). Sociological and political concerns about school effectiveness research: Time for a new research agenda. *School Effectiveness and School Improvement, 12,* 7–40.

Timperley, H. (2005). Instructional leadership challenges: The case of using student achievement information for instructional improvement. *Leadership and Policy in Schools, 4*(1), 3–22.

Timperley, H. S. (2008). A distributed perspective on leadership and enhancing valued outcomes for students. *Journal of Curriculum Studies, 40*(6), 821–833.

U.S. Department of Education, Office of the Under Secretary and Office of Elementary and Secondary Education. (2001, January). *School improvement report: Executive order on actions for turning around low-performing schools.* Washington, DC: Author.

Waters, T., Marzano, R. J., & McNulty, B. (2003). *Balanced leadership: What 30 years of research tells us about the effect of leadership on pupil achievement: A working paper.* Denver, CO: Mid-Continent Research for Education and Learning.

West, M., Ainscow, M., & Stanford, J. (2005). Sustaining improvement in schools in challenging circumstances: A study of successful practice. *School Leadership and Management, 25*(1), 77–93.

Whelan, F. (2009). *Lessons learned: How good policies produce better schools.* London: MPG Books Group.

Willms, J. D. (Ed.). (2003). *Vulnerable children: Findings from a longitudinal study of children and youth.* Edmonton: University of Alberta Press.

Willms, J. D., & Ma, X. (2004). School disciplinary climate: Characteristics and effects on eighth grade achievement. *Alberta Journal of Educational Research, 50*(2), 169–188.

Wolk, R. (1998). Strategies for fixing failing public schools. *Education Week, 18*(12).

Yukl, G. (1989). *Leadership in organizations* (2nd ed.). Upper Saddle River, NJ: Prentice Hall.

Yukl, G. (1994). *Leadership in organizations.* (3rd ed.). Upper Saddle River, NJ: Prentice-Hall.

Zollo, M., & Winter, S. G. (2002). Deliberate learning and the evolution of dynamic capabilities. *Organization Science, 13*(3), 339–353.

Index

Page references followed by *fig* indicate an illustrated figure; followed by *t* indicate a table.